A PILGRIM FINDS THE WAY

A PILGRIM FINDS THE WAY

(A walk from Barcelona to Jerusalem)

George Florian Walter

Typecraft Press Inc.
PITTSBURGH, PENNSYLVANIA

CREDITS

Cover and graphics by Ronald Patterson.
Photography by Ken Popchack.
Editing and proofreading by Kathe Siglow and Donna Wyeth

Library of Congress catalogue card number 88-50181

ISBN: **0-9620287-1-1**

Printed in the United States of America

TABLE OF CONTENTS

PART ONE: Pittsburgh — New Orleans

PART TWO: Two months in New Orleans

PART THREE: Crossing the Atlantic Ocean

THE FIRST STAGE of the Pilgrim's Journey saw him make his way from Barcelona on the east coast of Spain to Santiago on the west coast. In all it was a journey of about 650 miles. Since at this time he occasionally took rides when offered to him, he covered this distance in a period of four weeks. On it the pilgrim began to learn what it meant to be a pilgrim firsthand. He came to value the apostolic tradition and appreciate the importance of our forefathers in the faith. It was during the second week that the Lord favored him with the most singular personal grace of the entire year of walking.

THE SECOND STAGE of the Pilgrim's Journey consisted of a six-week walk from Barcelona, Spain to Paris, France. From Barcelona to the French border was approximately 300 miles and from there to Paris was another 450 miles. The pilgrim continued to take rides until he got out of Spain, but once into France, he committed himself to walking only and refused all offers to ride. During this time the pilgrim came to a deepening love of Mary, the Mother of Jesus and experienced her loving presence again and again. He also came to a deep appreciation of all that he owed his earthly father and mother and wrote to them at length, thanking them in detail for many of the ways they had shown him their love. And finally during the latter part of this stage he came to a deep surrender of his life into the hands of his heavenly Father, so that it no longer mattered to him whether he live or die.

THE THIRD STAGE of the Pilgrim's Journey began with a month's layover in Paris, and ended with a seven-week walk to Zurich, Switzerland (a distance of about 350 miles). This included a two-week stay with his cousins on their farm in

Enchenberg in eastern France, and a three-day stay with his cousins in Zurich. During this stage the pilgrim came to appreciate the wholehearted hospitality, simple family life and something of the roots of his natural family in their European environment.

THE FOURTH STAGE of the Pilgrim's Journey was a seven-week, 500-mile stretch, from Zurich to Rome, Italy. Here the pilgrim came to be impressed with the Alps in Switzerland and the Umbria Mountains of Italy. The mountains and the men and women of faith who had once lived in them turned his thoughts to the possibility of giving his life totally to God as a hermit.

THE FIFTH STAGE of the Pilgrim's Journey was a 750-mile stretch from Rome to Athens. Here he was confronted by the civilization and culture which had so shaped Western Christendom and yet whose finest philosophers and military heroes had to bow before the superior power of the Gospel of Jesus Christ. This paralleled his own personal experience of finding insufficient all the knowledge and wisdom of a liberal arts education and of discovering the deep richness of the foolishness and poverty of the cross.

THE SIXTH STAGE of the Pilgrim's Journey was the 1750-mile walk from Athens, Greece to Haifa, Israel. It took him the best part of four months. This corresponded to the journey of St. Paul who had left the Middle East and traveled to Asia Minor and Greece to preach the Gospel and to spend himself for the risen Lord Jesus whom he had met on his way to Damascus. During this time, as the pilgrim walked in the footsteps of the zealous apostles of the early Church, his own faith was rekindled as he was able to get behind all the historical trappings of his faith and touch it fresh as it sprang forth from the lives of the early apostles. He experienced a true death in the physical and spiritual desert of Lent and then life and resurrection in the celebration of Easter.

THE SEVENTH STAGE of the Pilgrim's Journey was the 200 miles he walked in the Holy Land — the goal of his year of pilgrimage. It would be the last four weeks of a full year's journey. Here he came to touch so many of the places that Jesus himself had known. Now his faith no longer depended merely on printed pictures, words in a book or secondhand testimony. It was all very direct and real, especially the climax of entering the city of peace, Jerusalem, and spending 24 hours in prayer at the site of Calvary in the Church of the Holy Sepulchre. Truly the tomb was empty. Jesus is risen. He's alive. Praise God.

FOREWORD

George Walter, an accomplished practitioner of the art of walking, walked into my life in the Chancery Office of the Diocese of Pittsburgh in June of 1971. George, an ordained deacon, had decided that God was not calling him to the priesthood, at least not at that time. We had obtained for him a dispensation from Rome which would free him from the obligation of celibacy and of reciting the Breviary.

George expressed the hope that by accepting the dispensation he would not preclude the future possibility of embracing the clerical state. I assured him it would not. George also expressed the firm intention to remain celibate and to continue reciting the Divine Office.

George began a new life. He felt called by God to be a hermit and to walk the earth. His home is a small, modest poustinia (hermitage) on the property of Saint Mary's Catholic Church in Glenshaw, Pennsylvania. There he prays and fasts and gets the strength for his trips on "Saint Francis' horses", his pilgrim feet. The author of this work is a genuine eccentric. He also looks the part. I can understand why as he walks in Western Pennsylvania, Western Europe, or the Middle East, he provokes interest, curiosity and bewilderment.

His gentle manner, however, soon assures people that he comes in the name of the Lord and that his journey is one of peace. God provides George with food and shelter on his way. Sometimes God gives George the luxury of hardship.

Since my first visit with him, George has remained in touch telling me of his work, seeking my blessing as he left on a pilgrim walk and, I am pleased to say, praying for me and for all of God's people.

This journal of the hermit's walk from Barcelona to Jerusalem is an interesting travelogue. But it is much more than the story of faraway places. It is also the story of the journey of a soul because George allows us to share his thoughts and meditations. The reader will be touched and inspired by George's reflections.

In one of my conversations with the author, he expressed hesitancy about giving a newspaper interview. His humility made him question the advisability of this. I assured him that we would all be enriched, and that his witness might touch many souls.

It is for the same reason that I encouraged the publication of this work. George has taught me, a bishop, many things. I pray that the story of his journey will help all readers, pilgrims all, on our journey to the New Jerusalem.

+MOST REVEREND ANTHONY G. BOSCO
Bishop of Greensburg

PREFACE

"Go, sell what you have and give to the poor . . .
and come follow me." *Mark 10:2*

Jesus of Nazareth originally spoke these words to the rich young man who asked Him "Isn't there something more to life than just keeping the commandments?" Jesus, the Son of God, has continued to speak these words ever since, by the power of the Holy Spirit, to all who have come to Him with a deep thirst for the truth about life. And *since that time* countless men and women have attempted to allow these words to shape their lives in one way or another.

The Journal that you are about to read is an account — 15 years after the fact — of how one person in 20th century America responded to these words by walking 4,000 miles from Barcelona, Spain to Jerusalem. The reflections contained herein were recorded on that walk and written over a period of one year from May 1970 to May 1971. The author let them lie dormant for a period of 15 years — placing them in the Lord's hands — even though his friends had often asked that he share them. Then in the fall of 1985, it seemed the time had come to bring them out into the light to make them more available to God's people. It is the author's hope that the Holy Spirit might use them to further the Kingdom of God in the hearts of His people by encouraging every child of God to leave all and set out on that journey back to the heart of the Father, whence he came.

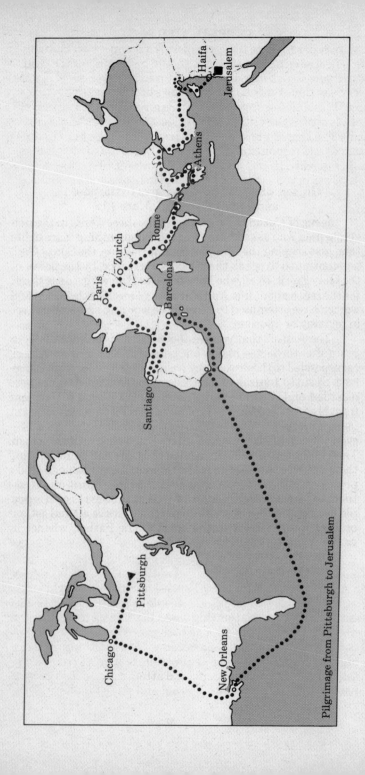

Pilgrimage from Pittsburgh to Jerusalem

INTRODUCTION

In order to place this year of walking and its accompanying reflections in perspective, it should be helpful for the reader to know something of what led up to it. After all, it is not every day that someone in his late 20's drops everything, takes up a Bible and sets out through foreign countries in search of answers to his deepest longings. The thought of doing something like this might cross a few people's minds, but circumstances and responsibilities normally cut off such imaginings rather quickly. In this author's case, however, his own need for an answer beyond what he could find in books and people, and the Lord's tremendous grace, made it possible. Here is how it came about.

The Fall of 1966 — a little over three years before this present pilgrimage — found the author ordained to the order of diaconate and beginning his last year of theological studies for the Diocesan Priesthood in a Major Seminary in Western Pennsylvania. It was his 12th year of seminary education as he had entered formation for the priesthood on the high school level right after completing eight years of Catholic elementary education. These years of training had gone by quickly and, for the most part, rather smoothly. The disciplined life and the intellectual challenge required by the seminary had not caused any major difficulties.

However, beginning with his studies on the theological level — which coincided with the conclusion of Vatican Council II — things became somewhat unsettled. It was a time when practically everything began to be up for questioning. Old forms and patterns of behavior were challenged and new ideas and ways of acting were at least considered, if not actually accepted and tried. These were the years of "the new morality" (situation ethics), "the new theologies" (death of God), "the new social conscience" (black voter registration in the South, etc.), and "the new liturgy" (Mass in the vernacular and facing the people, etc.).

Through all of this change, this future candidate for the priesthood began to feel like he was losing his bearings — that he was adrift on the sea and had nothing to stabilize or steer him in the proper direction. This led him to question both his suitableness for leading God's people as an ordained minister and even his own relationship with God — even to the point of wondering where this God he had grown up believing in had gone. The big question then became, "If everything is changing and I've lost my sense of direction, how can I commit myself to pastoring God's people and attempting to lead them to heaven? I'm no longer sure the old and more familiar ways of priestly ministry are all that significant or effective in accomplishing their purported goal. How can I go on?"

This state of mind reached a critical point around Christmas time of 1966 when it came time for each candidate for priesthood to sit down with the bishop and talk about his views on ordination, Christ, the Church, celibacy, etc. The Bishop, too, sensed an unsettled state of mind in this particular seminarian and agreed it was time for him to draw back for a while. Yes, he said, "it would be good to finish the academic year, but then in the Spring, set out on a pilgrimage; pray; keep seeking; ask God for the light; never give up hope that He will hear and answer; let the Spirit of the Lord heal, teach and renew you on new and deeper levels."

Upon completion of what was now 20 years of Catholic education, it seemed two basic paths lay open: one could get into some sort of church-related work or one could get into a strictly secular field. Thus there were thoughts of functioning as a deacon in some parish and also thoughts of joining Vista and Peace Corps. But toward the end of May, it became clear that no satisfactory decision could be made within the old environment. Something radically new was needed. There was a desire to put the familiar and safe aside and strike out into new territory. Somehow California beckoned as the place where one could get a new start, work out one's questionings and create a new life style in a way that hopefully would bring the much sought after peace and direction.

Thus was begun, "the life of a pilgrim". It was the first "break with the past". And though one could see the Lord in it upon looking back, there was no conscious awareness at this time of "a call to follow Jesus radically as a disciple." It was more basic than that: it was a desperate grasp to experience truth and reality at its fundamental source — namely God. It was more what has been called "the pilgrimage to the Absolute".

So with a small handbag and the offer from a newspaper ad for a rider to Los Angeles in return for paying half the cost of gas, this pilgrim set out for a city where he did not know a single person. And though the pilgrim had vacationed in some of the Western States several years before, this was a journey of a very different kind, and it was definitely not a vacation. It was more like a life or death search.

Arriving in Los Angeles, he rented a room in the downtown YMCA. He consulted the newspaper for possible jobs. After two weeks and various leads, it seemed to come down to a choice between an offer to be trained as a bank teller and an opening for a swimming instructor in a boys' club. But during

2

this time, the pilgrim's attention had been caught by something called "the diggers" who took care of providing food, clothing, and shelter for "the hippies" who were beginning to congregate in the Hollywood area. He sensed that this was more like the environment fitted to deep searching and questioning, for taking a regular job already tied one in too closely with the very structure and system one was questioning. So after two weeks, the pilgrim exchanged the straight life at the YMCA for the street life of Sunset Boulevard.

There he soon met up with a fellow who called himself "Plastic Man" — a young husband and father of two children in his late 20's who had just recently decided to "drop out" and join the hip underground movement in the Hollywood area. The pilgrim decided to invest himself and whatever savings he had in the bank into this particular movement.

So, for the next several months, the pilgrim mixed with the young people who were searching for new life in all kinds of strange ways: communal living, hallucinogenic drugs, Eastern meditation, sex without marriage, rock music, science fiction, etc. Contrary to what some surmised, there was never any evidence of the presence either of organized crime or of atheistic communism. It just seemed to be one of the extreme aberrations of advanced, humanistic, secular, technological, hedonistic culture. This was "the inward-looking branch" rather than "the outward-looking one". Thus there were "love-ins" rather than "sit-ins;" there was more emphasis on "grooving" (tuning into oneself, others, nature or God) rather than on changing the social structure.

But after a month and a half of housing runaway teens, organizing free "feedings" in the parks, writing and distributing a free underground newspaper; this pilgrim sensed he was not getting any closer to answering his questions here. And so, as they said of him there, "he split the scene" and set out alone to make his way on foot down the California coast toward San Diego.

Although the pilgrim had met many people in Los Angeles, he had not developed any significant or staying relationships. Several had invited him to join them in various adventures but he was not yet ready to form any partnerships and sensed the need to strike out alone to pursue this relationship with God that he sought so desperately, and which he as yet could not even clearly identify. Actually, by this time he had stopped going to church or receiving the sacraments. They were not providing what he was looking for in terms of personal encounter, and he was diving still deeper as it were — searching for the very rock bottom foundations of the whole religious

3

and social superstructure.

During the Fall of 1967, this dropout pilgrim continued making friends with artists in Laguna Beach, group therapists at Esalon Institute and the owners of "head (psychedelic) shops" in the San Diego area. His time was spent in a number of curious ways: working part-time for a landscaper; reading Marx, Tolkien, Heinlein, Huxley and the I Ching in a library; making silver jewelry at a friend's house; dancing to the beat of a bongo drum on a moonlit beach; typing for an underground newspaper; sitting for hours alone listening to the crashing of the waves on the shore; applying unsuccessfully for a three-month job on a commercial deep sea fishing boat; going on a month excursion with a fellow who had a map of a lost gold mine in Mexico.

By this time the pilgrim's uncut hair and beard had grown quite a bit. As winter approached, he came by a long blue Navy peacoat and a ridiculously long handmade tossel cap. Feeling quite at home in this foolish getup — for he was seriously questioning all of his society's standards — he decided to return to Pittsburgh and visit with family and friends.

Once back home, though, the pilgrim felt like a visitor from another planet — like a stranger in a strange land. His family and friends could not understand what had happened to him. Did he loose his mind? Was he on some kind of mind altering drugs? We he living some kind of weird fantasy? One of his relatives was sure he was living this way because of a bet for money. And so, although the pilgrim spent several months visiting with his former friends, he came to realize his search would have to continue in another place.

By Spring, the pilgrim was heading back west with a plan to stop in the Rocky Mountains near Boulder, Colorado, where someone had invited him to stay on his farm. Upon arriving, however, he could not find the place he had been told about, but discovered a group of about 30 other seekers (some called them "freaks") who were going to spend the Summer camping out in the mountains to "await the end of the world." He decided to join this group. He set up a little lean-to campsite and just spent his time enjoying the mountain scenery, "tripping" down the streets of the small college town of Boulder, and "rapping" with other people who were also trying to come to grips with what life was all about.

As the month of June came to an end, the world continued on its way with no obvious signs of catastrophic upheaval. The hippies left their campsite for wherever. This pilgrim headed for a higher mountain and a deeper confrontation with the mystery of life. Once again though, he would go it alone. For what

4

eventually turned out to be four weeks, he slept under the vast sky — clear blue all day and studded with bright stars at night. He baked his bread in a makeshift stone oven. He read Thomas Merton's "Bread in the Wilderness" and Chardin's "Pensees" and "Mass on the World." Inside he desperately cried out for God to show him His truth.

Here he began to understand more clearly that it was really GOD whom he was seeking. He came to realize that his restlessness and his inability to make longer commitments to particular jobs or persons was not so much due to a lack of strength or character weakness. Rather it was actually an unwillingness to stop short of meeting the only One who could fill the deepest desire of his heart — the Lord Himself. And so his lifestyle was the manifestation of a heart which was desperately crying out to God to reveal Himself to him.

And then one day it happened. A tremendous grace from the Lord penetrated the darkness and confusion of his heart and he met His Lord. His heart, as it were, shouted: "Oh, God, you are for real. You are here. You are my Father. I can see. Man did not make these mountains, plant these trees, stretch out this sky. You made all this. And You made me. That's where I came from. I'm not the product of some random evolutionary selection, of my culture, education, family, school, church, etc. I owe my existence to a unique, loving, creative act on the part of You, my heavenly Father. Thank you. Thank you, Thank you."

With that, the pilgrim realized he had touched the very rock bottom of the mystery of life and the foundation of every social structure (secular as well as religious) — God's existence. Now it was no longer merely a memorized answer to the catechism question "Who made me?" "God made me." It had become a first hand experience — a solid conviction — a faith alive and strong enough to support whatever the future might bring. With this truth so confirmed, the pilgrim could "return" to the society of man without fear or confusion — knowing now that he was a son of God. With his identity certain, his purpose became clear: life was merely a journey back to the heart of the Father who had made him in the first place.

The pilgrim knew it was now time to return to his former family and friends and especially to share with his spiritual father, his Bishop, how God was working in his life up to this point. But first he felt it appropriate to spend a week on retreat at the Trappist Monastery in Snowmass, as a kind of "decompression chamber experience" prior to re-entry into that world of surface structures — that is that world of social and religious symbols where most people live unexamined and routine lives.

The pilgrim arrived at the 400-acre Monastery the second week of August, unannounced. But true to their Benedictine principles that they treat every stranger who comes to their door as Christ, they welcomed him into the life of the brotherhood. He felt very much at home with the daily rhythm of prayer and work. Of course getting his hair cut and beard shaved was part of the re-entry ritual, but these symbols were easily laid aside because the peace in his heart did not depend upon such externals.

Upon his return to Western Pennsylvania, the pilgrim began to seek the Lord's will for his future. To help him in this he began to keep a daily diary, related to his family and friends and made a three day visit back to the Seminary which he had left over a year before. After prayer and consultation with his Bishop, who described him as "a kind of St. Francis of Assisi and gypsy", and who was willing to recommend him to a Trappist Monastery, the pilgrim decided to take an assignment as a deacon in a parish church in the diocese.

So on October 4, 1968, the Feast of St. Francis of Assisi, this "ex-hippie deacon," arrived at a middle class small-town parish to work with a pastor who was a monsignor and an assistant who had been a classmate in the Seminary. Here he hoped the Lord could begin reassembling all the pieces of his life and make it into a meaningful whole.

While stationed here, the pilgrim spent most of his time going from house to house, taking the parish census. He bought a used guitar at a pawn shop and taught himself to play simple chords to accompany the cries of his heart. He did not mind administering the Sacrament of Baptism but he could not bring himself to stand up on the pulpit yet and preach the Gospel. It seemed that he was not yet sure enough of the goal and means, to attempt to lead others to the Lord in a public and official way.

And then after six months, the Bishop said he would have to decide either to be ordained a priest or be laicized. He could not remain a deacon any longer. Since there was no strong conviction to go on to priesthood, but rather a real sense of the need for more searching, the pilgrim assented to requesting the dispensation from diaconate and he left the parish.

The question now was how to pursue the goal of getting to know Jesus. The Father was known to be the source and goal of his life. But he somehow had to better identify with the Father's Son, Jesus, who had been sent into the world to be man's way back to the Father (Jn. 14:6). So he decided to rent a small apartment near a large urban hospital and begin to seriously study the Bible and to pray for guidance.

For six months the pilgrim worked part-time as an orderly at the hospital: visiting people in the immediate neighborhood with a view to getting a first hand feel for their needs and concerns: reading the Bible; doing some summer theater with a group operating out of a local University; and entertaining a few friends in his $50 a month attic apartment. It was during this time that the idea of a pilgrimage to Jerusalem began to germinate in the pilgrim's heart. He had a close priest friend from seminary theology days who was living in Jerusalem and forming a Christian/Jewish kibbutz. He thought that perhaps he could better understand the Bible he was reading if he actually saw the places described in this ancient book.

But he also knew that he was not to go "the easy way" by plane or boat directly to the Holy Land. Rather, he was to make his pilgrimage "the long way" — via land — in imitation of his ancestors in the faith, the medieval pilgrims. These brothers and sisters, living in the 13th century ("The Age of Faith") seemed to be worthy models for this 20th century pilgrim. Also his itinerary would be set by the desire to retrace the spread of Christianity to the ends of the earth, only going backwards to its source in Jerusalem. Like the apostle Thomas, he needed to see and touch personally the evidence of the risen Lord (Jn. 20:25ff). Instead of the risen physical body of Christ, the pilgrim would touch the mystical body of Christ as it left its mark on the continent of Europe today.

Through reading, the pilgrim learned that Santiago de Compostela on the Western coast of Spain was, after Rome and Jerusalem, the third most important pilgrimage site during the Middle Ages. Since this shrine is dedicated to St. James the Apostle, whose feast day is July 25 and that also happens to be the pilgrim's birthday, there was a strong drawing to make this shrine part of the pilgrimage.

The first way the pilgrim thought of getting to Spain was to see if he could work his way over on a freighter. By checking around, it seemed one would have a better chance out of New Orleans than out of New York to deadhead (go one way) on a ship crossing the Atlantic. So the intinerary was roughly conceived and the pilgrim left his apartment on February 5, 1970.

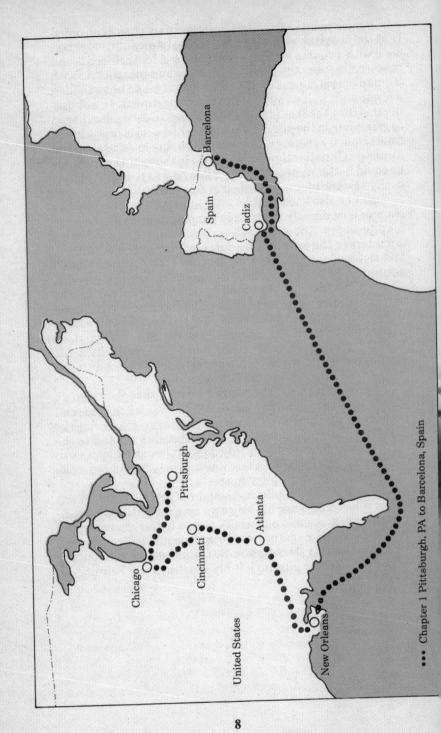

Chapter 1 Pittsburgh, PA to Barcelona, Spain

8

CHAPTER ONE
Pittsburgh, PA — Barcelona, Spain
February 5 - May 24
PART ONE: Pittsburgh — New Orleans

The pilgrim was now underway. He had taken to his parents' home a few boxes of his books and papers, terminated his job as an orderly and given up his apartment. He packed a small shoulder bag with a change of clothes, a "space blanket" given to him by a friend, and a copy of the New Testament given to him two years before by a Capuchin priest. Since there was no hurry or deadline to meet, the pilgrim decided to journey to New Orleans via Chicago, Dayton, Cincinnati and Atlanta where he could pay one last visit to old friends with whom he had kept in touch over the years. As usual, the mode of transportation was hitchhiking and this phase of the journey took up the months of February and March.

During this year-long pilgrimage, the pilgrim kept a small notebook in his pocket in which he recorded thoughts, insights, poems, quotations and dreams as they came to mean something special to him. On the average there might be one or two entries a week, although sometimes weeks would go by without any entries. These journal entries will be faithfully recorded here and will be tied together by placing them within their context along the journey with the aid of material drawn from some 14 long letters the pilgrim wrote to his parents as he journeyed along. Also each journal entry will carry a further reflection and comment dating from 15 years later. In this way it is hoped that something of the heart of the pilgrim will be revealed and read by those seeking enlightenment and needing encouragement for their own pilgrimage home to the Father.

The following entries were made during February and March from the time of setting out from Pittsburgh, Pennsylvania until arriving in New Orleans.

FEBRUARY 3, 1970 — THOUGHT — The PERCEPTION of one person (through the artistic expression of a vision) may become the dominating CONCRETE REALITY for a great number of people. The artistic expression brings the perceived vision into concrete reality.

COMMENT 1987: Isn't this what has happened in the history of the church in the founding of "religious communities" through the charism of their founder? Yet this seems to apply only in a very limited way to the charism of pilgrimage, except in those special cases where it blossoms into a full community as in the case of St. Francis of Assisi.

FEBRUARY 7, 1970 — THOUGHT — The thrust of spiritual guidance in the recent past tended towards self depreciation and self-hate; that of the present towards "self-respect" and "self love." Both seem open to dangers. Whichever is used, it is a matter of practical judgment. Today the danger of emphasizing only the good and positive elements of people is that one comes to distrust praise, knowing very well there are some downright evil elements in life and that those who are only full of compliments and optimism must be partially blind or unwilling to face the larger reality.

COMMENT 1987: *Actually neither emphasis is found in the Gospel of Jesus Christ. What is found there is "self-denial" but that is not "self-hate".*

FEBRUARY 9, 1970 — THOUGHT — One must first become part of and thoroughly involved in an institution before one can begin to be creative and original in the organization or situation within which this structure served it purpose. Only to the extent that one is familiar with the dynamics of the old forms can one begin to successfully build anything new.

COMMENT 1987: *This seems to be merely a piece of practical human wisdom, and is limited in application in the realm of church structures because the wisdom of God and the Holy Spirit are not bound by such dynamics.*

FEBRUARY 18, 1970 — DREAM — The pilgrim was tried in a court of law for his life. He told it as he saw it. Verdict was that he was insane and should be committed to a hospital.

COMMENT 1987: *Although the pilgrim "stands against" society, normally he does not do so in a way that makes it necessary for society to "put him out of sight", though they might like to, for he does disturb their conscience with a prophetic vision.*

MARCH 2, 1970 — THOUGHT — An important advantage of writing a book is that the reader is more likely to give his complete attention to you for a longer period of time than is possible in most day-to-day social situations. There you may get five or six readers to give you their complete and undivided attention.

COMMENT 1987: *Even pilgrims run the danger of giving in to the temptation of "wanting to be understood", and wishing they could "explain" themselves at least to a few other people they meet.*

MARCH 7, 1970 — THOUGHT — The United States — many people (especially the young and educated) are asking, "why are your garbage cans overflowing?"

COMMENT 1987: *A pilgrim has a different perspective on his society than those living within it. Thus he can see evidence of waste, greed, lack of respect for creation, etc. in a clearer light.*

SAME DAY — THOUGHT — How often does, "I love you," mean "you give me pleasure"?

COMMENT 1987: This is a reflection on how misunderstood the word "love" is in contemporary American society, where it is almost totally sense-oriented and ego-centered.

FEBRUARY 25, 1970 — THOUGHT — Only those who are lonely or lovers visit parks: Is there a connection? Seeking solitude: getting away from society, back to basics/nature? An intense awareness of an uncommon consciousness?

COMMENT 1987: A pilgrim walks alone yet he walks with One he loves. Is it any wonder he seeks out solitary places for his prayer and communion with his Lord?

FEBRUARY 26, 1970 — THOUGHT — "Introductions" of strangers to a group or another individual by a common friend are meant to "guarantee" the reliability of the stranger, taking the trust of the known friend as a basis for not fearing that the stranger will work harm.

COMMENT 1987: Pilgrims, for the most part, appear to be strangers. Only those who have discovered that they, too, are pilgrims on the way back to the Father recognize a fellow pilgrim as a brother and welcome him without the customary "introductions" that the world has found necessary to use for self-protection.

SAME DAY — THOUGHT — In emergency or crisis situations where there is no time to give detailed explanations of the situation and course of action, one might just say, "follow me."

COMMENT 1987: In this sense the Gospels report Jesus' public ministry as a "crisis situation". He knew he could not explain it all to his disciples, so they had to follow him by faith, even through death, so he just said to them "follow me."

PART TWO: Two months in New Orleans

And now the pilgrim arrived in New Orleans. The natural place to live there was in the French Quarter as this was where the street and night life of the city flourished, for it contained many shops, nightclubs, restaurants, tourist attractions and cheap housing. However, after a few weeks of inquiry, it became apparent that there were no opportunities for working one's way across the Atlantic Ocean. Instead a ticket would have to be purchased and so a job would be needed to earn the $230 required for passage on a freighter. Employment was soon found as a roustabout (common laborer) in the oil fields of Plaquemines County and reservations were made with a Steamship Company to travel First Class on a ship bound for Spain in late April.

In the oil fields the pilgrim did jobs like this: loading pipe onto barges with a crane; cleaning and scrubbing diesel motors and pumps brought in from the oil fields; living on and working off a tug boat laying pipe through marsh and swamps. Sometimes he would work 80 or more hours a week.

On his breaks from work the pilgrim would come into the city to observe life in this part of America. He bought his mother a picture of "Pirates Alley" he saw an artist painting, and sent it to her along with his first of what would be a series of long, detailed letters about his travels and experiences. Then, two weeks before his ship sailed, he moved into an apartment in the French Quarter and did janitorial work around the building in exchange for his staying there.

During these months the pilgrim was very much moving back and forth between two worlds: between the radically thinking element in the Catholic Church and the experimentally living element in the American culture. He was "on the fringe", as it were, about to set out on a journey that neither group could actually do but which required both radical thinking and a new style of living: namely, a pilgrimage on foot to the Holy City of Jerusalem.

In a sense it would be like a solo flight in a space probe orbiting the earth, that would enable the pilgrim to distance himself from the rest of the world — giving him a new and unique perspective — yet would in innumerable ways still depend on that world for life-support systems. Nevertheless, it would be at the opposite end of the spectrum: that is, instead of involving the most expensive, most complex, most recent technology; it would involve basically two simple items: a copy of the New Testament and the ability to walk.

The following were the journal entries the pilgrim made from March to May while living in New Orleans and preparing to make the voyage across the ocean.

MARCH 14, 1970 — QUOTATION — "The world as image: since the renaissance man has moved from an understanding of reality in which everything meant everything to a present understanding in which nothing means anything." Thomas Howard, *An Antique Drum*, Lippincott Co. 1969.

COMMENT 1987: This points to the fact that the pilgrim is preparing to leave the technological society in which nothing means anything, (that is everything is subjective and relative) and journey into a world (the world of faith) where everything means everything, that is where everything points to God who is everything.

MARCH 15, 1970 — QUOTATION — "Are we fooling ourselves? When we come to analyze what attracts us to St. Francis of Assisi, we may find that he represents to us a fantasy of escape rather than a true hero. He may actually appeal to the Rousseauist who is still alive in every one of us. In the mind of many people he has become a kind of nature boy who lives as the friend of birds and squirrels and does not have to pay any income tax. The fact that he experienced the agony of our Lord is small-point footnote." J.J. O'Sullivan, Leaflet Missal vol. XLI.

COMMENT 1987: This quote is a reminder to the pilgrim that there is a great danger in his way of life: it could stem largely from romantic fantasy rather than an authentic call from the Lord. His safeguard is to keep his eyes on his crucified Lord.

MARCH 17, 1970 — THOUGHT — How can a people so security conscious as Americans, ever come close to deep inner peace?

COMMENT 1987: Only those who are willing to chance letting go of every human support and security, can experience falling into the hands of the loving God who alone can give true inner peace.

MARCH 19, 1970 — THOUGHT — In a culture which constantly demands that one present a proper (marketable, attractive, acceptable) image, it is most difficult to experience that one is "proper" no matter who he is: that he is loved the way he is and was loved before he was (this love by God may of course be encouraging him to grow into greater unity with the truth).

COMMENT 1987: This thought points to the double aspect of Christian love; that it takes a person where he is on the one hand, but on the other hand will work to change the person into a perfect image of Jesus.

MARCH 29, 1970 — THOUGHT — Is it more difficult for those who can "banish darkness" with the flick of a switch, to accept the presence of evil than those who live with the daily cycle of light and darkness and arrange their lives accordingly?

COMMENT 1987: As man has gained control over his environment by technology he seems to have lost a sense of "powers greater than himself" — both evil powers and good powers. Thus also he senses less need for a "savior" to rescue him from the powers of evil, for he's done it himself.

MARCH 30, 1970 — THOUGHT — The "coffeebreak ritual": I have to have my coffee in the morning! It's reassuring. It ties one in with a familiar past: all is now allright with the world. "Coffeebreak" as "Angelus".

COMMENT 1987: Man loves and needs ritual. If he discards "religious rituals" like stopping his work at noon, turning his mind to God and reflecting on the tremendous mystery of His becoming man with the words of "The Angelus" then he substitutes a "secular ritual" like the "coffeebreak".

MARCH 31, 1970 — THOUGHT — There is no need for anyone to carry a cross in this day and age: we have machines to do the "heavy" and "dirty" work: evil is reduced to almost nothing, or at least to a more acceptable level.

COMMENT 1987: Technological man no longer "walks" and "works" his way through this "valley of tears" by the "sweat of his brow" but he "rides" or "flies" through it in his "labor-saving" machines. Thus his cleverness has "apparently" done away with the effects of original sin and the curse Adam got from God for his rebellion. Again, no need for a savior.

APRIL 4, 1970 — POEM — written while spending two weeks on an offshore oil rig in the Gulf of Mexico.

> "offshore oil rig" —
> steel and oil —
> yellow and black —
> valves and gauges —
> man and machines —
> no other living things —
> "laboring behemoth."
>
> "morning waters"
>   reflecting
>   sprinkled
>   sun-light:
>
>   catching
>   filtered
>   rays:
>
>   cleansing
>   nature's
>   waste:
>
>   nourishing
>   this day's
>   life.

COMMENT 1987: The "offshore oil rig" is a total manmade environment, and an apt symbol of the technological age. Crews of two to three dozen men "man" this machine which operates continuously. The crews change every week or two, but man's "creation" does not REST, unlike God's creation.

APRIL 9, 1970 — THOUGHT — How can men who "manhandle" machines, steel and plastic all day "humanly handle" other people (even one's spouse)?

COMMENT 1987: Man is changed by the kind of work he does. A farmer who works the earth all day will certainly have a different approach to life and others than one who operates mechanical devices.

SAME DAY — THOUGHT — Instead of our products coming to us today with a blessing, along the line of innumerable handlers, they have accumulated possibly dozens of "damns" and "hells".

COMMENT 1987: A pilgrim who is dedicated to the sacred, can only look with sadness on the mishandling of God's creation by unthinking man. Living a life of direct dependence upon God for his daily bread he is very conscious of pronouncing a blessing on all that his Lord supplies.

SAME DAY — THOUGHT — Maybe people want teenagers' hair and whiskers cut for the same reason they want grass and weeds cut — they cannot stand to see the wild, natural, untamed in the midst of what are supposed to be civilized areas.

COMMENT 1987: The pilgrim lives to a great degree "in the wilds" and so he tends to be sensitive to the efforts of others to "get him back" into a more "civilized" lifestyle.

APRIL 4, 1970 — THOUGHT — Those who today are fortunate to be able to see through the false gods of their forefathers and are rejecting them, seem to be in just as great a danger of setting up new gods and still being unable to see the one God.

COMMENT 1987: The pilgrim differs from the "social or political rebel" in that he has "dropped out" in order to better pursue a single-hearted search for the living God. This requires a constant attentiveness to the danger of getting "stuck" or sidetracked along the way and thus fail to succeed in his calling.

APRIL 14, 1970 — THOUGHT — One's name is a symbol of his inheritance from the past.

COMMENT 1987: If one does not like the name he has been given the reason could very well be that the person has not accepted who he is. Once one has come to terms with his past and becomes grateful for the gift of life he has been given then his "given name" can be "accepted" with thankfulness.

APRIL 15, 1970 — THOUGHT — One of the most important things on the radio is the time — every five minutes "the current time" is given.

COMMENT 1987: The pilgrim has absolutely no need to know what time it is. For him it is either dark or light. And even more importantly "now is the time of salvation" (II Cor. 6:2), and he lives in the constant awareness of the coming of the Lord.

SAME DAY — THOUGHT — People do not care about others

in today's society — advertisers and salesmen care about your money.

COMMENT 1987: It is a constant temptation for the pilgrim to slip over that fine line of distinction between the prophet and the cynic. Here the pilgrim seems to have gone over to the cynic's side.

APRIL 16, 1970 — THOUGHT — "Missalette" — everything is disposable — even the word of God.

COMMENT 1987: Since the pilgrim constantly has the Word of God abiding in his mind and heart, he naturally is very offended when he sees that word neglected, degraded and tossed aside. It pains hims to see something so precious and life giving "thrown out with the garbage."

APRIL 22, 1970 — THOUGHT — She's got love's discipline but not love's warmth.

COMMENT 1987: A pilgrim's heart is fired by love and he instinctively recognizes this love in others when he meets it. But often he meets people who have so walled up their hearts by "discipline" that none of "love's warmth" can escape to give life to others.

APRIL 25, 1970 — THOUGHT — The city is full of OTHER people.

COMMENT 1987: The pilgrim does not dwell or stay long in the city for the city is full of people who are working or shopping or recreating and since he does none of these things he is totally out of place there.

APRIL 29, 1970 — THOUGHT — People who are in a hurry usually find everyone else in their way.

COMMENT 1987: This thought came from observing cars passing slower moving cars and seeing the drivers scowling at the driver who was not "making time" or going fast enough to suit their purpose. It seems that being in a hurry invariably leads to anger, frustration and unhappiness.

MAY 2, 1970 — THOUGHT — "It's only a matter of time, sir, before someone else will have all that you now call yours."

COMMENT 1987: The pilgrim sees that all things in this world are passing, and thus observes how foolish it is to get so caught up in purchasing and accumulating so many things.

MAY 5, 1970 — THOUGHT — The new ritual for reminding people to clean up after themselves is "throwing a piece of trash in a waste can. It's no longer just a matter of "washing yourself". That problem has been solved. But there are now so many people that one's "waste" is almost directly dirtying another. Thus perhaps "throwing a piece of trash in a wastebasket" could replace the current "Lavabo" (washing of hands) at Mass. The appropriate chants would be chosen from current "litterbug" campaigns.

COMMENT 1987: Not all a pilgrim's thoughts are "holy". Sometimes he falls into some "strange thinking" as a kind of "diversion." In some sense this might help him not take himself so seriously. So this thought seems to be only "half serious" and said with "tongue in cheek".

SAME DAY — A "messiah" is he who can get it all together: that is, read all the symbolism and explain the meaning of life to everyone else through it.

COMMENT 1987: The pilgrim is far from being anything like a "messiah". Messiahs are more like your political leaders: those who have an ability for speaking in a pleasing way and able to get others to follow them. The pilgrim can "see" things clearly, but he is not called upon to articulate them so much as to live them out in a radical way.

SAME DAY — THOUGHT — There are basically two kinds of people: 1) those who "play games" with other people by selling them things or ideas, and

2) those who "play games" with their own minds and give everything away.

The latter are most likely to be the explorers and travelers: refusing to get "hung up" on some "local weed" (often offered by a woman) and settle down.

COMMENT 1987: This thought should at least cause a mild smile. It is obviously not a profound theological reflection. Rather the pilgrim seems to have again fallen over on the side of cynicism. At this point he had experienced a particular relationship which could have led to his "settling down" and giving up on his search for the personal relationship with Jesus that he desired. There indeed was a woman involved: "weed" was the curent word for marijuana, one of the effects of which is to get people to stop pursuing distant goals and just "sit down and get high."

SAME DAY — "milk and honey" — the sweetest, most delightful, nearly instantaneous transfer of total amount of raw energy to man, of all foods. When ground finely enough, everything approaches this superior quality of honey. "Chew a grain of rice 40 times."

COMMENT 1987: Some of the people the pilgrim was associating with at this time were into "health foods" and these thoughts reflect some of their theories. They probably have little scientific merit but symbolically the pilgrim is "on his way to a land of milk and honey" which means that all his spiritual and "heart" needs are met.

This concludes the Journal entries before sailing from New Orleans. These reflections show the pilgrim still very much influenced by the world, both the "straight" and the "hip" worlds in which he moved. He is still "shedding baggage" both mentally and spiritually, and it is obvious the "dirt of the earth" still clings to his spirit. He was not yet all that aware of the great things the Lord had in store for him. He only knew that he was willing to set out — alone, and as open to Him as possible — and to see what would happen. But now would come the two-week passage through the water — a spiritual crossing of the Red Sea: a leaving of the "flesh pots of Egypt" and a learning to live on "manna from heaven" in the desert pilgrimage to Jerusalem.

PART THREE: Crossing the Atlantic

The two weeks it took to cross the Atlantic Ocean from New Orleans to Barcelona became a time of quiet and solitude. There were only about ten passengers on the ship and there was no social life together except eating in the dining room three times a day. Thus the pilgrim kept to his room or went out on the deck and set up a schedule of prayer and quiet reflection.

His cabin with maid service and generous meal portions were more than what he normally sought as a pilgrim, but he thanked the Lord and rejoiced in these gifts. He enjoyed the two portholes in his cabin which he could open to leave in fresh air and the sound of the pounding waves. This helped overcome the roaring noise of the giant diesel motors which drove the ship. Thus all his "physical needs" were well taken care of and he had no work assignments or jobs to do. He had put himself into the bowels of this giant machine which was able to slowly but steadily pursue its goal of crossing the vast expanse of water.

For 15 days and nights, the droning of the powerful engines and the gentle swelling of the ocean surface, formed the context of his life. It was a totally new and different experience. Yet it seemed the perfect way to gain a firsthand knowledge of the distance that separated the old world of Europe from the new world of America. The pilgrim reflected that his grandparents and great-grandparents had made this passage many decades before — going in the other direction, of course — and they had traveled neither first class nor with such speed.

Of course the most impressive thing about the trip was the vast expanse of water. There was nothing but water: water to the right, water to the left, water to the front and water to the back. During the day the pilgrim would just sit out on the deck and watch the waves. He noticed that no two waves were exactly alike. The Lord was continually creating each one to be unique. And even though he was handicapped by his color blindness, he could distinguish the difference in the colors of the water from deep blue to deep green. He was told this was a "calm season" and as it turned out, there were no high waves or stormy seas the whole trip: just gentle bobbing or slight rocking and pitching movements.

Then there was the sky — endless sky. By day it was alive with giant billowy clouds and by night it was studded with a dazzling number of jewel-like stars. And then there was the most majestic creature and ruler of the sky, the sun. Its rising and setting were "the events" of the day. Like a king it called forth all hands to deck so that they might behold its glorious appearing and departing. This majestic ball of fire was so powerful it created the day by its presence and night by its absence.

Thus the water and the sky were appropriate symbols of the infinity of God. They were an invitation to surrender to the overpowering mystery of that which was beyond control. Man could "reshape" the land to some extent. But what was he to do with the ocean and the sky? He could do nothing but stand before them and behold them with wonder and awe. For the pilgrim it was like being present at the creation of the world as described in the book of Genesis. These marvelous creatures which God had made: the sky and the sea, the sun and the moon and the stars, the day and the night, were here to be experienced in all their pristine beauty, without the thousand and one distractions that come from living in the city of man-made structures.

And so it was truly like "starting over in life" — plunged into the chaos of the primeval waters, to be born anew — cast up onto the solid earth, upon which his feet would walk and upon which he would lay his body in sleep, till he would get to know firsthand, the Creator of all this world.

LIFE BUOY

I am a life buoy,
 anchored in the sea.
The wind and the waves,
 push me and pull me,
But I remain firm
 anchored in the sea.

I am a life buoy,
 anchored in the sea:
Most think it dull,
 not to move about
But I see all life
 from but a single spot.

I am a life buoy,
    anchored in the sea:
I know the unchanging,
    I know the changing:
And it's my role in life
    to keep them together.

— Atlantic Ocean, May 1970

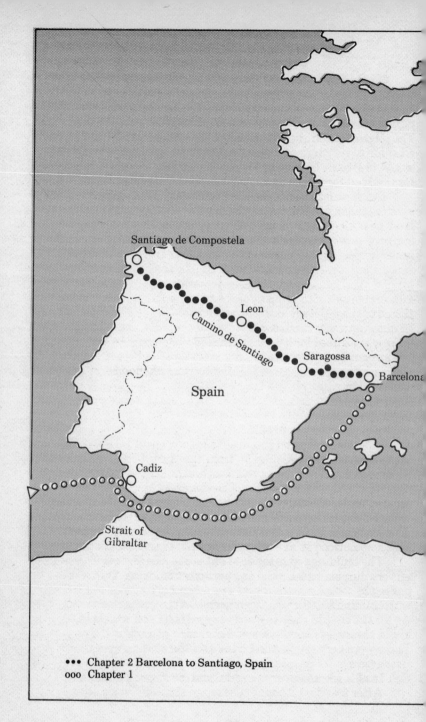

Santiago de Compostela

Camino de Santiago

Leon

Saragossa

Barcelona

Spain

Cadiz

Strait of
Gibraltar

••• Chapter 2 Barcelona to Santiago, Spain
ooo Chapter 1

CHAPTER TWO
Barcelona, Spain — Santiago, Spain
May 24 - June 20, 1970

On May 20th, after 14 days at sea, the Mar Adriatico — the ship on which the pilgrim was sailing — pulled into port at Cadiz, Spain. This was a small town that clung to the base of the cliffs at the edge of the sea on the southwestern tip of Spain. The pilgrim would spend two days here while the ship unloaded some of its cargo of wood, cement, hides and oil. Then he would finish the last leg of his sea voyage as the ship headed for the Mediterranean Sea.

But it was at Cadiz that the pilgrim got his first on the spot experience of Europe. As he walked off the ship onto the land, he noticed his legs seemed somewhat shaky. He was going very slowly and deliberately as if he expected the ground under his feet to shift and rock at any moment. Then he understood what it meant to have "sealegs". In the past two weeks his body had become accustomed to walking on a moving surface — the deck of the ship at sea. And he had become so conditioned to the different kind of coordination needed there, that he automatically carried it over on to the land, even though there was no need for it now. It amazed the pilgrim to see how the human body could take on a set way of behavior in two short weeks. He wondered if this physical phenomenon was paralleled by something in the spiritual realm, like carrying out old rituals or ways of doing things (as at sea) when the situation had completely changed (as on land) so that they no longer served their original purpose?

Now the sights and sounds of the "old world" made their first impression on the pilgrim from the "new world". Everything seemed so strange. It was not threatening; just different from what he knew in America. The change of language, which for most people would probably be the biggest point of difference, did not strike the pilgrim till he later tried to buy a stamp for a postcard. Rather, the first elements of the environment which he noticed as new were the buildings and the people.

The buildings were made of cut stone, tile and cement — all very durable, substantial and permanent looking. They were unlike the comparatively flimsy and temporary houses of wood with aluminum siding that were seen so often in the new world. As for the people, they seemed very relaxed and appeared to live in the streets, as there was a constant coming and going. There were very few automobiles and the streets were more passageways for people than roadways for mechanized vehicles. In all it seemed a very peaceful and contented atmosphere.

After two days, though, the cargo ship was ready to sail

and so put out to sea and headed for the Mediterranean. It was nighttime as the ship made its passage through the Straits of Gibraltar, but the pilgrim remained awake. He did not want to let slip by, unnoticed, the experience of a passage through this narrow channel which separated the two continents of Europe and Africa.

There was a strong wind blowing and that, in combination with the brakish waters and rocky cliffs, made a rather eerie and ominous impression. The pilgrim did not know what kind of special navigational skills were needed to sail safely through these straits, but he was aware that this was a particularly stressful point of conflicting tides and winds. He reflected on some of the historical crossings of this piece of water, especially the invasion of Europe by the Mohammedan forces during the Middle Ages when the whole of European culture and the Christian faith in the West lay exposed to possible destruction.

Another day of sailing on the peaceful Mediterranean brought the pilgrim to the end of his sea voyage. On May 24 the Spanish freighter came into the harbor at Barcelona on the northeastern coast of Spain and the pilgrim disembarked. He left his comfortable home on the sea and stood on the threshold of a walk which held few securities and many unknowns. But no fears, doubts or regrets entered his mind. His only concern was the next step he needed to take to begin his walk to Jerusalem.

It seemed most logical that one should seek out the cathedral church and there thank the Lord for safe passage and ask his blessing and guidance for what lay ahead. But the pilgrim was not at all prepared for the experience he had at the Cathedral of Barcelona. As he stepped through the doors and entered the vast spaces of the interior of the church, he felt his heart being swept up from him right to the top of the gothic arches which supported the ceiling. He had never seen or experienced anything like it. The whole interior of the church was bathed in a soft light as it filtered through the deep blue stained glass windows all along the sides of the church nave. It was like a physical prelude to the glory of heaven. The pilgrim sensed that here he had come in contact with an ancient element of his faith that he had never before experienced but was vital to answering the need of his heart.

After a brief prayer the pilgrim came back outside and stood on the steps of the ancient cathedral. He didn't know it at the time but years later he would learn that another pilgrim, St. Ignatius of Loyola, had stood on this same spot 400 years before, begging money to purchase passage on a ship sailing to the Holy Land. But the pilgrim was definitely being caught up in something very similar to the spiritual journey that the great founder of the Society of Jesus had himself experienced in his search for the meaning of life. For as he began to look around and familiarize himself with where he was, he saw signs indicating that he was not far from the famous monastery at Montserrat. This was no doubt a tourist attraction, too, but there was no reason why a pilgrim should not include it on his itinerary. And so setting off with his Bible in hand and small shoulder bag over his back, he headed on foot up the steep mountain pass to visit the Shrine of the Black Madonna.

Here the pilgrim kept mostly to himself as the place was thronged with busloads of pilgrims and tourists. As a matter of fact, he spent very little time inside the monastery chapel, as he found himself a little secluded area in the woods above the monastery — still within sight of the chapel bell tower — and there prayed and reflected on his own search. With that he felt he was ready to begin his trek across Spain.

Originally he had planned on heading South to Cordova and up to Madrid, but now he felt the Lord directing him a different way as he discovered that there was a road beginning right there in Barcelona called the Camino de Santiago (The road to the Shrine of St. James which lay on the western side of Spain). He took this as a sign that he should not so much be the tourist or visitor to historical sights (even religious ones) as a pilgrim making his way straight to his destination. Thus for the next 600 miles, he would have no need to be concerned about what road he must take or ask for next to get to his goal. All he had to say was "Camino de Santiago" or "Peligrino a Santiago" (Pilgrim on his way to the Shrine of St. James) and people would know what he was about and easily guide him on his way.

Very soon the pilgrim came to establish a sort of "modus vivendi" — a pattern of progress. Each day he would aim to walk about 30 kilometers or 18 miles in all. At this point in his journey he still took rides if offered to him (though after leaving Spain he got in the habit of refusing all such offers). So some days he made more than 30 kilometers. Each day he would try to end his walk just short of a town so that the next morning he could be there in time for an early Mass. To sleep he would look for a secluded place just off the highway among some trees or sheltering rocks as darkness drew on and there lay out his "space blanket" as a ground cloth and covering. By the grace of God there was always a place and never any trouble. Then once a week he would rent a cheap room, take a bath, change and wash out his clothes.

His daily rhythm went something like this. He would walk

about 5 kilometers (or three miles) and then rest beside the road. He could keep track of his distance by the stone markers along the side of the road which showed each new kilometer. During his rest stop he would first read the appropriate Psalms and Scriptures from the Latin Breviary he had along. Then he would eat a little bread and some fruit, cheese, oranges, etc., if he had any. Then he would practice learning how to play the soprano recorder* he had bought in New Orleans and had been led to bring along "for the company". Then he would get up and walk another 5 kilometers and repeat the same routine.

And what did the pilgrim see along the way? Actually he did not see many of the more famous museums, churches, monasteries, castles, etc. But he saw the country at a "human pace" — not in a speeding car or bus. He saw the farms and shepherds, the fields and mountains, the birds and animals, the sky and stars. He quenched his thirst from the fountains in the little villages of 100 or less families. He tasted their freshly-baked bread which he would purchase each morning or it would be just given to him free. He watched them sweep their streets in the morning with homemade straw brooms and sprinkle water on them from a bucket to keep the dust down.

He watched the little old ladies wheeling their wooden carts to the market or out to the roadside to cut fresh grass for fodder for their animals back home. He enjoyed the sight of young fellows or girls with their daily deliveries. He watched with amazement to see the women bent over their washing boards down at the "community laundry" which was often just the edge of the river. But he also noticed they used plastic buckets and modern detergents.

Also the pilgrim rejoiced in noting how the typical small town was organized. At the center of the village was the Catholic Church. There was usually a large plaza and central water fountain in front. The church tower had a clock and bells chimed the hours. It was physically so constructed that it was obvious that the church and the people's faith was the central fact around which their lives were organized. One could see the riches that past generations had lavished on the decoration of their places of worship — their churches. These physical signs, along with an experience of these simple people at prayer, responding to the acclamations of Mass and receiving from them the "sign of peace", told the pilgrim of their very real faith. The pilgrim had failed to find this kind of living faith in America, but it was the one thing which he so much desired to share in. He cried out with the Psalmist "My soul longs for the liv-

---

*a flute-like instrument

26

ing God, as a deer longs for running streams"(Ps.42:1).

The pilgrim's thirst for faith, however, was significantly paralleled by a physical thirst for water. The road he was following, the Camino de Santiago, lay through something of a desert area, and during this particular time, all Spain was suffering from a drought. Now the pilgrim had not originally provided himself with a canteen for water, but he soon found a four ounce jar and a piece of aluminum foil that could serve as a lid. This he filled up with water whenever he could and carried it in the top pocket of his plaid checkered jacket.

But before long, the hospitable Spaniards insisted on providing him with a *bota* (pigskin flask) that could hold about a quart of wine. But not finding the wine all that thirst-quenching, the pilgrim began filling it with water, and set aside the little glass jar. Often the Lord supplied water in the most amazing ways, as for example the day he saw a man out in his field and asked him for water. This man took him over to a well which was just a hole dug into the ground and not at all visible from the road or even from the field till one was right on top of it. Here the pilgrim got a drink, filled up his container, and learned how he would have to depend on others to provide for his basic needs.

But the pilgrim was thirsty for more than water for his body, and the Lord would soon quench that inner thirst too in a most unexpected way. This happened during the second week of his walk. He had been reading from the Gospel of Luke because this evangelist had cast his account of Jesus into the framework of a journey to Jerusalem. What Gospel could be more appropriate for the pilgrim to read on his own journey to the Holy City of Jerusalem?

And so, one particular day, after closing the Bible and continuing on his walk, all of a sudden it struck the pilgrim as it never had before: what Luke is writing about is true. This Jesus he is speaking about is not just a great historical person who lived 2,000 years ago in Palestine, went about preaching and doing good, was eventually crucified, rose and went to heaven. No, this Jesus is ALIVE — NOW — and He is right here with this pilgrim — in his heart. That's what the resurrection is all about. Jesus rose not so much so he could return home to His Father, but so he could remain here on earth in a new way with his disciples and followers.

The pilgrim now understood for the first time what it really meant to be a Christian. That it was not just to believe the Son of God came to earth to establish a church and then went back to heaven to await our coming home. But rather, it was to trust him as THE WAY to get back to the Father: that He became personally present and real to all who called upon his name and surrendered their whole lives into his care. And this was what the pilgrim had missed all these years. He had sensed there was something more and had set out in search of it without knowing until this moment just what it was he needed.

It would be several years before the pilgrim found the words he needed to talk about and describe this revelation and experience. But it was real enough at the moment to make a lasting impression on him. So although he did not make any journal entries around those days he would remember this grace from the Lord with an ever-deepening thankfulness and joy. It would be the sustaining power to keep him going through all the difficulties of the coming year of pilgrimage, for he now knew in an indisputable way that his Savior walked with him.

JUNE 15, 1970 — THOUGHT — Christ came to tell us about another life than the one of the flesh we know: in an age when the life of this world is so comfortable and attractive, why should anyone be interested seriously in some other kind of life? We no longer live in a "vale of tears".

COMMENT 1987: This single journal entry for the 600 mile walk from Barcelona to Santiago identifies one of the key difficulties of preaching the Gospel of Jesus Christ in our modern age. For in general people living in technological societies are satisfied with the standard of living already achieved or they place their goal just a little bit further up the social ladder, and not in a transcendent world beyond this one. If one builds an "oasis" in the vale of tears, then there is little incentive to continue on the climb up the mountain of spiritual perfection and reach the Kingdom of God.

The pilgrim arrived at his first major destination, the Shrine of Santiago de Compostela, or the Shrine of Saint James (the Apostle) on June 20. Here the pilgrim benefited by making contact with a tradition that took him all the way back to Jesus Himself, through his chosen Apostle James. For tradition had it that the body of James the Son of Zebedee (who along with Peter and John had formed an inner circle around Jesus during his ministry) was miraculously discovered by a 7th century Bishop at this very site in Spain. Realizing that this James was also the first to drink the master's cup of death and to be baptized with his master's baptism of suffering (Mk. 10:35-40 and Acts 12:1-3) the pilgrim received many graces for his own call to follow his master even to the point of being willing to lay down his life in testimony to His love.

It was here also that the pilgrim received two "souvenirs" that would prove to be very significant for his spiritual journey also. The first was the "scallop shell" which for so many pilgrims over the ages had been the sign that they had visited Santiago de Compostela. This the pilgrim proudly wore on his pack as a sign to those who knew its significance and also as a way of identifying with St. Rock[1] and all other holy pilgrims who had been led to make this very same journey of faith.

The other "souvenir" was a small, two inch high plastic, glow-in-the-dark statue of the Blessed Virgin Mary. This was handed to the pilgrim on the steps of the great Shrine by an elderly lady who appeared to just have that ministry of handing out these little images to whomever the Lord led to her. This the pilgrim eventually mounted on the peak of his aluminum hard hat which he had been wearing since working in the oil fields in Louisiana. And this would be the beginning of his realization of the special love and protection he was receiving from Mary, the Mother of Jesus.

[1] St. Rock (1295-1378) is a greatly honored saint in Italy and Spain. He is known for his care of the sick, his willing endurance of unjust imprisonment, and for his frequent pilgrimages to Rome and Santiago de Compostela. Statues in his honor show him with a pilgrim's staff, an ulcerated wound on his leg and a dog bringing him his daily loaf of bread. Many miracles have been reported as a result of his intercession and he is especially invoked against pestilence and plague.

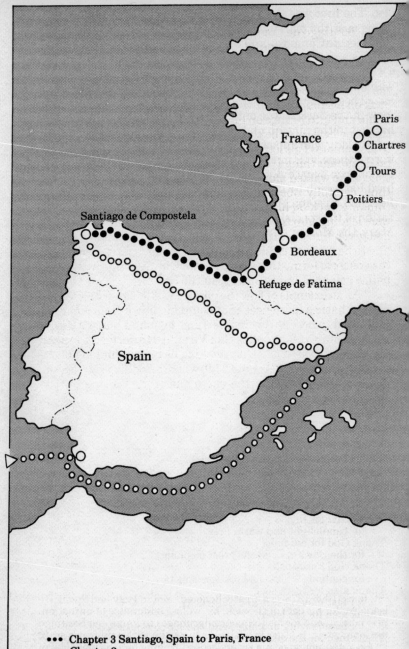

Paris
Chartres
Tours
Poitiers
Bordeaux
Refuge de Fatima
Santiago de Compostela
France
Spain

••• Chapter 3 Santiago, Spain to Paris, France
ooo Chapter 2

CHAPTER THREE
Santiago de Compostela, Spain — Paris, France
June 22 - August 3, 1970
PART ONE: Santiago — Bayonne

The pilgrim spent the next 20 days taking a route along the Northern coast of Spain that was something of a doubling back on his journey, but which was designed to get him out of Spain and into France on his way to Paris. Towards the end of this time he wrote the third of his long, detailed letters home to his parents. This letter and the next one gave evidence of two predominant things that were happening to the pilgrim at this time as he walked along. First, he was just kind of taking his time, carefully observing things around him, all the while thinking back on his past life. And secondly, these activities were leading him to a deep appreciation for what his parents had given him over the years of his life till then, and causing him to be truly grateful for all their love and care.* And one of the concrete forms this gratitude took at this time was a telephone call back to his parents in the States.

As an example of how the pilgrim was at times just out for simple, basic experiences that could be drawn from where he happened to be, one day in late June, he found himself near a small fishing village called San Vicente. He decided to spend the night on the beach. Upon waking he began thinking of the incident in the Gospel (John 21:9) where after his resurrection, Jesus had appeared on the shore and while waiting for the

---

*THANKING GOD AND MAN
Thank God for the sun;
    for its light and warmth.
Thank God for the earth;
    for fertile soil and bare mountains.
Thank God for water;
    for rushing streams and ocean depths.
Thank God for fresh air;
    for gentle winds and violent storms.
Thank God for fire;
    for candlelight and warm fires.
Thank God for animals;
    for the tiny ants and the great elephants.
Thank God for men;
    for contented souls and restless spirits.
Thank men for the wheel;
    for fast moving cars and big trucks.
Thank men for the lever;
    for labor-saving machines and speedy computers.
Thank men for the alphabet;
    for simple words and learned books.
Thank men for the city;
    for fine food and nice clothes.

— Spain, June 1970

apostles to come in from fishing, had started a fire and baked some fish. So he decided he would enter into the spirit of that scene by going down to the wharf and buying a fish. He brought it back and cooked it on an open fire he made there on the beach. It was just a way of allowing his meditation upon the resurrection of Jesus to take on a specific, concrete form.

But also the pilgrim could enjoy what at first sight could be considered a merely natural experience. The same day he took a plunge into the cold, foaming salt water of the Altantic lay in the sun drying off on the beach. This was not necessarily a profound spiritual experience, but not totally unrelated either to his soul's need to be immersed in and surrendered to the immensity of God's life (the water) and the desire to feel the healing life-giving rays of God's love (the sun) upon his soul (and body).

Thus, in his effort to hear God and become sensitive to God's working in his life, the pilgrim had turned to a deeper physical listening and awareness. He took time to notice details: to hear the sounds of the birds, to watch the activities of man and his machines, to note the movement of the tides, to observe the difference in textures of cheese and of bread (which he found to be coarse grained in Central Spain but light, crustless biscuits in the Northern areas), to be amazed by the intermingling of ox carts and diesel powered trucks on the same highway and to be amused by the buses jammed with people, their assorted baggage tied on top and everyone leaning halfway out the windows while going full speed down the road.

As it turned out, this 400 miles of his journey would be the last in which he would accept rides. He never solicited rides but at times he accepted them when freely offered, as for example by the young boy and his girlfriend, and the four secretaries on holiday from Madrid. But the most significant ride and the longest (perhaps 150 miles) was taken not far out of Santiago and was that given to him by a retired British couple returning to England after having visited the Shrine of St. James.

The pilgrim came upon them one afternoon about 2 o'clock. They had pulled their van over to the side of the road, and being accustomed to their daily "tea ritual" — even though on a camping trip — had set up their little propane stove and sitting on some rocks, relaxing amidst the beauty of the rugged mountains, were sipping their cups of tea. The pilgrim saw they were English and struck up a conversation with them. Thereupon they offered to take him to Ovieto which lay along both his and their line of travel.

What was most significant to the pilgrim, however, was that here he was sharing with people on pilgimage from a country (England) that from the early Middle Ages, had supplied an amazing number of pilgrims to the Shrine of Santiago. It was a direct linking of faith with pilgrims spanning 600 years or more. He thanked the Lord for supplying one more beautiful and surprising piece of the mosaic of faith that was beginning to fill in more and more before the eyes of the heart of the searching pilgrim.

Here are the Journal entries for this part of the pilgrimage:

JUNE 22, 1970 — THOUGHT — Animals have instinct; man has routine (less deliberate) and ritual (more deliberate). The further one gets from the beginning of either the more likely one is to loose their original spirit.

COMMENT 1987: The pilgrim here is still wrestling with the connection between "the way things are done now" and "how they got started that way". His hope was to pass beyond the way things are done now and go back to the original spirit and meaning, especially in matters of faith.

JUNE 23, 1970 — THOUGHT — Sure, one must work in this life. But the most valuable things are given to you free (faith, hope, love, friendship, etc.)

COMMENT 1987: Never far from the new pilgrim's consciousness is the charge "you're not working to support yourself", whether actually spoken by others or just part of his mental baggage. But having broken free from the compulsion to work and called a lie the dictum that with hard work one can get anything he needs to make himself happy, the pilgrim experiences life in its most important and lasting dimensions as gift and grace.

JUNE 28, 1970 — THOUGHT — I refuse to take pictures (or keep a detailed diary) for fear of missing what is there. Pictures (and words) are plentiful and cheap, but the feeling is rare and expensive.

COMMENT 1987: The pilgrim here is reflecting on the difference between a pilgrim and a tourist. A pilgrim comes humbly and stands in awe before the new places he sees and opens his heart to be nourished by the grace of the moment. The tourist comes with less sensitivity and tries to grab or capture on film the places he sees so he can take them back like trophies.

SAME DAY — THOUGHT — Realistically, considering the nature of man, it is probably ultimately better to have people safely stashed away in cars and buses than to let them walk, for to have such hordes moving from place to place on foot would wreak more damage to the land than the devasting armies of old could possibly have done.

COMMENT 1987: Again the pilgrim seems to have slipped

over onto the cynical side, or at least is jesting and poking fun at the busloads of the touring people he sees.

JUNE 29, 1970 — THOUGHT — Is my thing about pictures and writing more an indication of selfishness, of unwillingness to share myself with others, or is it more a desire to hold off, to first get it all together in one meaningful pattern, and then being selective rather than just spewing everything out that strikes my fancy, communicating something of greater value?

COMMENT 1987: The pilgrim here is revealing a bit of examination of conscience and admitting that his motives for not being like the tourists and journalists, etc., might not be all that pure. But it also shows a deep character trait in the pilgrim, namely the desire not to pass on to another anything that he cannot vouch for personally as being valid and true.

JULY 3, 1970 — DREAM — Last night I saw a man carrying a cross, He stumbled and fell. Second time I tried to decide whether to help him up or pick up his cross. I started to help him but a bystander motioned "No."

COMMENT 1987: Obviously this response of the pilgrim flowed from a part of him that did not immediately respond with compassion, but still looked for human approval of his actions.

JULY 4, 1970 — THOUGHT — Take time out from enjoying to communicate: take time out from communicating to enjoy.

COMMENT 1987: The pilgrim had spent the first 26 years of his life mainly trying to communicate. Now he was out mainly to enjoy, not just in a superficial and selfish way, but to experience deeply life and its meaning. This expresses the aspect of the pilgrim's life of "letting himself go" and surrendering to the all-embracing love of his heavenly Father, rather than centering on being the productive and faithful servant: the contemplative rather than the active.

JULY 5, 1970 — THOUGHT — Is it any wonder that people do not pay attention to sermons nor are they interested in "the way of God" when they have so come to distrust the "false words" and gimmicks of advertisers and salesmen, when they daily experience the breakdown of what was guaranteed. Nor does the authority of tradition mean much in an age when "the new is the best".

COMMENT 1987: This reflection shows the pilgrim's basic disillusionment with words as a way of communicating the overpowering reality of the Lord, and touches on how secular society conditions man against truly "hearing" the Word of God and trusting in His promise. This is perhaps one of the basic sources of the pilgrim's lifestyle which shuns words and explanations and opts for concretely living out the Gospel.

SAME DAY — THOUGHT — It is to be expected that one loses the "sense of the earth" and feels restless and alienated when he no longer tramps the earth with his feet but speeds over it on rubber tires or jet planes. When he no longer feels the steepness of a hill or mountain, but just tramps a little harder on the accelerator. When he no longer receives nourishment from water flowing out of a rock but turns a handle or pushes a button. When he no longer digs in the earth with a hoe but first experiences his food in plastic bags or on the table. When he no longer washes the dust from his clothes but throws them in a machine. When he no longer wipes real dirt from his body but scrubs invisible skin bacteria from his pale skin. When he does not feel in his hands the dampness of rainy days or the heat of a burning sun but encloses himself in climate-controlled environment?

COMMENT 1987: This needs little comment as it is fairly clear and to the point. Since the pilgrim lives close to the earth, he can better see how far technological man has withdrawn from it.

JULY 6, 1970 — THOUGHT — Who wants to be seen carrying a cross when the lighter the load — preferably a briefcase — you carry the higher your status?

COMMENT 1987: Again the pilgrim relates the Gospel mandate to pick up one's cross and follow Jesus with today's values and culture, contrasting the values held in the Kingdom of God from those held in the world.

SAME DAY — You are no longer in the hands of God but of "Allstate".

COMMENT 1987: The pilgrim sees that the world encourages man to look for security in monetary insurance whereas God demands that man look for ultimate security only in His faithfulness to being a loving Father.

SAME DAY — THOUGHT — Grant, Lord, that my life may not be taken from me before I have freely given it up.

COMMENT 1987: Here the pilgrim is aiming to imitate Jesus when he said that his life would not be taken from him but that he would freely lay it down, (Jn. 10:17f) thus showing that the whole purpose of our trial period on earth is to bring us to the point of surrendering our wills to the Father and to become completely detached from everything other than God.

JULY 7, 1970— THOUGHT — How does a society which loses its respect for the earth ever come to respect life?

COMMENT 1987: The pilgrim here shows the close connection that exists between all that God has created, from the lowliest element to man himself. To break the chain at any point harms the whole. And he likewise sees that modern society's lack of respect for human life is tied into its distancing itself from the natural life of God's creation.

SAME DAY: How does a society which is steadily losing its respect for food, throwing things away, consuming more food with less and less thankfulness — seeing eating as something to taken for granted and got in between other things — ever come to respect life?

COMMENT 1987: The pilgrim becomes aware of how hurriedly man in the electronic age engages in the "naturally sacred" act of eating and breaking bread together. Something that Jesus chose to be an instrument of giving His own divine life, has been functionalized into serving man's own limited temporal goals.

With this the pilgrim arrives at the end of his journey through Spain and he is ready to cross over into France. During the previous six weeks, the Lord had accomplished several important projects in the pilgrim's life. He had taught him about the basic rhythm of prayer and walking. He had shown him that He could take care of his physical needs just fine in spite of lack of ability to speak the native language, have a tour guide or provide himself with a full outfit of camping gear. But perhaps most importantly the Lord had begun to construct one of the two "spiritual legs" by which the pilgrim would be able to eventually pursue to completion, the call to pilgrimage. That is, the Lord had introduced him into a vital relationship with the apsotolic tradition through the apostle James and the evangelist Luke, which had in turn led him back to a firsthand experience of the master, Jesus Himself. Soon, as he passed into France, the Lord would begin construction on the other "walking support" or "leg", which would be a true devotion to His mother, Mary. These were two stabilizing factors that needed renewal in the pilgrim's life if he were ever to finish the task to which he had been called.

PART TWO: Bayonne — Paris

On July 8, 1970, the pilgrim entered France at its southwest corner. It would take nearly four weeks to walk to Paris. The passport check points were at the two ends of a small bridge that crossed over a river. The pilgrim sensed that this was a significant crossing and so he decided to sit down for an hour in the middle of the bridge to reflect on what he was doing. Others were passing quickly back and forth, on business or pleasure, and not taken up with reflecting very deeply upon their lives. But the pilgrim "sat by the stream (of Babylon) and wept" (Ps. 137), not physical tears but rather a deep groaning in his spirit that God's children were so satisfied with their lives in this exile and had forgot about their true home and the promise of the heavenly Jerusalem. He longed to arrive at his true home but he could find no like-minded companion for his travels.

Eventually he rose from his place of prayer on the bridge over the river separating the two countries and passed the customs station without even getting his passport stamped. If they were not going to make a fuss about it, he certainly was not going to pursue the issue. After all, it was a mere external legality. He was more interested in the Lord stamping his heart with his love and forming there a true reflection of His goodness.

Two days later the Lord used His Blessed Mother again to speak to the pilgrim, and show him that she would be his strong companion, (one of his two legs, as it were) so he could continue on this pilgrimage in safety. It was noontime Saturday (Mary's Day) and he was near St. Geours de Maremne, south of Bordeaux. The pilgrim heard bells announcing the time for the Angelus. So he stopped walking and said the prayers he had learned as a child (The Angelus) which recounts the annunciation of the angel to Mary that God wanted her to become the Mother of His Son.

As he started his walk again, however, he looked in the direction of the ringing bells and saw a sign which read "Ermitage de Fatima". He felt compelled to enter there, at least make a visit to the chapel. Coming in he found a group of about 15 people, mostly about his age, along with a priest saying the Liturgy of the Hours. He joined them wholeheartedly since they prayed in Latin, just as he was accustomed to doing.

After the service, one of the sisters who spoke English very well, introduced him to the priest who was the leader of the group. This priest was very cordial and took him to his office where he explained briefly that this was a small group of committed Catholics who were dedicated to spreading the message of our Lady of Fatima. He also drew for him a kind of "prophetic diagram" of what he felt God was saying to him and the direction of his life. It was in the form of a cross and indicated that after he visited Jerusalem he would return to this "Refuge de Fatima" before returning to the States. He then gave the pilgrim his own new pair of French paratrooper boots, some French money, and invited him to stay for supper and sleep there that night.

The next morning the pilgrim was off, very grateful to his heavenly mother who showed how she was looking after her son through these devoted children of hers. Though he was invited to stay on indefinitely, he really was not that tempted to end his journey there and join their community. But he was truly blessed and refreshed by this spontaneous and sincere act of Christian hospitality. And since he had no plans to detour slightly to the east and visit the famous shrine to Mary at Lourdes, he accepted this gift from his heavenly mother as her own special sign of her love for him.

It was not long after leaving the "Chapel of the Virgin" that the pilgrim experienced the first call to suffer persecution for his love of Mary. One day as he was walking along the road, a car pulled off ahead of him and an angry Frenchman came storming back to him shouting and pointing to the small plastic image of Mary that had been given to him in Santiago and which he had mounted on the peak of his aluminum hard hat. The man said it was a disgrace to wear this image like that and he ripped it off the pilgrim's helmet and threw it out into a newly plowed field along the side of the road. He then got back in his car and drove off, leaving the pilgrim free to go over and retrieve the small image and put it in his pocket till he could again mount it where it had been.

A few days after passing out of Bordeaux, the pilgrim met up with his first and only companion on his pilgrimage. As it turned out they would remain together for about six weeks — till the pilgrim left Paris on his own. His name was Pierre; he was 25 years old and spoke only French. He was a political refugee from South Africa — a man without a home or a country — though he had a French passport.

He was on foot, too, without so much as a change of clothes and said he had to get out of French Algeria because of his stand on the rights of black Africans. He said he would like to make the pilgrimage to Jerusalem also and although the pilgrim had his doubts about the wisdom of it — especially when he showed a great interest in drinking wine and courting the favor of women — the pilgrim did not send him away. He had said he would like to get a job in Paris and earn some money for the pilgrimage. The pilgrim put it in the Lord's hands and trusted that in time his true intentions and commitment would become clear. There was very little communication between him and the pilgrim: they mainly marched along in silence, speaking only about essentials like food, water, rest and direction.

About the half way point between the Spanish border and Paris, in his fourth letter home (July 18) the pilgrim expressed what proved to be a rather prophetic utterance concerning his own life and vocation. He wrote: "I think God has something greater in mind (than ordained diocesan priest); that is, He is asking an even greater sacrifice of me, and that will involve giving up even the respectability of a formally organized religious life. When one seeks eternal happiness, one may have to endure the scorn that may be attached to the way of life that leads you to that happiness. That way for me is not yet clear or permanent but right now it involves tramping through Europe like a pilgrim."

The pilgrim had also come to a great sense of detachment from his own will and from any need to plan and arrange his future. He surrendered his life totally into God's hands. It didn't matter to him if he got to Jerusalem or returned to the U.S.: whether he lived a long life or died today. His only concern was to "seek first the Kingdom of God." In his letter home, he said: "The substance of my life has become constant union with God through the aid of the Breviary, Mass and Rosary. The Scriptures are truly my daily food, and the only thing I find ultimately worth living for." He had found "the peace of soul that comes from discovering and following the will of God ever more faithfully."

He continued on in his letter: "most people are caught up in the cares of this life and do not take the time to slowly meditate on the Gospels. If only we knew what the Scriptures were really asking: what our faith is really demanding in its most radical calling, I dare say one would scarcely recognize the Catholic Church as what we know it to be today. For years we hear the message, read and sermonize on it and it never has much effect. Beware of allowing it to sink in; to really take it seriously; to spend much time pondering its message; it may mean a radical change of thought and life."

It was at this point that the pilgrim found himself philosophically and theologically changing from a "liberal to a conservative" in the area of moral responsibility. That is, he set aside the heavy emphasis on seeing things as determined by heredity and social environment and set squarely down on personal responsibility with its concomitant acceptance of guilt for sins and praise for virtuous action. This was perhaps tied in with the pilgrim's daily reading and meditation upon *The Imitation of Christ* by Thomas á Kempis, but it was no doubt also aided by the fact that the pilgrim was at this time experiencing more control over his life, thoughts and actions than at any other time before. And thus he came to understand that he and no other was responsible for what he did or did not do.

One other event before Paris that was significant for the pilgrim's growth in faith was his arrival at Chartres, some 50 miles southwest of Paris. At Chartres the great cathedral was dedicated to Our Lady, so she was still showing her motherly concern for the pilgrim's spiritual progress. As the pilgrim and his companion approached Chartres from the south, the twin cathedral spires already were visible from a point beginning about five miles away. So the pilgrim on foot was inspired and encouraged by being able to fix his eyes on his goal for the last two hours of his walking.

Later the pilgrim learned that this cathedral has for centuries been a favorite pilgrimage site for young people who walk in large groups to this shrine every year. Thus the pilgrim joined multitudes of other pilgrims who had walked in these same footsteps also seeking a deeper commitment to the Lord whose earthly house they made the goal of their walking.

As the pilgrim entered the gates of this house of God and of his mother, he experienced again a tremendous reinforcement of his Catholic Faith. These stones almost literally "shouted out praises to the Lord" (Lk. 19:40) even if the Lord's disciples had been silenced or spoke in an unintelligible way. This edifice of stone conveyed a sense of faith and love coming through those who had spent their whole lives, over a period of three centuries, to build this house to the Lord and worship Him in it, and to honor their mother Mary. These stones did this for the pilgrim now, centuries after the fact (of building the Cathedral and of Jesus' death on Calvary) in a way that books, reading and personal testimony had never been able to do for the pilgrim. The faith of the People of God who had gone on before, was being renewed in his heart now through these memorials in stone, just as the Apostle Thomas came to believe when Jesus presented him with the evidence of his wounds. So our Lord was continuing to strengthen the "leg of devotion to Mary" as He rebuilt the pilgrim's faith in Himself. Now the pilgrim would be able to faithfully complete his earthly pilgrimage. The following are the Journal entries for this stage of the walk through France:

JULY 7, 1970 — THOUGHT — "Bread" — that's for children — too fattening and I have to watch my weight."

COMMENT 1987: The pilgrim practically lives on bread and water as these form his staple food each day. Here he reflects on the contrast between his deep appreciation and thankfulness for bread and modern man's disdainful comment which he paraphrases for them.

JULY 21, 1970 — THOUGHT — Possibly "guided tours" are the only way today for acquainting large masses of people with the origin of processes and the things that go to make up one's daily life. "Guided Tours" — this is rather a superficial and impersonal knowledge when compared to the past, but may be all that's left — it might have something to say about the masses' knowledge of God and their awareness of their origin in Him.

COMMENT 1987: This reflection again indicates the pilgrim's personal need to go deeper into the origin of things than the average person who is satisfied with a quick "tour". But while he is willing to accept this state of affairs in the areas of secular knowledge, he is not ready to accept this superficial knowledge when it comes to knowing God, for here he knows God Himself wants much more.

SAME DAY: — THOUGHT — A possible interpretation of the Scripture passage, "Let your speech be yes, yes, and no, no" (Mt. 5:37): answer briefly and without complicated qualifications — these are so often the result of *an effort* to appear learned or a desire to impress.

COMMENT 1987: The pilgrim lives in a world of silence in the sense that he does not carry on normal conversation with others around him. Thus he is much more sensitive to words and how they are used.

JULY 22, 1970 — THOUGHT — "Institutional memory" — a form, a structure, an action which embodies an original valid insight but no longer recalls that insight to the person performing the action.

COMMENT 1987: The pilgrim here coined the phrase "institutional memory" to describe aspects of his Christian heritage that he was taught to keep and accept, for which he could find no meaning or understanding when he examined them more carefully.

JULY 24, 1970 — THOUGHT — The moon and stars no longer rule the night — electricity does, by giving us light.

COMMENT 1987: The pilgrim again, living close to nature, framing his day by the rising and setting of the sun, comes to know these natural creatures in a deeply personal and appreciative way. This is in stark contrast with the normal experience of modern man whose daily life is framed by manmade structures.

JULY 29, 1970 — THOUGHT — The purpose of memorization? Wise men found it nearly impossible to communicate to children the real meaning of life. They decided the only thing left to do was to get them to memorize certain key formulas with the hope that some day "the light may dawn" and that having "the words" they might be able to fit them to their experiences.

COMMENT 1987: As the pilgrim begins to experience anew the things that he had been taught to believe in as a child, he begins to be thankful for the words that now help him articulate his experience, and projects back to the wisdom of his ancestors who required him to "memorize".

SAME DAY: — THOUGHT — The reason for hierarchy? When you walk a narrow and difficult path, you cannot walk side by side, but must go single file.

COMMENT 1987: Being so familiar with walking the pilgrim naturally looks at things through this experience, and here comes up with a simple explanation of the hierarchical nature of the church which in his day was so analyzed, questioned and denied. His experience of walking seems to be cutting through a lot of intellectual haziness and enabling him to peacefully accept Scriptural truths.

SAME DAY — DREAM — After many rehearsals, I came to the dress rehearsal and I was the leading character and the first to speak. But I forgot the scene completely, so I looked for a director or prompter, but there was none. I shouted, "I don't even know my name in this play: how can I act if I don't know who I am?" So I just started to act naturally, doing what came to me and the rest of the cast joined in — choreography and all. As I went along I recalled parts of the play that I had rehearsed.

COMMENT 1987: This dream could be taken as a parable on the life of the pilgrim as he came to the end of his seminary training and was just ready to "make his appearance" to lead God's people on "the stage of life". It even notes his "identity crisis," and shows how he began to "act out a new play" which, however, still depended on the original one for bits and pieces.

JULY 30, 1970 — THOUGHT — All of man's work seems directed towards making things easier i.e., faster, with less effort — to prolong pleasure.

COMMENT 1987: The pilgrim, with his eyes focused on eternity, looks past the temporary goal of "pleasure". Yet he is able to see how much of modern man's time is consumed on this lesser goal, which, in turn, prevents him from "enjoying" the things of the Lord.

SAME DAY — THOUGHT — "He whose stomach is full does not think about food: he whose head is full, does not think." He who is hungry or disciplines his appetites, apreciates every bit of food: he who clears his mind or disciplines his thoughts, then has room to think. People can get "fed up" by hearing too much about religion.

COMMENT 1987: The pilgrim here expresses the reason he felt he could not "think" about God during the long 20 years of his education: namely, his head was too full of other people's ideas. His pilgrimage was a way of discipline or fasting, to "take off some excess weight," so he could begin to live as his Creator had intended him: fully conscious and appreciative of Himself and all His gifts.

AUGUST 3, 1970 — Our number one enemy is no longer the devil, but dirt.

COMMENT 1987: A somewhat cynical remark and really overstated, but still containing a grain of truth and like a pin could prick the conscience of today's fanatics about cleanliness.

SAME DAY — TV brings us an event which happened last year or a quarter of a million miles away. The liturgy brings us an event which happened 2,000 years ago. Some day TV may recapture events from long ago. TV can break the bonds of space and time, but it cannot break the bond of death.

COMMENT 1987: Here the pilgrim lays bare the basic powerlessness of the "secular sacrament" which is TV and the infinite superiority in the realm of the Spirit of the Church's Sacraments which make each succeeding generation of believers present at the redemptive sacrifice of Christ, especially as summarized on Calvary. Even should man "recapture" visually and audibly Christ's historical life, it will still take the gift of faith from the heavenly Father to enable the man viewing it to "see" any more than most of those present in Jerusalem on that fated day saw.

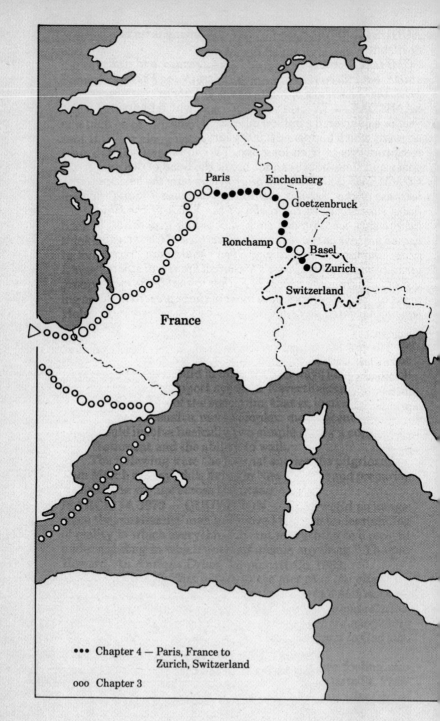

Paris

Enchenberg

Goetzenbruck

Ronchamp

Basel

Zurich

Switzerland

France

••• Chapter 4 — Paris, France to
        Zurich, Switzerland

ooo Chapter 3

44

CHAPTER FOUR
Paris — Zurich
August 4 - October 27, 1970
PART ONE: One Month in Paris

The first thing the pilgrim did upon arriving in Paris on August 3 was to look up the Youth Hostel whose address had been given to him and his companion by a nun outside of Chartres. The name of the Hostel was Association Maurice Maignen, and it was located at 99 Rue de Lourmel. Finding the Association was no difficulty, for his companion was a native Frenchman and he could easily ask directions.

Upon arriving at the Hostel, they found that it was run by a priest, and only cost $1.60 per person per day and this included *petit dejeuner,* a daily breakfast of a large bowl of hot sweetened milk, chocolate or coffee, with bread, butter and jam. This seemed to be a good arrangement and plans were tentatively made to stay for a month. Thus after two and a half months of walking and laying his head down in a different place on the earth practically every night, the pilgrim would — for the next five weeks — have a room to which he could return each night to sleep.

He and his companion were in room number 8 on the fourth and top floor. The modest room had freshly painted pastel yellow walls, a high ceiling, large windows on the east side, clothes cupboards, two single pipe-frame beds with coil springs, two desks with chairs, and a separate room with sink, mirror and closet. It was very much like the rooms the pilgrim was used to in his seminary days, though this one was much larger. He guessed that those seminary rooms were modeled on just such European rooms as this one in which he was now staying.

And so it happened that the Lord arranged to give the pilgrim a taste (unbeknownst to him at the time) of the life of a "poustinik". That is, in ceasing temporarily from his journeying he would set up a daily rhythm of prayer and study until the Lord called him forth again to continue on his way. Thus he would pray the Psalms according to each hour as specified in the Church's official prayer known as the Divine Office. These he read from the Latin Breviary he carried. Then like monks from the time of St. Benedict in the 6th century, he would engage in *"Lectio Divina"* or "spiritual reading" by taking a short portion of the Gospel to read each day as well as a chapter from *The Imitation of Christ.* He prayed the Rosary and attended Mass each day at 7 p.m. in the chapel which was part of the Youth Hostel.

In addition to this schedule of prayer, the pilgrim would

usually spend each morning writing up his reflections on the spiritual journey he had been on for the past three years. It was a kind of autobiography which he thought he might send back to the seminary where in 1967 he had finished his four year course in theology. And though he did complete the writing to his satisfaction, he never did send it back. In this long 9 page letter which he wrote "in the spirit of praising God for his mercy and faithfulness" he traced his journey from an unquestioned faith during his first 22 years of life, through the probing that led to doubt during his last four years of seminary life, to his coming to a sense of peace and identity now three years later. He showed how he sought with all his being for something that was permanent and stable to which he could commit his life and make this the only goal of his life. He recounted how he found the answer in the Rocky Mountains where His heavenly Father finally showed him that He was the Creator of all things and that He alone satisfied the craving for the permanent and unchanging ground worthy of a lifetime commitment. (A copy of the full text of this letter appears in Appendix II, A-3.)

In the afternoons, the pilgrim would then take a walk through the streets of Paris, visiting a church or two, though usually ending up and spending most of his time at our Lady's Church, Notre Dame. At the cathedral he would spend his time either inside praying or outside in the adjoining park (where he eventually came to realize one was expected to pay money for using the seats, or the street people here were just devising their own simple little scheme of getting a few pennies in exchange for some homemade "tickets" that were given in exchange.)

Spending so much time outside in the park just gazing at the magnificent gothic structure dedicated to the Mother of God, the pilgrim found himself beginning to sketch it in pencil from various angles as a way of taking the truth of which it spoke, and the faith of its builders, into his own heart. Inside he would pray quietly or join in the beautiful singing of the Mass or Vespers on Sunday, as the case may be. He knew enough French from the year and a half he spent studying it in the seminary to pray and sing along at Mass, and he was most edified by the devotion and wholehearted participation he saw in the assembled congregation.

On one of his afternoon tours, the pilgrim made a particularly significant visit. It was to the famous church dedicated to the Sacred Heart (Sacre Coeur) on Montmastre, where again he would (unknowingly at the time) make another connection with Ignatius of Loyola. For Ignatius had in this very place in the 16th century, taken his first religious vows with a small group of companions who would eventually be known as the Companions or Society of Jesus — the Jesuits. And even though the pilgrim would not be taking formal religious vows here, he did come to a clear understanding that his three-year search for a radical, total and ultimate commitment had ended. For he had found that the Lord his God was the one solid basis upon which to anchor his life. He was now willing to dedicate the rest of his life to listening to His word at all costs — no matter what others thought or said.

One of the things the pilgrim was very thankful for during his month's stay in Paris, was that it provided him a place where he could receive mail from his family back in the States. Even though he was being tremendously strengthened and built up on a spiritual level, he still experienced the need for contact and communication on a human level. As a "stranger in a strange land," not knowing the language and not having a close companion with whom to converse in English, he read and treasured the letters sent to him at the American Express Office by his mother and brothers, and even a letter from the chaplain priest at the Refuge de Fatima. They were as much food and sustenance to him as the physical bread was for his body and spiritual bread was for his soul. And what did he do for physical bread? The following incident will show how the Lord could take a possibly embarrassing or even troublesome situation and turn it into a humorous anecdote.

The pilgrim did not see any reason why he should spend his money on buying bread when he could just go to the back of any restaurant and collect good pieces of bread that had been thrown out. One day the gendarmes accosted him and told him to empty out his bag for them to examine its contents. As he dumped out his sack full of chunks of bread, his flute or recorder came tumbling out also. They exclaimed: "Oh, a musician" and being satisfied that he was not a criminal or a thief, wished him well and departed the scene.

In all, then, this month in the capital city of France was a time that allowed the pilgrim to see more clearly that his particular witness as a Christian was to be a pilgrim and point dramatically to the fact that all this world is passing away and there is a need to keep one's eyes on what lies ahead in eternity. He had caught a glimpse of the glory of the Father that lay ahead, and everything else that he and most other men hold as important and valuable in this world, appeared as dust and mere straw. His place in the Body of Christ had taken a dramatic shift. Rather than being a pastoral minister as he had been preparing for all those years in the Seminary, the Lord had called him to be a sharp sign of contradiction, pilgrimaging through life as though already enjoying the final state of blessedness. Although he could not assume the title of "prophet" he was certainly being called to a "prophetic lifestyle." And as the pilgrim wrote in one of his letters home, "God had heard his prayers, poor and infrequent as they were — hardly knowing what he was asking for. He not only heard, he read his heart and the true desires hidden there, and graciously bestowed His own gifts over and above anything the pilgrim had ever imagined."

While in Paris the pilgrim made the following journal entries:

AUGUST 11, 1970 — THOUGHT — Artists and creative people must live on the fringes of their societies if they are to have a special vision: they cannot become too entangled in the mass illusions.

COMMENT 1987: The pilgrim in some small sense is a "religious artist" in that the Holy Spirit makes of him a "visual image" of a spiritual truth that is not easily grasped through the ordinary symbols that God's People have available to them in their liturgy and traditions. This call sets him apart in some very obvious ways from church life as it is ordinarily lived and may even be viewed by the less reflective among God's children as "on the fringe" rather than "at the very heart" which is where the pilgrim's life should put him.

AUGUST 14, 1970 — THOUGHT — He who does not know the way or trust his own knowledge of the way or his ability to travel it makes the most willing follower. He who thinks he knows the way, feels he can get there himself, isn't interested in getting there, would rather go another way or does not trust the one who wishes to lead him, and is unwilling to follow another.

COMMENT 1987: The Christian life is basically one of following the Lord Jesus. Although the "lone pilgrim" might appear not to be following anyone but doing his own thing and seeking his own way, to the extent that he is an authentic Christian, he has a deep sense of "being led" by the Holy Spirit to walk in the footsteps of Christ. Especially in a foreign country he senses the need to depend on the Lord for daily guidance. Thus the Christian pilgrim needs to develop a humble sense of dependency upon the Holy Spirit to show him the way.

AUGUST 16, 1970 — THOUGHT — Since people no longer want smoke (incense) thrown at them, perhaps we should spray them with deodorant. The image of holiness or sanctity has changed from one of veiled mystery (the draped body) to one of frank statement (the revealed, almost naked body).

COMMENT 1987: The pilgrim here is reflecting on the loss of the sense of mystery by his contemporary technological society which holds nothing sacred or beyond questioning and analysis. He laments the fact that respect for and comfortableness with the unknown which is essential for a deep and living faith in the true God, has been replaced by disrespectful probing with weak human tools (human reasoning) into that which is by nature greater than man and not able to be "possessed" by his greed.

AUGUST 23, 1970: — THOUGHT — "Vanity of vanities, and all is vanity" — can one with a radically eschatological perspective ever be seriously involved in building the world? That's where I'm at now!

COMMENT 1987: The pilgrim here succinctly states the difference in roles within the Body of Christ, the Church, that is the difference between the call to be a pilgrim and the call to be a pastoral minister. The pilgrim points to the reality of the life to come, the pastoral minister points to the eternal significance of the world at hand. Both are true and both are needed. The pilgrim thought for years he was called to the latter, but now finds himself immersed in the former. He wonders how long his call to pilgrimage will last.

AUGUST 24, 1970: — THOUGHT — "Some day there will be so many people in the world with so much leisure time who want to travel, that only the most privileged with special permission will be able to leave their cells (homes). There will come the time when a change will be made from trying to interest people in traveling and touring, to trying to discourage them from physically moving about. The effort of advertisers will then be to sell people on the advantages of staying in their cells and viewing any place in the world they want on their "holovision screens".

COMMENT 1987: The pilgrim here is playing the role of science fiction writer by attempting to project a trend he sees developing in the present and drawing out of it an extreme conclusion. He is of course saddened by the prospect for he sees how much of life his brothers and sisters are missing even now through the acceptance of verbal descriptions and light images put together by someone else. And what disturbs him most is that mankind thereby not only forfeits a personal and experiential contact with the created world, but that he also loses a desire and ability to have a personal communion with his Creator and Lord.

AUGUST 29, 1970: — THOUGHT — "I think I shall be in the United States when the Third World War breaks out. I shall survive, but many will die."

COMMENT 1987: This does not seem to be so much a prophetic word from the Lord about what is going to happen as a gut feeling about the seriousness of the spiritual darkness which lies about and the personal assurance of God's love and protection that the pilgrim experiences and which not even the ultimate physical horror of war can dampen.

SAME DAY — THOUGHT — "I wonder if the laity at any time in history had the custom of offering incense in their churches as they now light candles, or has this always been the prerogative of our priests? (Pagan laity did offer incense to their gods.)

COMMENT 1987: Although on the surface this might seem to be just a bit of idle historical inquisitiveness, perhaps it is part of the pilgrim's wrestling with the difference between the "religious state" and the "lay state" and the implications of that for one's spiritual life and prayer forms.

SAME DAY — THOUGHT — "The idea of there being an "eternal law" which governs all things now makes more sense to me as I become more sensitive to powers around me that are not created or controlled by man. I understand better now how in former ages men attempted to get themselves back in rhythm and harmony with that all pervading order and that this is how they hoped to achieve peace. None ever succeeded completely, but the saints and wise people came close: from this perspective every single action and thought of a person's life had a "most proper form", a way in which it came closest to conforming to the divine intention, and how it could best fit into its assigned place in the cosmic order. Ritual and liturgy in this framework were man's attempt to come as close as possible through symbols to the ultimate reality.

COMMENT 1987: The pilgrim had struggled back in his seminary days with the concept of "the natural law". It had never made any sense to him then. Now he sees that perhaps it didn't make any sense because at that time he was locked into a one-dimensional universe because he had never experienced anything beyond what man had made and he could control. It wasn't till he broke through that barrier and discovered the world of the heart and of the Spirit that he could begin to know what was meant by "natural law" or even "supernatural law". Once that was discovered as real, and as desirable, life became "sacred" and was no longer just "secular" and the pilgrim experienced a real desire to conform his life to that higher law.

SEPTEMBER 2, 1970: — THOUGHT — To change something one must "get inside" it, but to know something one must get "outside it."

COMMENT 1987: The pilgrim here is reflecting on the current

wisdom that was going about in the days of change and renew-
al in the Catholic Church after Vatican Council II. He has come
to see that the common wisdom which says "stay in the church
and change it" is not sufficient. One must somehow get "out-
side" it, that is step back and get a more objective view, to really
"know" it and therefore work for the proper changes. A pilgrim
"steps outside it" in this sense since he is not intimately in-
volved in its day-to-day running.

PART TWO: PARIS — ENCHENBERG

As the month of September began to count off its days,
the pilgrim felt a strong urging to be up and on his way. Even
though his would-be "companion" wanted to work for a few
more weeks, he sensed it was time to be back on the road. To
stay in Paris any longer would be to risk missing the Lord's will,
and he could ill afford to do that.

On September 8 he left Paris and began the 200-mile walk
directly east that would take him into the region of Alsace Lor-
raine which carried many fond memories because of all his
paternal grandmother had told him in the 29 years that he had
so far known her. This was her birthplace and where she had
lived till the age of 16 when she left to come to America. He had
written ahead to his cousins who still lived there and told them
he was leaving Paris. Then from Verdun he had sent a card saying he should arrive in their little village of Enchenberg in three
days. He had to trust the Lord with what they might be thinking about this cousin from America, the land of the rich, coming to them so humbly on foot. Nevertheless, he had met one of
his cousins, Bernard, several years before when he had come for
a visit to the States, and so all of them would not be total
strangers.

Thus leaving "Pierre" in Paris to work for another month
and with an agreement to come by train to Enchenberg at the
end of three weeks, he set off from the big city to walk through
the departments of Marne, Meuse, and Moselle, heading for the
area just east of Sarreguemines which lay near the German
border. The following were some of his reflections on that leg
of his journey.

SEPTEMBER 10, 1970 — PRAYER — "Thanks be to God for
bread, the fruit of the earth, of the work of human hands and
of man's machines."

COMMENT 1987: The pilgrim here takes the prayer over the
gifts said by the priest at Mass during the Offertory time and
makes his own addition, which, living in a society that no
longer makes its bread or communion wafers by hand, he feels
should include giving credit to the machines which contribute

to man's daily livelihood.

SAME DAY — "The most complete following of Christ would involve just lying down in ecstasy without moving, until one died — total union with God, having no other intention but to be completely absorbed in His reality, not even moving a finger. Why did Christ not do this? Was he always TOTALLY absorbed in prayer to His Father?

COMMENT 1987: This reflection is somewhat embarrasing to the pilgrim 15 years later as it shows a heavy leaning to a non-Christian Eastern philosophy, and makes judgments about Christ through that way of thinking. Although there is room for "ecstasy" in our Christian experience, the only mention of it in the Gospels was on Mount Tabor when Peter, James and John just wanted to stay there with their glorified Lord. Although there may be momentary experiences of God's glory now on earth and a few of God's specially chosen servants share a mystical union now, it seems the time for full ecstasy as a way of life for most of God's people must wait for the other side of death.

SEPTEMBER 17, 1970 — THOUGHT — The Psalms are for "poor people," not for the rich and satisfied!

COMMENT 1987: The pilgrim of course was nourishing his spirit daily on the praying of the Book of Psalms in the Bible. As he identified with the author of these heartfelt songs, he realized that they can only be authentically uttered by one who recognizes his poverty, powerlessness and need. The rich and satisfied have no need to cry out to God.

SAME DAY — THOUGHT — Questioning can lead either to greater understanding or to doubt.

COMMENT 1987: The pilgrim is here reflecting back on his experience of his last four years in the Seminary where questioning was the "order of the day". Although it was meant to lead to greater understanding and a more solid and personal faith, it had in his case led to confusion, uncertainty and doubt. By the grace of God, however, it was now leading back to faith.

SAME DAY — THOUGHT — "I believe in God the Father almighty, Creator of heaven and earth." How can those who do not KNOW the heavens and the earth but only the city of man, KNOW God? If they do not believe in these visible things (signs and symbols) how can they believe in the invisible world?

COMMENT 1987: Here the pilgrim has hit a deep and persistent theme of his analysis of the cause of the erosion of the Christian faith in his contemporary technological world — namely alienation from the physical world of nature. Basically he is saying: if man knows firsthand the works of God, he will come to know God Himself. But if all he knows is the works of man, he will not come to know God.

SEPTEMBER 18, 1970 — THOUGHT — "Pictures" cheapen the reality which is photographed by making the subject more readily available to a larger public with less effort than would have been needed to see the subject in person. The subject is not as DEEPLY appreciated. It may have a wider range of being "known" but it is a more superficial knowledge. A picture may be worth a thousand words but BEING THERE is worth a thousand pictures.

COMMENT 1987: The pilgrim never seems to let go of this subject of taking pictures. It seems he is so dedicated to "firsthand experience" and "in-depth" that he has little use for "the secondhand experience" of pictures and those who indulge in them.

SEPTEMBER 20, 1970 — THOUGHT — For this reason God became man: to reveal man's unity with each other and with God: to break down the walls of ignorance and hatred and envy which had been built up.

COMMENT 1987: Although this could be interpreted in a Christian and Biblical manner it shows a rather Eastern and rationalistic bias. To bring it more fully in line with orthodox teaching about why Christ came to earth, one would have to include both the love of God and the sin of man.

Late in the afternoon of September 23, the pilgrim arrived in the little village of Enchenberg. As he passed the largest building in the town, the Catholic Church, he felt drawn to make a visit there. He prayed that he would be open to what the Lord intended to teach him here during his stay with his relatives. Coming out of the church he continued up the road. Up ahead on his right, he soon spotted a tall thin man eagerly looking his way and acting as though he was trying to identify the approaching pilgrim. Immediately the pilgrim sensed this was Mr. Rimlinger (Etienne), his grandmother's oft-spoken of cousin, and the head of the house where he intended to stay.

And so it was. The pilgrim's seminary courses in German had not been able to give him much facility in speaking the language, but that was no great barrier when Etienne warmly welcomed him with a hug and greetings in German. He then took the pilgrim to his modest but comfortable two-story home and introduced him to the rest of the family, his wife and five children ranging in age from 7 to 25. For the next two and a half weeks, this would be his adopted family and he would be given the privilege of living with a beautiful, simple farming family that was experiencing a change from a German into a French culture and from a self-sufficient way of life into a technological and independent way of life.

The pilgrim was given a comfortable bed in a spare guest room and much of the time over the next few weeks he would spend alone there typing up the rough draft of the nine-page article he had written in Paris the month before. Also when alone he would write letters back to the States and even made several tape recordings to send back to his family and friends. In addition he would continue his habit of daily playing the recorder, and he found this quite delighted the family. He would play both traditional melodies and ones that just came to him spontaneously. One that became a favorite he named "Complaint in the Night" as it seemed to express the groaning of his spirit as he cried out for more of the light of Christ.

But the rest of his time, the pilgrim shared in the daily life of the family. One of the first family activities in which he shared was the gathering of the potato harvest. They had planted nearly an acre of potatoes on the other side of town in an area where each family seemed to have its own field. This was a new experience for the pilgrim, but one he thoroughly enjoyed. He loved being out in the fields, working with his hands, picking the raw fruit of the earth. He marveled God had given the earth the power to produce food for man and beast.

Lunch out in the fields would be a "picnic" or "barbecue" as Bernard called it in translation and it was a very special moment. For at noon time the Angelus bell tolled from the parish church in Enchenberg, and although the workers did not bow their heads in prayer, the pilgrim could not help but recall the famous painting of the man and woman in the field, pausing to say the Angelus. As his thoughts turned to the Lord, he recalled all those who had gone on before him in the faith, joining him with that humble virgin who responded to that "First Angelus": "Behold the handmaid of the Lord: be it done unto me according to thy word."

At the day's end, 20 large sacks had been filled with potatoes and these were brought back to the house in a flat bed wagon pulled by a tractor. Then they were dumped into a storage bin in a building which served as the barn for their two cows. The potatoes would be food for the family and for the animals. Actually the barn had a common wall with the house, so the cows were like part of the family.

The daily life of the family naturally centered on the meals. In the morning Etienne would get up about 5 a.m., go out to the barn and get a pail of fresh milk from the cows. This he would bring in and sit on top of the wood stove so that it could come to a boil (thus "pasteurizing" it to some extent). Then the other members of the family would come into the kitchen, dip a bowl of hot milk for themselves and add to it sugar, or chocolate or coffee. Into this they would dip chunks of French bread and eat it with butter, jam, honey, sausage and bacon.

Noontime was the big meal with meat, potatoes, salad, wine or beer, and fruit. They had a plentiful supply of an unusually large vegetable which the pilgrim only knew of by name up till that time. It was called a rutabaga, but it was the source of an amusing family story that had been passed along to him by his grandmother. For she had told him that his uncle Steve, her brother, so much enjoyed these vegetables that the family began to call them "Uncle Steves".

At four o'clock, when the children came in from school, everyone in the house joined together in the kitchen to share the events of the day and have a large cup of coffee, bread and sandwich spreads. Then there was a final time to eat at about 8:00 p.m. when a large bowl of hearty vegetable or meat soup was served. Thus there was no need for snacks, fast foods or raids on the refrigerator. And meals were family-building events.

The Rimlinger household did not have a television, though they did have a radio which was only turned on for short periods of time each day, just to get the news. It was not allowed to play continuously, either as background music or for entertainment. There was too much of a serious atmosphere maintained in the home for that kind of use.

Thus there was a very real peace and quiet around the house. Oh, there were sounds, many sounds, but these were all made by life-sustaining activities like those made by the animals (the crowing of roosters, the mooing of cows, the meowing of cats or the barking of dogs) or by human beings (talking, hammering, singing, etc.). Occasionally one would hear a tractor hauling a load of wood, a chain saw cutting logs for their wood stoves; but there was no proliferation of machines, toys and gadgets, nor the waste of power exemplified by young drivers squealing tires or aimlessly riding motorbikes over the land.

One of the farming activities that the pilgrim had never imagined before was going out to one of the meadows and cutting fresh grass with a sickle bar on the tractor and gathering in a large pile of fresh grass to feed the cows. This saved having to take the cows out to pasture — the pasture was brought to them. Once there was no longer green grass available, no doubt they had to rely on hay to feed the cows.

Each of the family members did what he was able to do best to make the pilgrim-cousin feel welcome. The father was in charge and oversaw the general life of the family to make sure everything was fitting together and running smoothly, though he spent most of his time on farming chores. The mother remained quietly in the background carrying out her husband's decisions and making sure that all the children were doing their parts while she herself did most of the work cooking and cleaning inside the house.

The father and mother had to see that the pilgrim was taken around to visit all the relatives. They even outfitted him with "formal clothes" — a sport jacket to dress up in to make the visits with them. Thus he visited the butcher in Enchenberg, the shoemaker in Bitch who put new heels on his French paratrooper boots, and the priest Father Joseph who was also a third cousin. Included on the tour was the village of Goetzenbruck about five miles away where the pilgrim's grandmother had been born, baptized, raised, and received her First Communion. The church there was visited and her home was pointed out — it still stood and was in good repair, though no longer in the family. A side trip from there included the family burial plot in the cemetery in the village of Altorn.

The oldest brother was Raymond and he gave of himself very generously to the care of the pilgrim, even though he taught school during the day and being just recently married lived away from the family. Since he had his own car he took the pilgrim twice to Strasbourg, which lay about 60 miles to the east in order to visit various churches. Actually this would be the pilgrim's only time he would spend in Germany proper. On one of these visits, he bought the pilgrim a khaki-colored, full length hooded army coat in preparation for the winter weather which lay ahead.

Also he shared with the pilgrim that he had been in the seminary for a short time and upon learning of the pilgrim's interest in reading the Scriptures, gave him his Greek/Latin New Testament from his Seminary days. His wife Françoise, whom the pilgrim inadvertantly kept embarassing by mispronouncing her name so that he was calling her as though she were a boy, eventually gave him a piece of her wedding veil to carry with him on his pilgrimage. Once he got to Jerusalem the pilgrim cut out a "chi rho" symbol for Christ and mailed it back to her with a prayer as a token of his gratitude. One day Bernard took the pilgrim to his school and had him speak about his pilgrimage to the 5th grade children to whom he was teaching English, but it seemed to be a little much for them, and they did little more than listen politely.

The next oldest son was Bernard, and he was the pilgrim's official interpreter, as he was the best in speaking English. After the first week, however, he left for the Army. His 14-year-old brother Gerard, was also interested in speaking to the pilgrim, as he was studying English in school and was glad for the practice. Aloysius, the brother between Bernard and Girard, rendered the pilgrim service by locating a tape recorder by which he could send messages back to the States. The pilgrim learned when he got to Zurich, that Girard drove over 100 kilometers the second night after the pilgrim left, looking for him, as he thought it too cold to sleep outside that night. Praise God for a caring brother!

There were two girls in the family, but not having any sisters in his own family, the pilgrim was not too sure how to relate to them. Terese, in her late teens, was a maturing young woman, somewhat self-conscious and maintained a respectful, not overly-familiar relationship with the pilgrim. The darling of the family was Jeanne and at seven years of age, she was a delight to the pilgrim with her natural enthusiasm and spontaneous expressions of affection. She was in no way spoiled as she was given her own chores around the house, going to the store, etc., and each family member made her feel important. When she heard that the pilgrim had celebrated his 29th birthday two months before, she decided to make a birthday card and gave it to him. This he treasured and kept with his various souvenirs, eventually bringing it all the way back to the States.

One example of how the family accommodated the pilgrim was in the humbling experience the pilgrim had the first night there. When he woke up in the morning, he found that he had urinated in his sleep. Bedwetting had been a problem he had struggled with all through his childhood till the age of 11 or 12, and now here it happened again after all these years. He didn't know if it was due to sleeping outside (as Mrs. Rimlinger suggested), to something he ate, to a urinary infection or, as Etienne half jokingly offered, due to the fact that his system could not handle the powerful "schnupps" that he had been given to drink the night before. No matter what the cause, his hosts made light of the accident, even in light of the damage to their mattress.

As the days went on, the pilgrim set up his daily routine. He would begin the day with Holy Mass at the Parish Church. This was quite a familiar experience for him by now and he felt quite at home with the responses in French, etc. But when Sunday came, he was quite surprised by several things. First was the orderly seating arrangement. All the children sat up front — not with their families. All the men sat on the right side of the church and all the women on the left side.

Also, some of the liturgical changes which the pilgrim had encountered in other parts of France, like communion in the hand (which had not yet been permitted in the United States in 1970) were not practiced here. And all the women wore head coverings. But this was understandable as this was a village somewhat removed from the mainstream of the society and traditions tended to change more slowly. Even in the matter of language, there was a mixture of French and German for the older people spoke only German, but the children were taught French in the schools, and this village now lay within French borders.

As the second week of the pilgrim's stay with his cousins neared the end, he began to make plans to be on his way. Of course everyone tried to persuade him to stay in Enchenberg for the winter (and take Bernard's place). But the pilgrim had "made a vow" to walk to Jerusalem and he did not want to have to excuse himself to the Lord about putting off its fulfillment. Also he missed the freedom of the open road, where there was no need to accommodate one's self to another's needs and desires.

In a letter he wrote to his parents from Enchenberg, the pilgrim reflected on his need to be alone. He felt this was the only way he could pursue his overriding interest in prayer and meditation on the Gospels. Thus he could not even imagine a religious community that would help him pursue such a goal for all such communities that he had known were too actively involved in the affairs of the world. Thus he resigned himself to "walking the earth among foreign people who did not bother to talk to him."

He saw himself becoming less and less a part of the world around him. His thoughts and actions, he felt, were becoming further and further removed from those of "normal people" and he was participating less in the everyday affairs of men. He projected that some day he might find it necessary to withdraw completely (psychologically and physically) even to being a hermit in the desert.

All in all then, the pilgrim's stay with his cousins had allowed the Lord to do much for the pilgrim. It had brought him into touch with the roots of his physical life and cultural background by a firsthand experience of the kind of life which had nourished his father's mother and father. It allowed him to experience an older and alternative family lifestyle than the technological one he had known up to that time. He had had time to pray, reflect, write and come to identify the call to solitude more clearly than ever before. Now it remained to see the next lessons the Lord had in store. During these days, the pilgrim had the following reflections:

SEPTEMBER 27, 1970 — THOUGHT — Pictures only capture the surface details, unless they are carefully (artfully) composed, developed and displayed to indicate a deeper meaning.

COMMENT 1987: Here the pilgrim seems to be not so harsh in his judgment on picture taking as he allows a possible useful kind of picture taking that is done with sensitivity and awareness of the reality beneath the external visible image.

SEPTEMBER 29, 1970 — THOUGHT — Once technology reaches the point where everyone is guaranteed a minimum income, sufficient to sustain their physical lives, then people will not "have" to work: then they will either work because they enjoy it, want a higher standard of living or are inspired by a Christian faith to bring all things under the rule of Christ.

COMMENT 1987: The pilgrim here is projecting a future welfare state, and whether that happens or not, the thought being presented is that there needs to be a better motive for working than mere physical need for this reduces man to being a slave. And though in a sinful world man may work out of greed and to satisfy his lower pleasures, the Christian faith calls one to work in order to build up the Kingdom of God.

OCTOBER 5, 1970 — THOUGHT — For many, the practice of religion is a convenience; for some, it is a matter of conviction.

COMMENT 1987: The pilgrim is able to see this distinction because he has experienced passing out of the first stage and on his way into the second. No doubt he hopes many others will discover the same truth.

SAME DAY — THOUGHT — Have we stopped talking about the Christian ideal as something unattainable by our own efforts because our people have been conditioned by the modern world to believe that EVERYTHING is within their grasp if they work HARD enough or save long enough and because we do not want to arouse in them feelings of guilt and insufficiency which might impede the "building of the earth," the "progress of man" and the "growth of business?"

COMMENT 1987: The pilgrim here is questioning the trend to "secularize the Gospel" and make it serve a merely human goal. He seems to be digging around at the root of the cause of the present lack of a strong faith in God for who He is in Himself and man's desperate need to trust Him. He himself has caught a glimpse of the Kingdom of God and now looks askance at all efforts, even by people in religion, to divert man's attention away from heaven and towards the earth.

SAME DAY — THOUGHT — How is it that I who have always refused to attempt to commit myself to something I did not think I could do well or finish, have committed my whole life to a goal — total union with God — which I know I cannot attain through my own efforts alone? Is this an aspect of faith?

COMMENT 1987: The pilgrim here is marveling out loud about the mysterious ways of God's grace — how it can turn one around 180 degrees, as it were and use for His glory, what the pilgrim refused to put to the service of man's glory.

SAME DAY — THOUGHT — Isn't it strange that those who we say "are close to God" are those who realize themselves to be so far away from Him?

COMMENT 1987: This thought expresses the truth that there is a vast difference in viewpoints between those who look in human terms and those who look in God's terms. Just as to the human eye stars that look far away and "close to God" will be seen by the scientist and astronomer as relatively close to the earth in comparison with other stars.

SAME DAY — THOUGHT — I found it easier and more meaningful to "give up" my desires than to try and satisfy all of them.

COMMENT 1987: The pilgrim in trying to satisfy his carnal desires came to realize he always craved more, and thus discovered the spiritual principal and Gospel truth that true peace is found in disciplining and curbing our flesh. "Blessed are the poor in spirit, for theirs is the Kingdom of heaven" (Mt. 5:3).

OCTOBER 9, 1970 — THOUGHT — Since food is basic to life, anyone interested in understanding life and its origin must become aware of farming, and the earth. The best way to do this is by living on a farm for a while.

COMMENT 1987: Obviously the pilgrim was learning some important lessons during his three-week stay with his cousins and sharing in their simple life as farmers. It was part of his need to be in firsthand contact with the roots of his life — even physically and geneologically.

OCTOBER 10, 1970 — THOUGHT — CHILDREN: for them everything is a "game". They are "deadly serious" about everything. They do not "worry" about food, clothing and shelter. What they need they just ask for, and keep asking till they are satisfied, whether it be material things or attention of affection. They "trust" everyone instinctively. They speak right out what they are thinking. They are inquisitive and searching. To them everything is new and wonderful. They ask questions not because they have doubts or because they want to gain control, but in order to learn and understand. They need to be constantly reaffirmed about their worth and value.

COMMENT 1987: The pilgrim here seems to be meditating on Jesus' command to become like little children if we desire to enter His Kingdom. We can learn from this how we should relate to our heavenly Father.

SAME DAY — THOUGHT — Will there appear in the United States "a new crop of contemplatives" to match "the new crop of activists?"

COMMENT 1987: The pilgrim here seems to be not just asking a question about the future but stating the need for more prayer and contemplation in the Church in America.

And so the pilgrim was ready to press on to fulfill the vow he had made to pilgrimage to the Holy City. But his "friend" Pierre from Paris had not arrived. What was he to do? Then a note arrived. It was in French. The best the pilgrim could make out it said he would be coming in another week. That was too long in the pilgrim's mind, and he determined to set out the very next day, October 12.

PART THREE: Enchenberg — Zurich

It dawned a clear but cool October day. Everything was provided for the pilgrim's journey: a long army coat with hood and warm lining that was bought specially in Strasbourg: a French army backpack that was in the family: a lightweight French air force sleeping bag; a few days' supply of food; a bottle of vitamin B tablets sent by his mother; and even a little bottle of schnupps for cold nights. Etienne offered to drive the pilgrim part of the way south in his car, but this was politely refused: the pilgrim had vowed to walk, and would do so as long as he was able.

The pilgrim was finally on his way again. He had in a sense picked up much baggage at his cousins in comparison with how lightly he had traveled since his first four months. But he knew he was heading for the Alps and winter was approaching so he took it as the Lord's way of providing and caring for him.

It was only years later that the pilgrim learned that the Lord was guiding his steps during this part of the journey in a very direct way. He was told that Pierre had come from Paris later the very day the pilgrim had left Enchenberg. Etienne had put him in his car and driven him down the road looking for the pilgrim, but to no avail. Thinking back to this time, the pilgrim could recall the distinct impression that something like this was taking place. For he remembered that there were very few cars passing him on the road south.

At one point, he felt he should get off the road and up into the trees and shrubs along the side of the road to take a rest stop and to pray. But just as he was up there and out of sight, a car went by and though he did not know what Etienne's car looked like exactly, nor why he might be driving that way, he sensed the Lord did not want any encounter with the people in that car. Looking back, the pilgrim realized the Lord was also protecting him from a possible companion who would not further the pilgrim's purpose of a pilgrimage to Jerusalem. Praise be to God.

The pilgrim would spend ten more days walking through eastern France on his way to Basel where he would eventually enter Switzerland, But from his seminary days, the pilgrim remembered his professor of modern church architecture talking about a pilgrimage chapel of abstract design built by LeCorbusier in 1944 called "Our Lady of the Height — Ronchamp." Looking at his map he saw this famous shrine was near Belfort which was not that much out of his way. So he decided to make it a part of his journey.

This was in keeping with the pilgrim's choice to pass up such renowned shrines as, say, that of Lourdes, and seek out less conventional ones like this one which had an " — architectural appeal" rather than a "devotional appeal". It seemed that spaces, shapes and monuments of faith were able to touch the pilgrim's spirit in ways that prayers, sacraments, and words had thus far not been able to do.

As it turned out, the pilgrim spent almost two days at Ronchamp, for the priest chaplain — although not speaking any English, and using Latin as the best common language with the pilgrim — treated the pilgrim very hospitably. He invited him to dinner and let him stay in the pilgrim's hostel for the night. And although the chapel itself was not at all moving or inspiring to the pilgrim as was Chartres and Notre Dame in Paris, he found it a fitting enough place to pray. There were no more Summer tourists and it was just he and the chaplain at the morning Mass which was considerately said in Latin for the pilgrim's benefit and to his great delight. Then on the following day the pilgrim accepted a ride of about 20 miles with a sculptor who was a frequent visitor to the Shrine and offered to drive the pilgrim as far as his home, which lay right along the pilgrim's intended route to Basel.

As the pilgrim reflected on his experience at Ronchamp, he sensed that the Lord had ministered to his search for faith through several free and spontaneous gestures of hospitality by brothers in the Lord. In this case it was not so much the "architectural statement" that spoke of faith to the pilgrim, as acts of practical Christian service, meeting the pilgrim where he was at, caring for his need of food, shelter and love.

Also this seemed to be a confirmation that this pilgrim was not the "modern spirit" he had thought he was, but that he was closer in temperament to "the medieval man". For the chapel at Ronchamp portrayed a "modern" attempt to express man's faith in God. And although the pilgrim was encouraged by learning that pilgrims had been coming to this site at least since 1274 and that the "miraculous virgin statue" was from the 17th century and was rescued out of the destruction the shrine suffered in the Second World War, he found that his faith was not greatly built up by the concrete forms and shapes that were so much a part of this building.

This shrine seemed to him to be a monument to man and his technological ability rather than a structure which glorified God and his compassion. It was not like the medieval cathedrals which were the work of countless faithful souls over centuries of time painstakingly putting together a house of the Lord. Rather it appeared to be the creation of a famous architect and a few crews of workers who "quickly" erected a structure that would attract the attention of men. It gave the appearance of ostentatious pride rather than humble anonymity. Not that the pilgrim was rendering a condemnatory judgment upon the building at Ronchamp. For he admitted that perhaps if he were to live in the vicinity and come here day after day, he would adjust to these abstract forms and meet his Lord here in the sacraments. It was just that the present architectural statement did not give him the vital contact with the faith of his ancestors that he was seeking. Here are the thoughts of the pilgrim's journal during this part of his march.

OCTOBER 15, 1970 — THOUGHT — Is the traditional function of authority being undermined today, partly because now many people are "experts" and "authorities" and "teachers" about things they have never experienced but only know through the mediums of print, pictures and TV? Does this kind of knowing not lead to a lessening of confidence? The knowledge may be vaster in extent and more numerous in detail, but it is less deep in the emotions and total impression.

COMMENT 1987: The pilgrim here returns to his theme of searching out the root cause for his own, and supposedly others' lack of trust in what his teachers and mentors had told him. He is coming to realize that nothing can beat firsthand experience, especially in the area of contact with God. When so-called teachers merely hand on what they have read in a book they begin sounding hollow and lose credibility, something like the scribes and Pharisees at the time of Jesus.

OCTOBER 16, 1970 — THOUGHT — The contemporary demand for "authenticity" is partly a cry for a new symbolism. The old verbal symbols are found to be too far from the sensed truth, and new verbal symbols which more closely approximate the reality are sought.

Thus in an age when life was "hard," Christian preaching took the form of drawing on the symbolism of punishment, death, health and rest. Today when life is easy, it must change its proclamation and speak in terms of resurrection and life. In the former age there was no problem encouraging people to work — it was taken for granted. In the present age, if people do not understand the Christian urgency to "build the earth" there is a danger the human race will tire of its so-called "fast life" and completely throw up its hands in despair about ever becoming completely satisfied. Today, Christianity must witness to TRUE joy, TRUE peace, TRUE life, which is not exactly the same as that which the world offers and seeks.

COMMENT 1987: The pilgrim here is trying to put his finger on the reason why religious language has recently undergone such a radical change so that instead of looking heavenward, it now looks mostly towards the earth and the city of man. The danger here of course is that theology and preaching will merely follow the fashion of the age and lose sight of the revelation of Jesus Christ. It's the perennial balance of being in the world without being of the world.

OCTOBER 20, 1970 — QUOTATION — "en batissant cette chapelle, j'ai voulu creer un lieu de silence, de pricr, de paix, et de joie in interieur," Le Corbusier, July 25, 1955 spoken about his chapel at Ronchamp.

TRANSLATION — In building this chapel, I wished to create a place of silence, of prayer, of peace and of interior joy.

COMMENT 1987: The pilgrim was obviously struck by the architect's goal in building the shrine to our Lady of the Height, which corresponded so well with his own personal search, though to the extent that the author forgot that all these treasures could only be ultimately found in Jesus Christ and not in some material construction of concrete and glass, he was being misled.

And so the pilgrim now headed for the country of Switzerland. As he came into the town of Belfort, though he would not know it till years later, he crossed the path of another pilgrim, Hilaire Belloc, who almost 70 years before, in 1901, had walked this way and written it up in a book called *"The Path To Rome."* Superficially perhaps the two pilgrimages looked very different as Mr. Belloc was not struggling with the foundations of his faith. Nevertheless, they shared a common spirit in the vow to walk, and in the choosing of the earthly center of the Catholic Faith, Rome, as their goal.

On October 22, the pilgrim came to the border of France and Switzerland. Here he met his first harassment by the police, for the French border guards suspected him of smuggling drugs when they searched his pack and found a bottle of "vitamin B tablets". They crushed the tablets, sniffed them and passed them around to one another trying to decide whether or not they were illegal drugs. Obviously they were amateurs at this sort of thing and since none of them spoke or understood English, and the pilgrim could not explain very well in French, there was not much communication. But eventually they decided he was harmless and could be allowed to pass.

The pilgrim was upset by this false judgment and tried, to no avail, to get the police to write a note saying he was searched but let go. He had not yet learned the job of suffering unjustly in imitation of his savior, Jesus, and remaining calm in the midst of such accusation. Nevertheless, the feelings of resentment quickly passed after a few miles of walking and the pilgrim now opened his mind and heart to whatever experiences the Lord had in store for him in this new country during the two weeks' sojourn there.

One of the first things that struck the pilgrim was the heavy German influence he saw all about him, including the language. Thus when he stopped at a Catholic Church the evening of his third day, just before arriving in Zurich, he found a church full of devout Swiss praying the Rosary in German. This sign of faith was very encouraging to the pilgrim and he was thankful that he had learned the Our Father, and the Hail Mary in German during his high school seminary days, so now he could join right in with them.

That night when he got to the Schibli residence, he found them all eagerly awaiting his arrival. Unlike their cousins in Enchenberg, they did not live in a small village or have a farm. They lived a more middle class life in an apartment in the large city of Zurich. They lovingly cared for all the needs of the pilgrim from serving him generous portions of food to preparing his bath and washing his clothes. They immediately telephoned their cousins in Enchenberg to let them know of his safe arrival, for there had been constant concern about him for the past week.

During his three day visit, the pilgrim was taken to see some of the other relatives and got to see something of the city of Zurich. He noted how very neat and clean the city was kept. There was evidence of the Protestant Reformation in the prominent statues of Calvin and Zwingli set up at various points around the city. And of course he noticed the prominence of very large and ornately decorated clocks on many of the public buildings. After three days though he knew it was time to be on his way. Of course his hosts didn't want him to set out again on his own, but seemed to sense something at least of the pilgrim's commitment and respected his decision even while not fully understanding it. They needed a new measure of faith as well as the pilgrim.

Switzerland

Zurich
Einsiedeln
Lugano
Bergamo
Como
Florence
Assisi
Norcia
Cascia
Rome

Italy

••• Chapter 5 Zurich, Switzerland to Rome, Italy
ooo Chapter 4

As the pilgrim headed south, he walked the Eastern shore
of the Zurich Lake, with his next desination being Einsiedeln,
and it lay ahead a two day journey on foot. The name of this
town and shrine had been given to him both by his grandmother and uncle in the States, as well as by his cousins in Enchenberg and Zurich. So it seemed he should not pass it up
when he was so close and at least see what the Lord might want
to show him by it all.

A brief write-up about Einsiedeln proved very interesting
to the 20th century pilgrim. It said "Einsiedeln" means hermitage. Next it mentioned that its "black virgin" along with
the one at Montserrat make it one of the main pilgrimage
spots in Europe. Supposedly the first hermit here, St. Meinrad,
a Benedictine, arrived about 828 with the statue of Mary. And
throughout the Middle Ages, Einsiedeln was a great spiritual-
cultural bastion of the Christian world.

All of this was very well and good, but the pilgrim was not
out to just collect worthless, if interesting, historical facts. He
was concerned with being personally moved and inspired to
greater faith. Regretfully he did not find it at this shrine. Not
because the richly decorated interior of the basilica with its
gold ornamentation, marble statues and giant frescoes could
not speak words of faith from their makers. Rather he was not
moved to faith here because this magnificent basilica had become surrounded by bustling hotels, restaurants, and all that
goes with a growing tourist trade. And inside, the atmosphere
was anything but fit for prayer and recollection as a skill saw
buzzed and hammers pounded as workmen — seemingly oblivious to the place in which they stood — were busy construct-
ing a stage up near the altar.

It all seemed a far cry from the original inspiration of a
hermitage. And though it was dedicated to "Our Lady of Hermits" the pilgrim wondered how many visitors in the past year
received graces along these lines by stopping off at this shrine.
In that vein, it seemed much more appropriate to be off alone
into the mountains to pray in peace. So after telephoning his
cousins in Zurich as they had requested and using the money
they had given him "to have a meal at Einsiedeln," the pilgrim
was quickly back on the road and heading for the pass over the
Alps.

Upon leaving Einsiedeln, heading toward the city of
Schwyz and eventually over St. Gotthard Pass, the pilgrim

decided to leave the main road and try out one of the many marked footpaths he found. Actually he observed that the Swiss so valued walking and cycling that they went to great lengths to provide an abundance of footpaths as well as specially paved walkways along the sides of all the roads for pedestrians and also a special part of the road was reserved for bicycles. He was especially glad for this provision as he often found himself walking a few hours after sunset now that there were only 11 hours of daylight and he did not need 13 hours of darkness for sleep.

The day after he left Einsiedeln, as the pilgrim approached Schwyz, he saw a sign indicating a trail up a high mountain called "Gross Mythen," which he judged by the altitude quoted to be about 6,000 feet above sea level and no doubt stood out well above most of the surrounding mountains. Even though he knew he would probably have to come back down the same path he went up and so far he had not "backtracked" a single mile of his over 1700 miles walked, he felt so drawn to making this climb part of his pilgrimage he hardly had to give it a second thought or prayer. It seemed to be part of the Lord's forming the "hermit" aspect of his heart and a testing of the willingness to go the more difficult route rather than just pursue the shortest and easiest way.

Sight-wise the pilgrim was more than amply rewarded for his effort. After about an hour and a half climb along a carefully shoveled out two foot wide path with four foot walls of snow on each side of him as he neared the top, he came to a point within a few hundred feet of the summit beyond which he could not pass. For a man was working up ahead of him with a shovel to clear a recent snow slide which had completely blocked any further progress on his path. Accepting this as the Lord's saying "this is far enough" he scouted around for a place where he could clamber off the path and find a private little spot to gaze upon this beautiful creation of the Lord.

This he soon found and immediately became spellbound by the sight of looking out over the top of snow-capped mountains for as far as he could see in every direction. It was like the Lord's special gift to him — and anyone else who was willing to make the effort to climb "the Lord's mountain". Here he could experience something of "dwelling with the Lord of creation" in a way not possible anywhere else in the world. To celebrate such an occasion he prayed a few psalms from the little pocket New Testament he had with him and played a few tunes on his flute. These seemed appropriate to gently pierce the silence with a reverent cry of thanksgiving for the wonders the Lord had made. Then the pilgrim returned by the same path and descended once again into the valley and "the city of man".

The pilgrim was now heading for St. Gotthard pass, which he would reach in two days. Since it now was almost November, the pilgrim wondered if he would find himself in the first new snowfall of the year. All around him he saw evidence of last winter's snow. At Andermatt, about 10 kilometers from the top of the pass over the Alps, there was still last year's snow and ice in the streets and on the sidewalks. But it was not cold, for the sun made it warm during the day; so, for example, on Sunday the men wore just their suit coats when going to Church. Then during the night a prevailing wind from the south brought warm air from Italy and the Mediterranean Sea. Thus the pilgrim could still sleep outside.

On Sunday night, November 1, the pilgrim slept on top of St. Gotthard Pass. There were no trees or bushes that high up under which he could take shelter for the night, but the Lord provided a very nice, dry, grassy spot between several big rocks which was open enough to let the sun shine on and melt the snow away. The pilgrim was especially thankful to the Lord for the clean air and clear sky at night for, as he beheld the heavens above him, he saw a countless number of "new stars" that he never before had been able to see anywhere else on the earth. And so he remembered God's promise to Abraham (Genesis 15:5) and reflected on the truth that one had to be willing to follow the call of the Lord to leave one's homeland and set out alone to climb "heights" both "physical" and "spiritual" to experience the special presence of the Lord that alone could satisfy the hungry heart of man.

Crossing over the top of St. Gotthard Pass, the pilgrim passed through the little town of Ospizio. By Tuesday, November 3, in the afternoon, he had come near Lavorgo and decided to take time out to write a letter home detailing to his family back in the States his travels since his last letter which he had written from Enchenberg. Since it was rather chilly, the pilgrim had to find a place in the sun so his hands would be warm enough to hold a pencil and write. He ended up sitting in a river bed with huge granite boulders, lots of sand and sparkling waters all about. But he had to keep his ears and eyes alert, for he saw a sign on the river bank in German, French, Italian and English, warning that this river was subject to quick changes of water flow due to the hydroelectric plants near by.

After writing the first two pages of his letter, the pilgrim picked up and walked another 5-6 kilometers till he came to an ideal place where he could make a fire and cook a hot meal. This would be one of those rare occasions when all the circumstances necessary for such an event would be just right: namely, a remote enough area away from civilization with lots of trees and so an abundance of dead wood for a fire; a good supply of drinking water; he would have along something that needed cooked. The first two conditions were ideally fulfilled in this part of the Alps and his relatives in Zurich had given him bouillon cubes, ham and salt pork, potatoes and coffee. So these he prepared into a "pilgrim feast" and rejoiced in the goodness of the Lord who so wonderfully cared for this "wandering Aramean."

Then on Wednesday night, November 4, the pilgrim found himself in a small village where there was an evening Mass scheduled for 7:30 p.m. It was the first Mass he attended in the Italian language but he was pleased to find his knowledge of Latin made it very easy to follow along. And his heart was so uplifted by the beautiful way the people — mostly women of course — sang; even in harmony. And the church was almost full. What a testimony to the faith of these people to find such devotion when it was not even Sunday!

On Thursday, his last day in Switzerland, the pilgrim wrote the last four pages of his letter to his family. In it, as he reflected on his climb over the Alps, he expressed the thought that he was really "a hermit at heart" for he was finding he would rather be alone than with people. He didn't mind joining with others in prayer — no, this was a tremendous support. But he felt an aversion to the idle talk and activities that seem to fill the times when people live their daily lives together at work, at home and at play. He was beginning to feel himself drawn away from such "diversions" as he heard a call to penetrate deeper and deeper into the mystery of God's presence and love for man. Thus he could end his particular letter with a wish that those who read it would find the "peace" that he had found, under the protecting love of Jesus and his mother.

The following are some of the thoughts that the pilgrim recorded on his walk through Switzerland:

OCTOBER 27, 1970 — THOUGHT — Do not most people "work", more to satisfy the appetites and needs of their bodies, than in order to transform all things for the Kingdom of God?

COMMENT 1987: The pilgrim here continues to wrestle with the basic reason for working, or "doing something that contributes to the general welfare." He finds he must have a spiritual basis for working and will not settle for any utilitarian or merely temporal reason.

OCTOBER 28, 1970 — A LIST OF WHAT OTHERS THINK ABOUT THE PILGRIM:

1. An American girl visiting Notre Dame Cathedral in Paris: "And beside us we have a miner."

2. A French woman to her neighbor in St. Die: "He's a soldier."
3. A young Spanish country lad: "Perigrino, perigrino!" ("Pilgrim, pilgrim.")
4. A neighbor of Schibli's in Zurich: "Is he a doctor?"
5. His cousin to a nosey tenant: "He's a professor of theology."
6. A young boy in Northern Italy: "Are you a boy scout?"
7. Fr. John Boyer to the American Express Office in Paris: "The man with the aluminum hat."
8. The chaplain at Ronchamp: "Are you a priest?"
9. A gendarme on the road: "Are you a student?"
10. A fanatic Frenchman: "Do you think you are starting a new religion?"
11. A young Spanish lad in Toledo: "Are you a geologist? a prospector?"
12. A private detective searching his bag in Paris and finding his soprano recorder: "Oh you are a musician?"
13. A tourist seeing him sketching the rose window at Notre Dame Cathedral: "He's an artist."
14. The gendarme searching his pack in Altkirch: "He's an army deserter. He's smuggling illegal drugs."

To those who hurl nasty remarks as he passes by, he is a tramp.

To those who look and wonder, he is a fanatic.

To those who see the effort and sacrifice, he is a saint.

COMMENT 1987: The pilgram can hardly not notice what other people think of him, even though he knows he cannot allow anyone else's judgments to sway him from the vow he has made to the Lord. Nevertheless, he finds an element of truth in every comment that comes his way, and by the power of the Holy Spirit, he seeks to hear the Lord he serves speaking to him through all these judgments and words.

NOVEMBER 1, 1970 — THOUGHT — I am not interested in what other people are doing. I think those who say "I'm interested in everything and everybody" are not really, truly and deeply interested in anything. To be passionately absorbed in only one thing, means that all other things assume less importance and take up less interest.

COMMENT 1987: Here the "singlemindedness" of the pilgrim and every searcher for the Lord comes through. The pilgrim is not a dilettante. Rather he directs all things to further his one single goal, and everything else he leaves aside.

NOVEMBER 3, 1970 — THOUGHT — Today's generations have less a sense of receiving life, property, skills, knowledge, etc. from their fathers than previous generations. Therefore there is less a sense of respect, thankfulness and gratitude.

These attitudes have been changed and transferred from the level of a single benefactor — the father — to corporate benefactors — the firm, the association, the corporation (that which pays one for his work). These are what seem to give one his life and it is to them he commits himself, striving to please them and conforming to their expectation of him.

COMMENT 1987: This thought continues the reflection on the loss of respect for authority in the modern world and also points to a root cause of the disintegration of family life in a technological culture: the father is no longer the source, the head of life except in a basic physical sense and very tenuous ongoing sense (others can easily substitute for him) as the children grow up.

NOVEMBER 4, 1970 — THOUGHT — Why I do not go to movies: if one knows and lives life himself, he does not need to experience it vicariously through plastic film and recorded sound. For life in itself is simple: only in its accidental forms is it varied and complicated.

COMMENT 1987: The pilgrim continues to view everything through the narrow lens of ultimate reality and direct personal contact, eliminating all but what is essential for making progress along the straight and narrow way to eternal life.

NOVEMBER 5, 1970 — THOUGHT — Today we do not so much have the feeling that one or two — father, mother, God — people "made us", gave us all we have and so we do not so much feel "we belong to them" but we are "made" by many and so do not feel we "mainly belong" to anyone.

COMMENT 1987: The pilgrim here traces the source of modern alienation and identity crisis to the breakup of the close-knit family unit and the expanding role of social institutions on forming the modern man.

SAME DAY — THOUGHT — In former ages when almost everyone did the same kind of work — farming — one received his uniqueness and identity from "where he was born" and who his relatives were. Today the place of origin and family line is not as significant for these are growing more and more alike while work is becoming more and more specialized, so that is what distinguishes one from another.

COMMENT 1987: Continuing on the theme of where one gets his identity, the pilgrim contrasts the way identity was gained through family before the proliferation of specialized jobs with the way identity is gained now by what one does. Uniqueness no longer flows from being part of a family but now flows from standing apart from it and being independent.

NOVEMBER 6, 1970 — THOUGHT — We are a generation that looks to the future, rather than to the past. We are not so interested in how it used to be done as how one can do it better. Very few spend time trying to understand the lives and customs of our forefathers. And so we do not look to the past for patterns of behavior, nor are we so willing to accept the old way of doing things.

COMMENT 1987: The pilgrim in his own personal search for the roots of his family, his forefathers in the faith and his true identity, sees that he has pursued a path that few moderns are likely to take. The craze for novelty and rejection of the past seem to fuel modern man's whole lifestyle.

PART TWO: Como — Florence

And so the pilgrim was ready to pass out of Switzerland after two short weeks. After Einsiedeln, he had set his next goal as Bergamo in Northern Italy, about 150 miles away, for he wanted to visit a Montessori school for junior high students there. Since he had no detailed map of this region, at Schwyz he stopped at a travel agency and they kindly wrote out the names of the towns he would have to pass through. Thus in Switzerland, he should go through Brunnen, Altdort, Andermatt, Gotthard, Bellinzona and Chiasso.

It was Friday, November 6 when he passed out of Chiasso, the last city in Switzerland and came over to Como, the first city in Italy — that land so rich in the Catholic faith he was seeking to experience. For some reason his passport got marked at the Italian checkpoint "October" 6 instead of "November" 6. Whether this was their way of deliberately shortening his stay in Italy (from the normal 3 months allowed a tourist to only 2 months) — though this would not be typical of the Italians as a people — or whether this was just an oversight, he would never know. As it turned out he was in Italy just a few days under two months. Anyway he trusted the Lord would take care of all the necessary details. He was just happy to be now on a nearly direct path to Rome.

The pilgrim found Northern Italy to be highly industrialized. Still, there were plenty of small villages in the countryside and it was in this area that one night he was shown beautiful hospitality. It happened like this. One evening as the pilgrim was walking along the road, a young shepherd in his early 30's by the name of Georgio, saw him and came up to greet him. Upon learning that he was Catholic and on his way to Rome, he asked him to his home for supper and to stay for the night, for he thought it was too cold with the ice and frost to sleep outside.

Thus the shepherd brought the pilgrim into his rather large one story, stone home. As they entered the large kitchen, they found the whole family gathered there. His family consisted of his wife, who at the time was nursing the baby by the hearth, two other small children and his mother. The first thing Georgio did was to bring in more wood and build up the fire. Then his mother cooked a delicious meal on the open fire, first frying potatoes in a skillet of deep oil and then frying eggs in the same oil. Cheese, cold cuts and a special kind of Sicilian bread made up the rest of the meal.

Then Georgio took the pilgrim down to see his sheep where he got some milk for the children. He also pointed out to the pilgrim how valuable the female sheep were because of the milk, whereas he was quite disappointed when he saw how many of the newborn lambs were males. Arriving back at the house everyone was gathered around a small portable television in the kitchen. The pilgrim found the television so incongruous in such a rustic setting, amid what looked like poverty, considering the scantily furnished room, but apparently a television was not a luxury for even a simple shepherd family in this part of Italy.

Georgio then explained that he was Calabrese, from southern Italy, and that his people there are known for their hospitality. He said no "northerner" would have taken the pilgrim in, but he considered it his "sacred duty" to offer the pilgrim everything he had. Such generosity called forth a reciprocal gesture on the part of the pilgrim, as he dug through his pack and found little "presents" to give to each member of the family.

The pilgrim was then shown his room off the kitchen. It had a large bed, clean sheets, and "tons" of warm covers to ward off the cold from the unheated room. The pilgrim thanked the Lord for this experience of sharing with a simple shepherding family and learning firsthand how all men everywhere lived before the advent of the modern age.

The next morning all shared coffee made on a stove using bottled gas, and cookies. They packed the pilgrim some food to take along. Georgio insisted on carrying the pilgrim's pack over the fields on a shortcut to the road again where he parted and the pilgrim continued on his way in gratitude.

After Como the pilgrim passed through Lecco and then on to Bergamo. In Bergamo he spent a few hours at the parish church where Pope John XXIII had grown up and then went to look up the Montessori school he had heard about. He found that this was quite a college town and that there were many American students living there. He was allowed to sit in on some of the classes for junior high school students and had some of Montessori's educational philosophy explained to him in English. For some reason that was not yet clear to him, he was interested in alternative ways of educating young people — perhaps because he had found such a gap in terms of faith experience in his own seminary training. Years later he could also look back and see that the Lord was preparing him for some future work among young people.

Leaving Bergamo, the pilgrim headed down through the central part of Italy, via Bologna and Florence. One of the blessings from the Lord for which the pilgrim was thankful during this time of his journey was the weather. Crossing the Alps and now heading through the Apennines in early November, he thought it might already be too cold to sleep outside and even that he might run into some snowstorms. But the Lord favored him with good weather and the only snow he saw in this part of Italy, was from the previous year and that was high up on the mountains. So he still was able to walk his 20 miles a day and sleep outside wherever he ended his march for the day.

However, there were some days of rain and dampness. One such night was November 19, as he neared Bologna. It had rained off and on all day. His boots and socks were water-filled so that as he walked he heard "slosh, slosh". He was as the saying goes "soaked through to the bone." But though "chilling the body", the rain could not "chill the soul", for he remained light-hearted and joyful.

Nevertheless, the Lord chose to refresh his body, as well as his soul, through an example of genuine Italian hospitality. He felt he could not sleep outside in such a condition without "tempting the Lord" in regard to his health, so he searched out and found an inexpensive *pensione* where he got a room for the night and where he could wring out his things and hang them up to dry somewhat. But the innkeeper, seeing his condition, generously brought up a towel and a basic of hot water in which the pilgrim could soak his feet. It was such a simple gesture, but one which signified a deep Christ-like love of a total stranger. It seemed to be a literal carrying out of the Lord's gesture with the towel and water as he washed the disciples' feet at the Last Supper.

By November 22, the pilgrim found himself in Firenze, which he came to realize after being in the city for three hours, was in English called "Florence." Though he knew this city was famous for its culture, museums, Renaissance art and architecture, he was only inspired to visit two places: the Cathedral of St. Mary of the Flowers, especially its baptistry where he spent some time examining the biblical scenes on the bronze doors; and the Accademia which was a large hall built around a single sculpture, Michaelangelo's "David". He was totally fascinated by this particular work of art, and spent a long time just looking at and admiring this "living" piece of marble. He found in it such grace and beauty, such warmth and presence, as he had never seen before in anything manmade. It was in "a world apart" and captivated him for well over an hour. He viewed it from all sides, slowly walking around it as it sat on a ten foot pedestal in the center of the large hall. Finally he made his way out of the building, which he noticed in passing, had other "unfinished" sculptures by the same artist.

As he reflected back on this experience, he realized that it had made a deep impression on him — it had in a real sense "changed him". It had touched something deep within that had never before been stirred. It was so unlike all modern abstract and geometrical art, and it seemed to speak to him from an age in which faith was expressed even in carved stone figures.

Being that the subject featured was the young David, he could not help but make the connection with Jesus who was from the line of David and fulfilled and surpassed all that David stood for. It also seemed to convey something of the patience, the love, the faith and the devotion required of the artist who created it. This sculpture was not a "statue" like what the pilgrim was so used to. It was not "poured from a mold." It was not "mass produced" or made on an assembly line. Rather it gave witness to a vibrant faith, reaching out from many centuries before, and still contained the power to ignite a spark of faith in this 20th century pilgrim's open heart.

Following are some of the thoughts the pilgrim recorded during these several weeks in Italy.

NOVEMBER 8, 1970 — THOUGHT — America has nothing to offer that I want — neither does any other country I have visited so far.

COMMENT 1987: The pilgrim has set his sights on "another city" (the heavenly Jerusalem) and nothing else has any attraction for him.

SAME DAY — One will defend his "life" to the extent that he does not believe in God, for if he believed completely in an eternal life, he would not want to prolong his present life.

COMMENT 1987: The pilgrim's faith is so strong and he so desired to be with God face-to-face that death is welcomed as the gateway to Paradise.

SAME DAY — In a generation when everything is NOW or in the FUTURE, a Christian must stand apart as one who places the most value on something PAST — Christ's entry into history 2000 years ago.

COMMENT 1987: Contrasting the world's stance with a Christian's stance, the pilgrim sees how there must be a sharp line of demarcation and the Christian must not become so merged with the world that he takes on its values and so fails to point to the Lord Jesus.

SAME DAY — With our growing use of and dependence upon television, movies, etc., it will become increasingly true that only that will be considered "real" which we see and hear on the screen — how then will it be possible to "believe" in Christ?

COMMENT 1987: Lamenting the fact that modern man, especially children and youth, tend to judge everything by how it measures up to what they have known from seeing it on television (seeing it live they remark "It looks just like on television") the pilgrim sees a problem for modern man to come to faith which is based on the authority of those who have believed and not on the ability of man to capture on film.

SAME DAY — "Nature" speaks to me of a power greater and previous to man, but not of Jesus Christ. This knowledge comes to me through the Church and I am reminded of it mainly by the symbols of that faith as found in our "old" churches.

COMMENT 1987: The pilgrim here is manifesting his "conservatism" in that he finds his faith more built up by the ancient and traditional symbols than those more recently created by the mind of man.

NOVEMBER 9, 1970 — THOUGHT — "Earth" — a nice place to visit, but I wouldn't want to live there (forever).

COMMENT 1987: The pilgrim takes a familiar saying of travelers to other cities and applies it to the realm of the transcendent so that he once again expresses his dissatisfaction with this world and longing for the world to come.

SAME DAY — THOUGHT — Americans give money "to build a new church" (which might require tearing down, destroying, the old one). Europeans give money for the "restauratio" (restoration).

COMMENT 1987: Walking through Europe the pilgrim often noted the work of restoration: the respect for the old and the desire to preserve it and incorporate it into the new. In his home parish in Pennsylvania and much of America he experienced the tearing down of the old to make way for the new. The way physical buildings are treated, shows an inner attitude that the pilgrim here brings to light. In the same way, he had experienced the tearing down of his faith by the modern theologians he had read, rather than an incorporation of the old into the present.

NOVEMBER 12, 1970 — THOUGHT — I am in Europe, not "to study" but "to absorb".

COMMENT 1987: Many people who saw the pilgrim seemed to think he was just another "American student abroad to study and travel." Thinking about this assessment, the pilgrim saw that this was not an adequate assessment of his purpose. Rather he was there to observe, absorb, and be nourished in his spirit by the evidences of faith in the Lord Jesus that he saw and experienced.

SAME DAY — THOUGHT — "Going to church" for a visit should be seen more as a "rest stop" than as a "filling station" where one goes to "get something" and then immediately leaves.

COMMENT 1987: Coming from a "self-oriented" society and one that is in a hurry, the pilgrim sees how this affects one's attitude toward God and religious practices. When walking all day long, day after day, one realizes how essential it is to stop for rests: not to just "take in food or water" but to be recreated in every aspect of ones heart, mind, soul and body. Indeed, the whole pilgrimage could be seen as a "rest stop" on the journey of life, in which the pilgrim did not engage in the normal activities of work or pastoral responsibilities.

SAME DAY — "The more a thing is given out of love, the harder it is to refuse — most things are given with very little love, but more out of a sense of duty, necessity, pity, etc.

COMMENT 1987: The pilgrim is often offered help along the way, from food, to money, to a ride, etc. Each time he must pray and discern how the Lord wants him to respond. If he has enough food for the day, he usually must say no. Since he desires to remain poor, he usually says no to taking money. Since he is committed to walking, he usually refuses rides. But occasionally there are situations where the other person truly needs to give something and the pilgrim may not refuse it out of some kind of rigid obedience to a "rule" he lives by. Thus the pilgrim must learn to read the heart of the giver, sense their need to give or receive love, and respond as guided by the Holy Spirit.

NOVEMBER 13, 1970 — THOUGHT — We have discarded everything else of our fathers — their way of dressing and moving about, of living and thinking, of working and recreating. Why should we not also discard their religion?

COMMENT 1987: The pilgrim is again reflecting on the current age's jettisoning of the faith that has been handed down, and ties it in partly with the modern penchant for what is new. There are other factors involved also like plain old rebellion and sin, the envy of the devil, etc. But the "spirit of the age" seems to be a significant contributing cause to the current erosion of faith.

NOVEMBER 14, 1970 — THOUGHT — Is it any wonder that men "work" with less "attention" and devotion today than formerly, considering the fact that the products of their efforts are very likely to be thrown away quickly, rejected, destroyed and are "little valued" whereas formerly the things that men used were treasured, preserved and treated with respect?

COMMENT 1987: The pilgrim here is noting that modern values of "throw-aways" and built in obsolescence and mass-produced items lead to a lessening of value placed upon the fruits of the earth and of man's toil. Since it costs less in human effort, it has less value, and this in turn leads to less enthusiasm for creating objects of utility and beauty. Formerly a sickle or a hoe was a valued instrument that was cared for and proudly passed on to the next generation. Today they are cast aside for "more advanced and more efficient tools".

SAME DAY — PHRASE — "The dis-United States."

COMMENT 1987: This little cynicism perhaps rises out of the countercultural roots that still partly supply the energy for this particular pilgrimage.

NOVEMBER 16, 1970 — THOUGHT — I have "all the time in the world" plus "eternity" to accomplish my goal!

COMMENT 1987: Again with a clearly eschatological focus, the pilgrim has found a way of summarizing his philosophy of life or "justifying" his way of life to those who object to his purpose and means. His goal is to know, love and serve the Father, Son and Holy Spirit; this begins on earth, and will continue for all eternity in heaven.

NOVEMBER 17, 1970 — THOUGHT — Man no longer has a "body" to remind him of his weakness and poverty. It is so pampered and satisfied that he can almost forget it.

The body is a symbol and sacrament of the spirit. The purpose of penance was and still is, the purifying of the spirit.

"Thinking with my body" — not "imagining" things but "feeling" things; allowing my eyes and ears to assume a second place and the sense of touch, smell and movement, a first place. Kind of like a dance: leaving sights and sounds in the periphery; allowing the body (footsteps) to lead. I am "feeling" my way through the world; not like a blind man but more like a baby, with an absorbent mind (Montessori's expression).

COMMENT 1987: These reflections show another source of the energy that drove the pilgrim onward, namely, a need to "get in touch with the real" through means other than the mind. Reading, thinking and studying had not satisfied parts of his being that hungered and thirsted to be touched. He here generalizes from his personal experience and attempts to make application to society at large.

NOVEMBER 20, 1970 — THOUGHT — We are allowing ourselves more and more to have our daily actions dictated by machines — clocks tell us when to get up, eat, work and retire; cars, buses, airplanes move us from place to place; "labor saving devices" have directions — we read them and follow their programs. This is death to the "spirit", to the soul and to creativity.

We are losing the ability to dance, which is movement springing up spontaneously from the depths of our soul — we only know how to move in response to our machines, pushing buttons, pulling levers. The solution is to learn how to play with our machines — paint our cars in psychedelic colors — they must become our playthings, not our masters.

COMMENT 1987: This sounds like some of the typical criticism coming from the countercultural revolution of which the pilgrim was a part in the late 1960's. But having purposely removed and distanced himself from his contemporary culture, he could see more clearly than ever how technology was having a detrimental impact on the well-being of mankind. But in addition to all of this, he was standing in a true Biblical perspective where one finds God warning His people about idol worship. That is, things created by man — even sophisticated robots and R2D2's that can "see, hear, smell, feel and walk" — may not be worshipped or served. To let what is below man rule over him is an affront to the heavenly Father because it degrades man to a position below inanimate matter.

NOVEMBER 30, 1970 — Movies, by "condensing life" lead people to speed up their own lives, hoping to experience as much in as short a time as possible.

PART THREE: Florence — Rome

Upon leaving Florence the pilgrim was now about to enter the Umbrian district of Central Italy. This would be the district that would eventually come to hold in his heart the position of the second most beautiful spot on the face of the earth (the most beautiful being his home State of Pennsylvania). Here he would come to agree most definitely with those who called this area "The Galilee of Italy." And actually the Galilee he would visit in a few months in the modern state of Israel would have little of the lush green vegetation, gently rolling hills and most of all, the quiet air of peace and almost tangible sense of God's presence, that this "Galilee" of Italy had.

But the pilgrim suspected this area of "the boot" was named the Galilee of Italy more because of its spiritual and mystical qualities than because of its physical and natural resemblances. And this would be testified to by the long list of canonized saints who were born and lived in this region. It has been said that per square mile more recognized saints come from this area than from any area of comparable size in the rest of the world. However, even if this could not be substantiated, the pilgrim felt it deserved the title from the mere fact that two great apostles stemmed from this area: namely, Benedict and Francis. And Francis alone, who so much resembled Christ, even to gathering men around him and sending them out two by two to preach the Gospel to the four corners of the earth, would be reason enough to compare this land to the hometown region of Jesus, the Savior.

After three days of walking through Tuscany, having passed through Arezzo and Cortona on his way to Perugia, the pilgrim came along the northeastern shore of Lake Transimeno on November 27. This Lake was made special by St. Francis who once made a 40-day Lenten retreat on an island in the middle of it. The pilgrim was not moved to imitate Francis at this point and so pushed on to Perugia, the first major city which lay within the region of Umbria and which served as its capital. Perugia was also a significant place for Francis for it was here in one of its prisons that he was held for months as a prisoner of war where he became deathly ill. Once back in Assisi, while recuperating from this sickness, he saw the futility of this world and turned his heart firmly to the things of God.

Two days later the pilgrim began to make his way down the Umbrian valley toward the eastern exposure of Mt. Subasio, catching his first glimpse of that picturesque city which was known the world over as the home of St. Francis. Here was his beloved Assisi. It lay halfway up the side of the mountain, surrounded by high stone walls, centuries old. Standing out in clear view from a distance, at the northern end of the town, was the series of massive arches that supported the basilica of St. Francis and its accompanying plaza.

The pilgrim would spend two days in and around this compact city of narrow streets, pink and white stone houses with tile roofs, and buildings going back not only to the 13th century and the time of Francis, but even to the time of Rome and before. He would visit all the major sites: the ruined castle on the top of the hill overlooking the city; the carceri or hermitage a few miles distant further up Mt. Subasio; the basilica with its upper and lower churches richly frescoed by the best Italian painters of the 13th century; San Damiano which Francis himself labored to repair; the home of St. Clare and her sisters; down on the plain the original hermitage at Rivo Torto and the first permanent foundation of hermitages at the Portiuncula of Our Lady of the Angels. All these hallowed spots were quietly visited by the pilgrim with the secret hope that the Saint would impart to him something of his share in the peace and joy of the Savior himself.

Having drunk of these spiritual riches to the extent his heart was open at this time in his life, the pilgrim set out in the direction of Rome once more. But seeing that he was not far from the town of Norcia, he detoured slightly to the east, in order to also touch something of the spirit of the Great Saint of the 6th century and Father of Western Monasticism, Benedict. Benedict was special to the pilgrim both because he had four years of theological training by Benedictine priests at St. Vincent Seminary and Archabbey in Latrobe, Pennsylvania, but also because he sensed a spiritual kinship with the man who fled the pursuit of learning in the universities and hid himself with the Lord as a hermit in the mountains.

The pilgrim spent only a few hours visiting the monastery at Norcia and praying at the tomb of St. Benedict there. He sensed a greater simplicity and plainess here than in Assisi where the Franciscan spirit was more earthly and urban, being mixed in with the life of the city of man. The Benedictine spirit was more rural, removed from the everyday life of the people and lived in a more conscious awareness of the heavenly city of God. Again, as at Assisi, he remained alone and as no one engaged him in any extensive conversation or deeper sharing, he had to go on what he knew from his past and what the Lord was doing in his heart directly by the Holy Spirit.

Upon leaving the homeland and heritage of the monastic family of Benedict, the pilgrim, still in the peaceful region of Umbria, headed for Leonessa, which would point him directly towards Rome. He had left Norcia in the middle of the afternoon of December 3 and had walked a little over 10 miles by the time it began to get dark. It was about 8 p.m. as he climbed a long, gradual slope alongside a mountain, and then all of a sudden, as he rounded a bend in the road, he beheld a beautiful little city lit up like a jewel, set against the dark hills with the crescent of the new moon, clear and bright, just ready to move behind the highest peaks of the mountains.

He had intended to walk a few more kilometers before looking for a place off the side of the road to sleep, but as he considered the sudden appearance of this appealing little city and he saw within it a beautiful church, he decided to sleep near the city so he could go into it for Mass in the morning. This turned out to be an inspiration from the Lord, for a wonderful surprise lay in store for him in the morning when he discovered where he was.

The name of the city turned out to be Cascia. This didn't mean anything special to him until after Mass he learned that the church he had seen lit up the night before and where he had come to share in the Lord's body and blood at the table of the Eucharist, was the basilica of St. Rita. Now St. Rita was the patron saint of his mother who is named Mary Rita. So he took this as a sign that the Lord was guiding him through the love and prayers of his earthly mother and through St. Rita whose holy life in this city in the 14th century had left such a rich spiritual legacy for the whole church of Christ.

Picking up a brochure available to visitors, the pilgrim learned that St. Rita was born in 1381 in the nearby town of Roccaporena. Her parents had her marry a violent man who caused her much pain for 18 years till he was murdered one day. When her two sons died within the year, she was able to fulfill her childhood desire of being a nun, though it took much persistent pleading to waive the rule that only virgins could enter the Order she chose. But once accepted, she lived an exemplary life of obedience, love and service to the poor. For the last 16 years of her life, she suffered a great deal from an open wound in her forehead as though from a thorn in our Lord's crown. This forced her to be secluded and live practically as a recluse. Thus in St. Rita, the pilgrim met a sister who bore the cross of Jesus with perfect joy and through a life hidden from the prying eyes of the world, received a glorious crown from the Lord she so well served.

From Cascia the pilgrim headed down the valley of the Corno River with its sparkling clear waters, into the region of Latium and on to Rome. It had been almost two weeks of spiritual formation by the natural beauty of the Umbrian Valley and the supernatural beauty of some of the Lord's most faithful disciples. The Valley had struck a note of deep resonance in the heart of the pilgrim, possibly because it was so much like his native Pennsylvania where he grew up: it had similar rolling hills. Only instead of wheat fields and pastureland, it had olive trees and grapevines. But now he was beginning to learn how to allow these natural gifts from the Lord to be instruments to help him in prayer and meditation. And these, along with the examples of men and women who had responded to God's grace with all their heart and soul, were now helping to restore and make personal, the faith of his fathers.

The following are some of the entries in his journal during these two weeks of pilgrimage:

NOVEMBER 23, 1970 — REFLECTION — Why am I walking to Jerusalem?

1. It seems to be the will of God;
2. In reparation for the sins, suffering and death caused by automobiles;
3. As penance;

4. An exercise in *patientia* (patience);
5. For peace;
6. To "work up an appetite";
7. For my own health;
8. To earn my bread and right to life;
9. To "get my head straightened out";
10. To get mind and body together;
11. To "know" the distance;
12. To have time to absorb;
13. To see what lies along the side of the road — what is thrown out;
14. To have time to look around;
15. To learn how to pray;
16. To get the feel of the earth;
17. To purify my mind and body;
18. To have time to pray;
19. To find my final goal in life;
20. It is the more primitive way of traveling;
21. A "purgation";
22. To allow my mind and body to slow down — to rest;
23. An intense examination of conscience;
24. For meditation and contemplation;
25. To "see" what we "miss" by going faster;
26. To "digest my past life";
27. To be more subject to the natural environment;
28. I prefer to "crack the nut" myself; to cut the meat off the bone myself; to dig out the marrow and chew up the gristle; to eat the apple core;
29. To know my own culture and faith better by the contrast;
30. A voluntary poverty;
31. To give my eyes a rest;
32. To sharpen my perception so that when I get to Jerusalem I will truly "see" what is there.

COMMENT 1987: The pilgrim has come up with 32 different ways of expressing the purpose and meaning of his walking. Often he is saying the same thing but in different ways. Basically there seem to be 10 different categories:

1. FOR HIS HEALTH — This is expressed in 7, 9, 10 and 5. This is mainly his mental, emotional and spiritual health, expressed by phrases like "getting his head together" "harmony of body and mind" and finally as just "peace". This of course is a very self-centered motive, a need to find the meaning of his existence and meet an unfulfilled hunger and thirst at the core of his being.

2. SIMPLICITY — This is expressed in 20 and 30. To aid him in his search the pilgrim has felt it essential to return to the sim-

pler ways of old, putting aside man's newest inventions which tend to complicate and obfuscate the inner truth of life. This could be called "voluntary poverty" for the sake of inner peace.

3. EXPERIENCE — This is expressed in 16 and 27. The pilgrim was coming from an environment which greatly valued "firsthand experience", probably because modern technological society gives mainly "secondhand experiences" whether in dissemination of information, or in the obtaining of food.

4. OBSERVE — This is expressed in 11, 12, 13, 14, 22, 24, 31. Obviously here we have touched an important reason for the walking. The pilgrim feels the need to observe and absorb. To go at a slower pace in order to better appreciate what lies about him. And this leads into the next point which is one of the reasons for observing.

5. PENETRATE — This is expressed in 28 which indicates the pilgrim's desire to get to the bottom of things. To pursue an object till it renders up its inner secret; not to be satisfied with a superficial knowledge.

6. ANALYZE — This is expressed in 27 as "to digest the past". The pilgrim is making a long reflection on what has happened to him so far in life in order to get a better sense of what he has to work with and then proceed to the future.

7. PLAN — This is expressed in 8. He wants to have a solid basis for his future and "know from experience" what he says or shares with others. He refuses to hand on to others what he himself has not first completely tested himself and found true.

8. PRAYER — This is expressed in 15, 18, 19, 23, 24. All of this is laying a basis for a life of prayer and contemplation. Although this is not yet completely focused on the Lord and his life, but rather on the pilgrim and his relationship to the world around him and himself, he is learning the basics of openness of spirit to what lies beyond the ordinary and first impressions.

9. PENANCE — This is expressed in 3 & 4. With reflection on the past the pilgrim cannot help but see sin and guilt and find a need to make reparation for the harm done. Eventually he will move from a more natural plane, namely the harm done to the environment and creation, to the supernatural and the relationship between man and God and man and man.

10. WILL OF GOD — This is expressed in 1. Though the pilgrim mentioned this first, it could also be listed last as it is a fitting summary of all the proceeding and will hopefully become the true center of all his seeking.

SAME DAY — Our minds have become so alienated from our bodies, we must take psychedelic drugs to prove to ourselves that we still have emotions and passions and a spirit. These drugs can help people who have lost their bodies — they turn their minds on to their senses again.

COMMENT 1987: The pilgrim here is speaking in the name of those who justify experimenting with hallucinogenic drugs. Unaware of the means the Lord has provided for the healing they need, they turn to a chemical substitute in spite of the dangers and illusions it carries with it. The pilgrim is beginning to realize that the traditional aides like fasting, prayer, sacraments, grace, the Holy Spirit, etc. are the only true means for coming back into wholeness with our Creator, with oneself and with all of creation.

NOVEMBER 24, 1970 — THOUGHT — In the beginning Adam gave the animals NAMES; today we would assign them NUMBERS.

COMMENT 1987: This is a reflection on the move from a more personal engagement with reality typical of man up to the present, towards a more impersonal relationship that is typical of the analytical, categorical, statistical approach of a technological society. Although as expressed here the pilgrim is not relating this to the realm of faith and religion, it could be transferred in the sense that modern man will be tempted to think that God acts like he does, and merely considers man as a number, rather than as knowing him by name.

SAME DAY — THOUGHT — One can "see" things from a distance, but he must "get up close" to smell and taste them.

COMMENT 1987: The pilgrim here again gives evidence of his need for firsthand experience and his disenchantment with "video" — thus he points out the limitations of a society that has become predominantly "visual".

SAME DAY — THOUGHT — The contemporary restlessness within religion may be due in part to the fact that this is a generation that can only conceive of goals that are realizable BY HUMAN EFFORT and NOW; traditionally religion has presented an ideal NOT realizable by human effort alone and only AFTER death. Thus some have been tempted to lower the ideals (secularists) while others have attempted to realize the impossible (idealists, hippies, etc.) In the past the mystics came closest to realizing the ideal and there were enough people who believed in them to support them — psychically and materially. Today, few believe such "withdrawal" could be a worthy ideal!

COMMENT 1987: Here the pilgrim returns to his eschatological emphasis of the Christian faith, showing how the transcendent and supernatural must always be a part of an authentic Christianity. Since modern man does not normally look beyond the present, the concrete and the verifiable, he will have a hard time valuing the promise of eternal life. And those who witness to such a future life (pilgrims, vowed religious, etc.) will be scorned and written off by such a society.

SAME DAY — THOUGHT — Perhaps today, just as the old type of whole wheat bread would give most people indigestion, so, too, the raw message of the Gospels would not be able to be digested by most minds.

COMMENT 1987: The pilgrim here shows a surprising pastoral sensitivity; something not too common to one dedicated to an eschatological and prophetic charism. That is, he offers something of "an excuse" to modern man for not being open to the promise of eternal life through the death of Jesus and taking up of one's daily cross, saying that his "digestive system" (his thought processes, heart sensitivity, etc.) would be "overloaded" by such input.

NOVEMBER 25, 1970 — THOUGHT — When one exceedingly values a "result" he will dedicate himself to learning all the detailed steps that have gone into producing that result without questioning them; e.g. the rubrics of the Mass.

COMMENT 1987: This reflection perhaps uncovers something of why the pilgrim was not able to ask for ordination at the end of his theological studies. That is, he was not convinced of the worth of the result of the Mass. How could he value what he did not experience? How could he pass on what he himself did not find real or significant? Why go through the rubrics (the words and actions) of the Mass if they did not accomplish their intended result?

SAME DAY — THOUGHT — Today when people no longer fear any evil power as greater than them, or beyond their control — for they can accomplish all they desire (warmth, food, clothing, luxuries, etc.) just by "working hard" and saving or borrowing money — so they no longer find any need to rely on any "good power", namely God. With the number of commodities available practically infinite, they are sure the full meaning of life must be contained within one or more of them.

COMMENT 1987: Basically this seems to be an updating of what has been always true of fallen man and was pointed out by the Lord God, Yahweh before the Israelites crossed into the promised land (Dt. 31:20ff), namely, that God's people are always tempted to forget about their Creator in times of prosperity. When there is an abundance available, man begins to think he is pretty clever, pretty self-sufficient, and pretty secure with not much need to recognize or depend upon the real beginning and end of his life. Thus part of the modern problem of faith is not all that new: "man mesmerized by the works of his hands", even to the point of idolatry. That is, he puts his trust in creatures rather than in the Lord God.

DECEMBER 1, 1970 — THOUGHT — We no longer venerate

the saints — or even people living today — because the machine has made all people EQUALLY VALUELESS. We no longer believe some people are better than others, that some are closer to God than others, for we no longer experience any power but that of the machine.

COMMENT 1987: The pilgrim is here pointing out how modern man has been changed by his growing use of machines. It has caused him to loose touch with the world of the spirit and of the heart and those supernatural gifts that are dispensed by the Lord as He wills and which point to His goodness, and the mystery of His plan. These are not qualities that can be programmed into a machine and they tend to be ignored more and more by people whose lives become increasingly tied up with numbers and statistics.

SAME DAY — THOUGHT — If a new "apocalypse" is to be written, it will employ the "literary form" of science fiction.

COMMENT 1987: It doesn't seem the pilgrim is really expecting a new piece of Scripture to be added to the already existing Canon, but he is rather adverting to the fact that the book of Revelation in the Bible is a particular literary form, just as today science fiction is a recognized literary form with its own rules of interpretation and meaning, etc. If the Sacred Author were working with today's literary forms, he might choose science fiction as the most appropriate to express the truths of the Gospel about the fulfillment of God's plan of salvation in the final judgment.

SAME DAY — Those who truly value or reverence someone or something, will not immediately touch or grab for that reality, but slowly allow it to reveal itself.

COMMENT 1987: The pilgrim is here revealing his own approach to life more as one of standing apart, patiently waiting, and quietly reverencing. He has noticed others approach life very differently, for example in impulsively snapping pictures of something new they see, or in immediately trying to pick up a little baby and cuddle it, or in purchasing and buying things that they do not really need but which strike their fancy.

DECEMBER 2, 1970 — THOUGHT — It is important to fast (and discipline all one's appetites) in order to remind oneself that the "body" is not our master and first consideration.

COMMENT 1987: Pilgrimage in itself is an ascetical discipline, and so through it the Lord is teaching the pilgrim the importance of some of the traditional ascetical practices which he had not understood previously. In a society which measures everything by the pleasure it brings to the body, this call to discipline is surely going to sound strange and be a bitter medicine.

SAME DAY — If we are doing the will of God, we are doing everything, no matter what we are doing. If we are not doing the will of God, we are doing nothing, no matter what we are doing.

COMMENT 1987: This is the pilgrim's understanding of the importance of doing the will of God. Many (and perhaps the voices of his mentors which still echo within him at times) charge the pilgrim with wasting his talents and time by not using the education, etc. which he was given. He, however, has heard the Gospel invitation to sell all, give to the poor, and come follow the Lord. This is the will of God, believing in Jesus and the Father. Without this basis, nothing else, whether it is teaching great numbers of people, building churches, ministering the sacraments, etc. has any value in God's eyes. And conversely, the smallest hidden action, like putting one foot ahead of the other on a pilgrimage, done out of love for the Lord, gives much glory and pleasure to the heavenly Father.

SAME DAY — THOUGHT — Who suffers or gives of herself more than a mother?

COMMENT 1987: Becoming acquainted with suffering first-hand, the pilgrim begins to see other vocations in the same light. This could refer to his own mother and other mothers, as well as to the mother of Jesus.

SAME DAY — THOUGHT — In all ages past up to the present, life was a struggle because the world was a hostile environment — a vale of tears. In that world the meaning of life was to work hard (just to survive) and to believe in a benevolent superior power.

Today, when it is no longer necessary to "work hard" to live, the meaning of life is different and it actually becomes meaningless — witness the restless search for new exciting things.

Chardin sensed this development and believed only Christianity offered a hope which "transcended" all human effort (which leaves the heart unsatisfied) sufficient to carry on the task of building the earth, or else the whole Western world was in danger of collapse from boredom and a strike would be called in the noosphere (the world of human consciousness).

COMMENT 1987: Here the pilgrim is examining one of the main roots of the dissatisfaction he discovered in his own heart and takes it to be symptomatic of the malaise of modern man. He had "dropped out", "called a strike" from ministering, working, producing in his society, partly because he had never come face to face with "the struggle to keep alive" — with real sacrifice. Everything had been given to him without cost, as it were. This had led to a sense of not "deserving" life — for some-

how he sensed that anything worthwhile had to involve a strug-gle. What is gained easily is not valued. Thus the generation born into affluence cannot appreciate the gift of life until they come face to face with their inner poverty of spirit and need for a savior and meet Jesus who struggled to the death to bring them freedom and life. Pretechnological society offered man-kind a concrete image of sacrifice in the physical struggle to "keep the wolf away from the door". Day by day life experience helped him understand the Gospel message about waging war in the spirit against sin and Satan. Modern man does not have the aid of that material image, but he still needs to know and experience the spiritual struggle if he is to come to truth, free-dom and salvation.

DECEMBER 5, 1970 — THOUGHT — Perhaps we have less a sense of sin today because we have less a sense of any goal that we are aiming for and of therefore "missing the mark"; all things are "permitted" and "right".

COMMENT 1987: The pilgrim here makes use of one Old Testa-ment word used for sin, which literally means "to miss the mark", to reflect on the decline of a sense of sin in Christian preaching and in the practice of Confession. Since most Christ-ian preachers have changed from an eschatological emphasis to an incarnational one, the goals are now earthbound (a just society, etc.) and supposedly attainable with enough effort. When God's commands are explained away to the point where just about anything is permitted, is it any wonder man no longer feels the prick of conscience?

SAME DAY — THOUGHT — Follow your conscience, yes, but make sure it is an informed and upright conscience."

COMMENT 1987: The pilgrim here clarifies the cries of so many modern theologians and popularizers of the "follow your conscience" teaching, so that it is brought back into line with traditional Christian teaching. Thus he cuts away the implied principle in the shortened formula which would allow one to do anything he doesn't think is wrong.

SAME DAY — THOUGHT — People who have never ex-perienced real hunger for long periods of time, tend to regard eating as merely satisfying an appetite and not as strengthen-ing the body for activity and work.

COMMENT 1987: The pilgrim knows hunger on his pil-grimage, and thus comes to know and value the true meaning of food and nourishment. He experiences in his own body, fa-tigue and the power of food to revive him so that he can con-tinue on his way. His daily bread is his daily strength. He never knew this when he was given three meals every day and his appetite could easily be satisfied with snacks and such any time he felt like it.

DECEMBER 6, 1970 — THOUGHT — It often seems that for many people, taking pictures (especially "snapshots") shows an insensitivity and disrespect for the object captured, for it means that one is not willing to spend the time it would take to get to know this reality, but is satisfied with the superficial, surface aspects and wants these in a hurry: they show a "grabbing" mentality

COMMENT 1987: This reflection is very similar to a previous one on picture taking and keeps surfacing in the pilgrim's thoughts as he continues to dive deep and not be satisfied with the quick, surface aspects of reality. He is holding forth for a more contemplative approach rather than to a functional or self-centered accumulating approach.

And so the pilgrim is ready to enter the eternal city of Rome. He had now completed the fourth stage of his walk, from Zurich to Rome, a distance of about 500 miles. His total mileage was now about 2,250 miles but at the time he never once gave thought to this fact. He had no inclination to look back, to calculate or to glory in what had been achieved. Rather his whole heart was compelled to press on, keeping his eyes on the goal of Jerusalem.

During the six weeks it had taken him to traverse this distance he had come to be impressed with the Alps in Switzerland and the Umbrian hills in Italy. With these experiences his thoughts were turned to God in a new and powerful way. It was as though the mountains and the saints he had come to know there beckoned him to leave the valleys of the earth below and ascend up to the heights. Yes, even if this meant "going it alone". And so were planted the seeds of the life of a hermit. And indeed somewhere along this part of the route, the pilgrim had been given a picture holy card of St. Romuald, the founder of the Camaldolese — an order of hermits stemming from the 11th century. Only the future would reveal the details of this call.

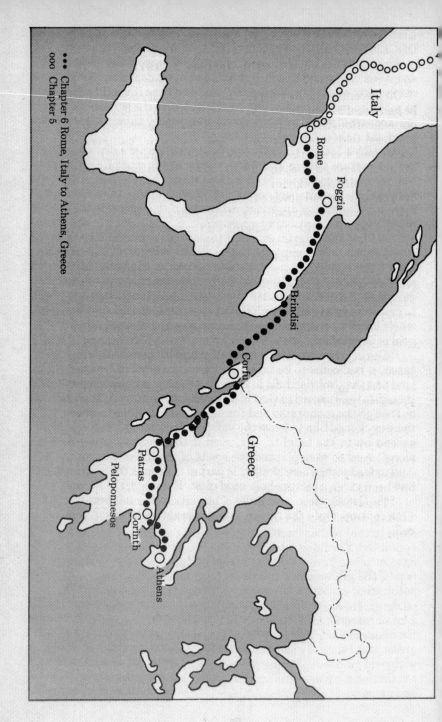

Italy

Rome

Foggia

Brindisi

Corfu

Greece

Patras

Peloponnesos

Corinth

Athens

CHAPTER SIX:
Rome, Italy — Athens, Greece
December 7, 1970 - January 21, 1971
PART ONE: Two Weeks in Rome

On December 7, the pilgrim entered that city whose name he had heard over and over since the days of his childhood Catholic education. Here was the source of that authority which he had been told came right from Christ, through Peter and his successors, and was therefore the arbiter of his faith. Here ruled the chief shepherd of all those who professed the Catholic faith.

Actually the pilgrim need not feel a stranger to this city, even though he had never before set foot within its walls. For he had "seen" it secondhand many, many times in picture books, framed paintings hanging on the seminary walls, and in 35 mm slide reproductions. He was familiar with the shape of the Vatican, the Coliseum, the Pantheon, the Arch of Constantine, etc., at least in miniature. But what would be his impression when he stepped into these monuments in real life?

The pilgrim headed right for St. Peter's Basilica and Vatican City, as this certainly would be the proper place for a pilgrim to visit and pray. He found the via della Conciliazione, the long straight avenue which led up to the front of the Basilica, and began to walk towards the great facade of St. Peter's. Then as he left the via della Conciliazione and stepped into the piazza, with the towering obelisk directly in front of him, he sensed a powerful maternal welcoming. Yes, again it was the architecture which conveyed the spiritual sense of "mother church". The long curved colonnades on each side of the piazza opened like the arms of a welcoming mother, and as he continued walking toward St. Peter's they actually appeared to be closing around him in an embrace which as much as said to the pilgrim: "Welcome home my son; it's good that you are here."

Thus the pilgrim felt a tremendous sense of peace, of belonging, and of acceptance. He made his way up the dozens of steps to the basilica itself. But once inside, he was greatly disappointed. The huge interior (large enough in which to land a light airplane, some said) the giant marble statues of bygone popes, the gilt ornamentation and baroque architecture, did nothing but convey to him the sense of a giant sepulchre or burial vault. He did not see a tabernacle or a crucifix until after a lot of searching, so there was little indication that this was the house of God. There was no public prayer or liturgy in progress: just tourists gawking and talking and taking pictures with paid guides explaining all the history of the place. And so, not finding it a place conducive to prayer, he soon made his exit and came back out to the piazza.

One of the people he hoped to see while In Rome was his former bishop, and dear friend, John Cardinal Wright. So he called on him at his residence which was actually just off one of the colonnades along the piazza. The cardinal, now overseeing the Congregation for the Clergy and responsible for 450,000 priests throughout the world, welcomed the pilgrim with open arms. He looked into the pilgrim's eyes and immediately made a positive assessment of the pilgrimage, saying: "Your eyes are bright and clear: I can see you've found the peace of the Lord." His next words were: "Do you have a place to stay in Rome?" "No, Your Excellency" said the pilgrim. "Then you'll stay here in my apartment as long as you like. Here, let me introduce you to the sisters who take care of me and this place."

And so the pilgrim who was used to sleeping out along the road at night and trusting the Lord to provide for his needs day by day, was being shown beautiful hospitality by one of the top prelates of the church, and successor of the apostles, in the very city of Peter. The sisters who would be taking care of his physical needs were of the same order as those who had taught him throughout his Catholic Grade School education, the Sisters of Divine Providence. And the cardinal made it clear he could come and go as he pleased and was free to join him for any meals he cared to while in Rome; just let the sisters know ahead of time.

And so the pilgrim settled into a daily routine of prayer, reading, and visiting the various places around the city. His reading during this time was from a book of Meditations by Dorothy Day, given to him by the Cardinal. Whether or not the Cardinal was trying to steer him in the way of the Catholic Worker movement he did not know, though he did jot down a few of Dorothy's thoughts, mostly having to do with prayer and community, rather than having to do with work and action. He continued to practice on his recorder and even played a few melodies for the Cardinal, who, however, quickly made known his preference for a traditional melody rather than a spontaneous improvisation. So the pilgrim played him "Jesu Joy of Man's Desiring" to his satisfaction and approval.

As the pilgrim visited various places around the city, one of his favorite spots was the Coliseum. Here he knew that countless martyrs had shed their blood for their faith in Christ in the days of imperial Rome. Somehow this place spoke to his need of a revived faith more clearly than the many churches and monuments throughout this great city. Here he seemed to be more directly in touch with an unadulterated, unembellished expression of a vibrant faith that was willing to go the whole way. He did not deny that those who created the ornate shrines and temples erected to honor these martyrs and other such witnesses to Christ also had faith. But somehow there was an air of finality, boldness and directness proclaimed by the arena of the martyrs' combat that ministered to the pilgrim's own need for a renewed faith.

One church, however, did succeed in captivating his ongoing interest. It was not one of the major basilicas listed in every tourguide of Rome as a must. As a matter of fact the pilgrim could not even remember the name of it years later, but it was a little dungeon-like structure off a back street. One had to go DOWN several steps to enter it. It supposedly contained a shrine honoring the pillar Jesus was tied to when He was scourged. But what kept him coming here day after day was the fact that there was continuous adoration of the Most Blessed Sacrament here and an order of religious sisters kept vigil two by two, day and night.

Here he found a quiet place to pray, undisturbed by tourists and by sacristans chasing him out so the building could be locked. Here the Lord was available to His people all the time, where one could "come as you are" into His most intimate presence — His very body and blood, soul and divinity — in the lowly little piece of white bread. Here amid the splendor of Rome with its proud past and bustling modern commerce, lay a power which nothing could destroy: the gift of eternal life which alone could give life to the heart of man: the throne room of the Creator of heaven and earth. All this was available to the meek and humble who would come on bended knee crying out from the depth of his heart "Lord, have mercy on me a sinner."

And so for two weeks the pilgrim tramped the paved streets of the mighty metropolis of Rome. He visited a friend from his hometown who was in Rome studying art. He spent a day with Archabbot Rembert Weakland, OSB who was the former Abbot of the Monastery/Seminary where he had done four years of theology. But mainly he was blessed by just being able to live and pray in this city of man which the Lord had chosen as that place from which the Gospel of his love would go forth to the whole world. Just to recall who his fellow travelers were over the centuries from Peter and Paul to Augustine and Benedict, to Francis and Dominic and Ignatius — the whole glorious list of faithful servants of the Lord — this was a great inspiration to him and source of building up of his faith.

On Sunday, December 13, the pilgrim was in the piazza with the large crowd that customarily gathered there for the Papal blessing. Pope Paul VI had come to the balcony for the Angelus at noon, had given a brief talk, and imparted his papal blessing upon all who stood below. This seemed to the pilgrim as the Lord's sign that now the time had come to continue on his pilgrimage. He had seen the Vicar of Christ on earth and was signed by him with the cross of Jesus in the name of the Father, the Son and the Holy Spirit. It was like the Lord now saying: "It was good of you to come. Now go forth in my name and authority and proclaim the love of God to all creatures. You have my blessing. I'm behind you the whole way. Be safe. Be healthy. Go in peace."

With this word planted deeply in his heart, nothing could change the pilgrim's mind: neither the suggestions of his parents that he stay in Rome for Christmas, nor the offer of the Cardinal of a place to stay. The pilgrim was content to accept the Cardinal's advice not to attempt to go up along the Adriatic Sea and down through Yugoslavia in the winter but to head south and cross into Greece from Brindisi. He also accepted money for the boat passage from the Cardinal and then took his leave of the eternal city.

The pilgrim made no personal journal entries during his stay in Rome. But below are two quotes from Dorothy's Day's book of *Meditations*, subtitled "Justifications and Challenges," which he had been reading while staying in Rome. QUOTE " . . . life itself is a haphazard, untidy, messy affair. Unless we can live simply, unquestioningly, and solitary, one might say, in the midst of a mob, then we cease to be a personalist. The more we live with people in community the more we must look to ourselves and regard the beam in our own eyes. The more we live with a babbling crowd, the more we must practice silence. For every idle word we speak we will be judged." (February 1943)

COMMENT 1987: The pilgrim here seems to be identifying with the alternate balancing of living alone and living in community. In doing this of course he would not be striving to be a "personalist" but to "live according to the Gospel of Jesus Christ." The emphasis on purification of one's own heart ("eyes") is another developing of the seed of the hermit life in his vocation.

QUOTE: "More than ever am I convinced that the solution lies only in the Gospel and in such a leader as St. Francis. Peter Maurin has been talking these past two years of recruiting troubadours of Christ. More and more am I convinced that together with our purely material efforts of building up hospices and farming communes, we need these fellow travellers with the poor and the dispossessed to share with them their poverty and insecurity and to bring them the reminder of the love of God." (May, 1940)

COMMENT 1987: This reflection seems to point more to the pilgrimage aspect of the developing vocation of the pilgrim. In it he is imitating Christ who "did not have a place to lay his head" (Mt. 8:20) and thus in a concrete and radical manner is testifying to Christ becoming poor so that we might be made rich (II Cor. 8:9). This vocation was dramatically lived out by the 18th century saint, Benedict Labre who lived on the streets of Rome, sleeping with the derelicts and eating out of the same trash heaps as them.

PART TWO: Rome — Brindisi

Upon leaving Rome, the pilgrim had as his next immediate goal to "get to Brindisi and catch a boat for Greece." Brindisi lay about 350 miles south on the eastern side of the heel of the boot of Italy. The land in between Rome and Brindisi was merely "to be crossed over." There were no shrines, sights or people he desired to visit, though he was open to whatever the Lord might want to show him along the way. One thought in his mind as he set out of course was, how he would spend Christmas and the celebration of the Lord's birth.

In these three weeks of walking, the pilgrim would come to know and experience genuine hospitality as well as mere curiosity. The farther south he got in Italy, the more open and spontaneous people seemed to be. This was so much the case that he even began to find it a nuisance as his desire was to be left alone to walk, think and pray. This routine was continually being interrupted when one Italian after another stopped to offer him a ride, give him money, feed him, invite him into their home, etc. Thus for example even a group of little children in Naples who were playing on the street, went around and collected what amounted to about 30 cents to give to the pilgrim.

This Italian hospitality was well typified by his experience of celebrating Christmas about a two days' walk west of Foggia as he headed east to get to Barletta on the coast of the Adriatic Sea. About three p.m. Christmas eve the pilgrim began looking around for a cheap room in a third class hotel so he could get cleaned up and go to midnight Mass (supposing that was the custom here in Italy as it was back in the States). But he could find no accommodations in the town he was in, so he decided to continue on his journey. Very soon, however, it began to rain. So he looked for some kind of a shelter. Spotting a bridge over a small creek he found a grassy bank under the bridge out of the storm and decided to "set up camp" there for the night.

But he had not calculated on the river rising and possiblity of his being right in the path of the water flow of a rain-swollen creek. So not long after falling asleep on the soft grass, he suddenly awoke to find himself laying in a puddle of water. He quickly gathered his things together and got up on higher ground but still under the bridge and out of the pouring rain. He watched the display of lightning and imagined the thunder to be the voices of the angels (Rv. 19:6) singing "Glory to God in the highest, peace to men of good will (Lk. 2:13-14)." And so he thanked the Lord for sending his messengers to wake him so he could keep vigil on this holy night. Like the shepherds out in the fields that first Christmas, he was not attending an elaborate liturgy in a brightly lit and colorfully decorated church. But he was grateful for the opportunity to watch and pray and welcome his King and Lord to earth as a tiny helpless infant in this simple and humble way. He then fell asleep and got a few more hours of rest before dawn.

Upon waking, the pilgrim rejoiced in a gentle warm breeze and shining sun. But this didn't last long. Before an hour of walking had been completed, it had clouded over and began to rain again. Now what was he to do? Just then he heard some church bells ringing. Taking that as a sign that the holy sacrifice of the Mass was about to be celebrated there, he quickly headed in that direction.

When he arrived, he found the church full and had to join the crowd of men standing in the back entrance way. But he could hear and see what was going on. Thus, even though the Mass was in Italian and the people let three young girls accompanied by a guitar do most of the singing, he had no trouble participating in the Mass. He was deeply aware of how great a gift the Father had given to him in sending His only Son to be offered up for his healing and reconciliation.

After the liturgy the pilgrim was preparing to depart, when a man came up to him and said he was welcome to come to his house for something to eat. The pilgrim went along with him, rejoicing to find such genuine hospitality offered to him, a perfect stranger (except for the fact that they were brothers who had just worshipped their Lord together in church). As it turned out this man seemed to have some standing in the town for many, many people stopped at his house to enjoy his hospitality and food.

Though he could not communicate verbally with his host, the pilgrim was able to say something to the children of the house who were learning English in school. As he sat down to the table he saw many different kinds of dishes: baked spiced fish eaten cold; peppers stuffed with nuts and raisins; wild rabbit, and of course bread and wine and Christmas cookies. Also he noticed that the room was heated by the fireplace in which a fine fire was kept going; this also provided the heat for cooking some of the tasty dishes. In addition, under the table he found a brazier that was kept hot with coals from the fire and which had a little wooden ledge running around the outside for people to put their feet on to get them warm. How homey, cheerful and pleasant.

About noontime the pilgrim took leave of his generous host, who as a final good will gesture, filled his plastic "Happy Christmas" bag with goodies from the table so the pilgrim would have something for the journey. Thus the pilgrim left physically nourished and with a heart filled with thanksgiving to the Lord for the blessing of such a reception. He prayed that all men, himself included, would be as open and hospitable to their Lord when He came to visit their hearts.

The pilgrim's next destination was Foggia, which he judged lay about 30 miles to the east. Normally speaking this would be too much to make by the end of the day, but as far as the pilgrim was concerned there was no rush — at least as far as he could see. Nevertheless, the Lord had other plans of which the pilgrim could know nothing, and a trial and testing was about to occur for which the previous hospitality would serve as a needed reserve of strength.

The first three hours after lunch were very pleasant walking, even though it was rather cool. The pilgrim figured it might be in the low forties, but with the lined long army coat with the hood up, plus the heat generated by his walking, it was quite comfortable. Then about three o'clock the rains began again. Now he began to wonder how he would spend the night outside with all his things already soaking wet. Then the rain changed to snow.

It began to snow huge wet flakes and very quickly the whole countryside was transformed into a "winter wonderland". Now though this was a beautiful sight to behold with the eyes, it did not do much for the body, especially when about 6 o'clock he began asking about the availability of rooms and could find nothing. He was told there would be nothing available till Foggia, and this lay at least another 15 miles or about 6 more hours of walking. That seemed like more than the pilgrim could physically handle, and then how could he expect to find a room at 12 midnight? So he prayed to the Lord to rescue him.

And of course the Lord did. Within a half hour He sent along an "angel" who offered him a ride in his car, all the way to Foggia and right to a third class hotel. There, for $2.50, the pilgrim got a large clean bed, plenty of heat, and a good hot shower. Besides all that the landlady there delighted to use the little English she knew. And so the Lord had prepared a place for the pilgrim. It just took a greater amount of trust and endurance than normal to find it, and he had to put aside his spirit of independence and accept the help of a stranger to give him a lift, even if it meant he could not walk this part of his pilgrimage.

From Foggia the pilgrim headed for Barletta on the coast. From there he would go south along the coast to Bari and to Brindisi where he could get a ferryboat over to Greece. On this stretch of some 150 miles one very significant and prophetic event occurred in the life of the pilgrim, and it was this.

One day as he walked along a valley floor with mountains on both sides, it came time to take a rest stop. As he looked about for a suitable place he glanced to his right and far up the side of the mountain he spotted an old church building. So he decided that would be an appropriate place to rest and pray.

As he began seeking a way up to the structure, however, he found that the only apparent access was an old abandoned road, much overgrown with trees and bushes. When he got to the building itself, he found that the church was in total disrepair. The doors were off, parts of the ceiling had fallen in and debris lay all about inside. His heart immediately went out to his Lord whose temple had been so abandoned by His children.

Finding a place to kneel, the pilgrim began to pray and worship his Lord. He asked for forgiveness for all his brothers and sisters everywhere who had abandoned their faith in God and gone off seeking happiness in other places. He asked for forgiveness for himself, as he, too, had for a time walked away from the practice of his faith and sought the meaning of life in the pleasures of the world. He prayed that all who still strayed might quickly return to their Father's house.

Then as he prayed, the thought came to him. Does the Lord want me to stop my pilgrimage and settle down in this place? Is He perhaps calling me, as He called St. Francis of Assisi, to rebuild his church and begin with the physical repair of this abandoned building?

The pilgrim considered that he could send for some money from the States to get started and then he could just live on the alms from the people. Here in a foreign country, he would be a stranger and be able to live the quiet life of a hermit. He asked himself: was this what the Lord had in mind all along in getting him on this pilgrimage?

The pilgrim remained for a few hours — much longer than his normal time for resting — and considered well where this thought was coming from: the Lord, the devil or himself. Eventually he discerned that the thought was from the Lord but that He did not intend the pilgrim to settle down here at this time. Rather He was planting a seed in his heart and giving him a desire to retire from the world and live a life of abandonment and prayer. This incident was merely a way of concretely fixing this calling in his heart. In another day and place it would come to fruition. So the pilgrim arose from his place of prayer and made his way back down the mountainside, continuing on his way.

By January 3, he had arrived in Brindisi and found a ferryboat that would shuttle him across to Greece for the small, fair price of $12.50. As he prepared to take leave of this land of his Catholic faith, he reflected on his walk in the past two months. In this land he had come to touch the heart of His Lord in canonized saints who had already finished their pilgrimage and won their crown of glory after living lives of heroic virtue here on this earth. He had also come to know living saints of the mystical body of Christ today who had welcomed him, a stranger, and shown their live in simple practical concern. He had been privileged to live and pray in the city of Rome where Peter and Paul had ended their lives of witnessing to the resurrection of their Lord Jesus Christ. They had planted the seed of faith which nothing in the past 2000 years had been able to overcome. As a matter of fact, this faith had been faithfully handed on even up to the age of the pilgrim, so that he, too, had heard the same saving message of God's love and reconciliation in Jesus Christ as had the first generation of Christians. All of this was both reassuring and enlightening to the pilgrim as he sought to find his way on his spiritual journey home to the Father.

The following are some of the thoughts the pilgrim had and recorded during these three weeks:

DECEMBER 16, 1970 — THOUGHT — I wonder if Christ was ever tempted to "hate" all men for the suffering they were causing him to undergo?

COMMENT 1987: The pilgrim, as he takes on some of the suffering of Christ as he walks along on pilgrimage, has this "human" or "fallen" reaction which is typical of the sinful human heart, namely to resent those who cause one pain and wish them an appropriate harm. Jesus certainly never felt this way because He was without sin, but as man the Father somehow mysteriously allowed him to be tempted as all other men (Hb. 4:15).

DECEMBER 17, 1970 — THOUGHT — There is no one who can understand another perfectly and it may be very misleading to say "Our Lord knows us completely for he never "knew" or "experienced" sin. Though he knew their effects more deeply

101

than anyone else, he never knew them as an agent and personal cause.

COMMENT 1987: This is a continuation of the previous day's reflection and again is answered by St. Paul who says that God allowed Jesus to be sin (II Cor. 5:21) and know that alienation from the Father on the cross as he cried out "My God, my God, why have you forsaken me?" (Mk. 15:34).

SAME DAY — THOUGHT— Before the advent of mass education (French Revolution) it was "natural" for the majority of people to look up to and respect those privileged few who knew more and considered them as fit to rule and guide and make the laws. People would attach temselves to one stronger than they in the way of a slave or vassal with the idea that this was the only way they could survive, being too weak to support their own life. So also, Christ was cast into this light as a king and lord. Today everyone has the right and access to all the information there is in the world. So mere knowledge does not inspire the old kind of respect or dependance. With the extent of knowledge being so vast, the listeners are sure the speaker is not aware of vast fields of information. What then is the basis of power? What gives priests their "potestas"?

COMMENT 1987: The pilgrim here is digging around once again at his own identity crisis as a seminarian and candidate for priesthood. Here he is still in the questioning stage as he has not yet entered the realm of faith which would eventually show him that the power comes from Christ as a pure gift to those who are empty of self and open, humbled and broken by affliction: open to the Lord's pouring in his grace and healing and life for others to receive through him.

DECEMBER 18, 1970 — Touring and vacationing appeals to a man's desire for power — to possess the whole world — to go out and see it and capture it on film.

COMMENT 1987: The pilgrim here seems to be once again coming up against one of the deep roots of Western Civilization which he finds in himself, but with which he is not comfortable and from which he wishes to disengage himself: namely Western man's penchant to dominate and use what he finds about him in the world to serve his own misguided appetites and sinful passions. Thus the pilgrim finds himself personally drawn more to a comtemplative stance towards the rest of creation around him; to live and let live, to not disturb but to take as is and let it be.

DECEMBER 19, 1970 — THOUGHT — People who are unsure of themselves and feel life to be insecure and threatening, find meaning and content in knowing or believing in a superior power, a divine order that guides the seemingly chaotic mess — like the power or laws which govern the stars and planets and seasons and growth of life; PRAYER in this context is man's effort to fit himself into this divine element.

COMMENT 1987: As the pilgrim experiences deeply the rhythms of nature and becomes aware of the pattern and order of it all, his faith in a divine lawgiver and master workman begins to be rekindled. This Lord of creation begins to attract his heart as he senses His beauty and allows his heart to be drawn to him in worship and praise. Thus prayer for the pilgrim is no longer so much asking for things that one desires or thinks he needs, but surrender to an all-encompassing beauty and good.

DECEMBER 21, 1970 — THOUGHT — Possibly God became man in order to renew his sense of dignity, to give him hope, show him a worthwhile future: He came in an age when men PHYSICALLY felt their poorness and helplessness in the face of nature and other men. The Jews, by considering themselves a chosen people could at least salvage the hope of a better future despite the most humiliating poverty of their present circumstances.

COMMENT 1987: As Christmas and the celebration of the Lord's birth draw near, the pilgrim's thoughts naturally turn to the mystery of the Incarnation. He highlights the truth that God came to resue the poor, the oppressed, the imprisoned. The Jews at the time of Christ felt this physically from their Roman rulers, but this was merely to be the external sign and context of the Lord's redeeming all people from spiritual poverty, complete bankruptcy and eternal damnation.

DECEMBER 22, 1970 — THOUGHT — Most people think I refuse to work for a living because I am lazy and don't want to exert myself. They do not realize that no work is hard enough or challenging enough for me to dedicate my whole life to except the work of union with God.

COMMENT 1987: The pilgrim here shows how he is still subject to being sensitive to what other people think of him and his way of life. Nevertheless, he turns it into an opportunity to express his complete dedication to the things of the Lord and not just offer a rationalization for his life.

DECEMBER 24, 1970 — THOUGHT — Once one comes to discover the plan of God for his own life and begins conforming his thoughts and actions to that plan, he has tapped an inexhaustible source of power and nothing, as long as it is in line with that plan, will prove too difficult. Actually there is a constant growth in strength, so that what earlier would have proved too difficult, later becomes possible.

COMMENT 1987: The pilgrim here is identifying the source of power or motivation which is keeping him going and giving him the energy and drive to meet one difficult situation after another. It is the awareness that one is in God's will and if God is for him, who can be against him? (Rm. 8:31). Thus there is not ever the fear anymore that God will eventually ask something too difficult, for there is the assurance that His grace will be sufficient when the time comes (II Cor. 12:9).

As Christmas drew near the pilgrim looked at the way he had experienced it in years past from a new perspective. Here are his reflections:

The Christmas story goes on and on. Year after year we celebrate a birth. We draw on the past and repeat the old and familiar. Where's life gone? Where is it going?

Emotions run high: "'Tis the season to be jolly." Special songs are brought out and dusted off; played over and over till all sounds so hollow.

It's time to give: Children's Hospital you know. Who can refuse? Let's see who can give the most. What about love? Does it get lost somewhere on the bank balance statement?

What about church? At least there we'll find the truth. Get out the ornaments: put up the tree. "It wouldn't be Christmas without all the decorations." Dress up the kids: parade the choir boys: Turn out the lights: sing "Silent Night".

Lord, can't we stop and get down on our knees? All you ask is a minute of time. Who will call us out of dead traditions past? And light the fire of love so you can come again alive?

What will my Christmas be this year? Lord, how do I please You? How do YOU want me to spend it? Do I have a choice? What does it mean to celebrate? Does the world really know what it's all about?

Please give me, Lord, The faith to see past all the thick facade, And find again the love that made The Word become our flesh.

Who in this world of sin and death can hold Your light up high? Till war and greed are put to death And love reigns over all?

COMMENT 1987: At first sight there appears to be a great deal of cynicism apparent in the reflections of the pilgrim. Yet they show how he has been challenged to his roots to step aside from all the old and familiar and get a fresh perspective. Hopefully, it is the Lord's instrument for teaching him the true meaning of it all.

Here are some further reflections, entitled
SOME THOUGHTS ON CHRISTMAS
Have you ever wondered just what it's all about?

- shopping for a dozen gifts
  things that will be soon forgotten:
- glittering tinsel, twinkling lights,
  striking the eye, by-passing the heart,
  hiding the hollow emptiness beneath.
- Christmas trees and colored balls,
  no longer reminders of the fruitful earth:
- miniature trains and make-believe world,
  still within the hands of man?
- Santa Claus and "What do you want?"
  as if a toy were it:
- wishing for a fresh white snow,
  thinking IT may still the land:
- "how many days are left to shop?"
  not one to stop and rest:
- sparking chains and spinning tires,
  nature still holds some untamed power:
- friendly visits, throwing parties,
  mainly fronts for worn out gossip:
- special foods and expensive drinks,
  "down the hatch" with hardly a thought:
- Christmas carols and midnight Mass,
  ancient customs we still observe:
- rushing here and rushing there,
  no time to stop and think and wonder.

SO MAYBE THAT'S THE MEANING
AND WHAT IT'S ALL ABOUT

In battle lines around the world,
men give themselves in hope,
  - so maybe that's the meaning and what it's all about.
In some poor home, the fire is life, the only warmth and light,
  - so maybe that's the meaning and what it's all about.
In some poor slum
a child is born
and given a mother's warm embrace,
  - so maybe that's the meaning and what it's all about.
In Roman times
a child was born
they said He was from God,
  - so maybe that's the meaning and what it's all about.
The city sleeps, the lights go out,
a man looks up and marvels,
  - so maybe that's the meaning and what it's all about.
The church is quiet,
the rich have gone

only the whisper of a faithful soul,
- so maybe that's the meaning and what it's all about.
A child at work, hours on end,
building castles in the sand,
- so maybe that's the meaning and what it's all about.
A child picks up a broken doll,
and shows it love and care,
- so maybe that's the meaning and what it's all about.
A grain of wheat, a kernel of corn,
dying, they rise
and give more life,
- so maybe that's the meaning and what it's all about.

COMMENT 1987: Again, standing apart from the world's celebration of Christmas, the pilgrim is confronted with the deeper meaning of all the traditional outward forms of the Christmas season. He will never be able to "get back in the swing of it all" ever again.

DECEMBER 27, 1970 — THOUGHT — Why did the first 25 years of my life seem so unreal? Because they were so easy and programmed, when real life is not that way? Considering the course of evolution, can life in the future be anything but the less real — less like it used to be (untidy, difficult, precarious)?

COMMENT 1987: The pilgrim here shows how naive he still is about life, due, no doubt to a great extent, to the fact that he had not met any great trials or crises in his life up to this time. For it is these kinds of difficulties and crosses that show one life is not so neat, easy and prepackaged but rather that there is a rawness, an unknown, deep down within. Projecting this upon the course of progress he sees about him in the technological world, he seriously questions whether it is real wisdom to try and make life to comfortable and easy for oneself and the up-coming generation.

DECEMBER 28, 1970 — THOUGHT — Prayers that are old and familiar can be a centering and stabilizing device amidst the ever-changing details of daily life. God alone remains the same, though our experience of Him constantly changes. He does not change because He is single, simple and without parts.

COMMENT 1987: Here the pilgrim discovers a "practical" purpose for memorized and recited prayers. This leads him to cast off the theory of process theology which talks about God changing, and go back to the traditional thinking which placed all change on the side of man, the creature and created. Thus the Lord can become that stable point about which the changing circumstances of his life break and in Whom he can find his refuge at any moment.

DECEMBER 29, 1970 — My main hope now is that I will rise and live with God after my death to this life.

COMMENT 1987: The pilgrim's heart has been purified now to the point of discarding all other plans, hopes, and goals, except the all important one of safely arriving at his eternal destiny, life with God forever.

SAME DAY — THOUGHT — Nowhere have I found a spirit like unto my spirit. Many were willing to laugh and rejoice with me — no one to mourn and weep, to watch and to pray.

COMMENT 1987: The pilgrim here reveals something of the loneliness of the vocation of the pilgrim. Before he left the city of man and took to the highway to the city of God, he could find many so-called friends who were willing to party and have a good time with him. But now that he finds himself called to weep and mourn for his sins and the sins of the world, he stands alone with no companions willing to pick up the Cross of Jesus and carry it to Calvary.

DECEMBER 31, 1970 — THOUGHT — Is it only because of SIN that the world goes on? If men disciplined their appetites as Christ asked on the Sermon on the Mount, all would give up their present plans and ambitions and wait for His coming. Maybe that's all it will take for the end of the world: all men LAY DOWN THEIR ARMS and join in one ecstatic prayer of union.

COMMENT 1987: Here the pilgrim expresses the solution to the world's problems from the eschatological perspective — namely repentance from sin. He sees that all the problems of the world stem from greed, from self-will and personal ambition — namely sin. If men would turn from sin the Kingdom of God would truly be made manifest.

SAME DAY — THOUGHT — Historically, the church seems to have chosen to follow Christ's later command to "take swords" (Lk. 22:36) and armed herself with weapons (structures) of the world, thus interpreting His eschatological discourse as applying only to His own lifetime and the end of the world.

COMMENT 1987: The pilgrim here is reflecting on the institutional aspect of the Church which very often seems to hide and distract from her eschatological nature. Since the Church is in the world, there is the constant temptation to take up the things of the world, forgetting to depend totally upon the Lord. That is why the Lord continues to send saints and prophets to remind the Church that she is to live by faith and she needs to repent and be purified.

JANUARY 1, 1970 — THOUGHT — The situation of telling someone about something they do not know: Christ telling us about heaven. The more the speaker is aware of the unfamiliar reality, the less of a problem it will be. He must also be aware of the experience of the listener: there can never be a perfect communication, for the speaker must always adapt and conform to the prevailing knowledge and myth, to some extent. At best he can give hints through symbols — parables.

All our actions in this life are only SYMBOLIC: none can perfectly attain the REAL! So our present existence is a matter of selecting the symbols we think most appropriately point to the reality which lies beyond.

So, too, the matter of RESPECT for life. The ultimate symbol here might be refusing to even take a step (let alone complete abstinence from food) out of a desire not to destroy the plant and animal life on the ground beneath our feet.

COMMENT 1987: The pilgrim here is reflecting on the problem of communication, especially the difficulties in trying to speak about eternal truths to time-bound man. He therefore sees the Lord Jesus' reason for the choice of parables and symbols, especially the teaching symbol that His whole life, death and resurrection became for man. His final comment on the symbol of not taking a step or eating food would make sense except for the fact that the Son of God became man, came to earth to live, die and rise again, and became THE ULTIMATE SYMBOL and only powerful and successful vehicle of true respect for life. In the physical chain of life, the lower form gives up its life and dies to sustain the life of a higher form. Jesus became the lowest form spiritually, taking on the death of a criminal, suffering as an outcast for all the sins of the world, in order to give life to all who eat of his body and drink of his blood. Thus the Sacrifice of Calvary and Communion of the Eucharist are now the ultimate sign and sacrament of RESPECT FOR LIFE.

JANUARY 2, 1970 — THOUGHT — For most people, conversation seems to be mainly an antidote to boredom; eating as well. These distract them from the emptiness they would feel in silence and rest.

COMMENT 1987: Having had such a profound experience of the VANITY of all earthly realities, the pilgrim takes a dim view of all merely HUMAN activities. This, of course, can lead to cynicism. But it can also be a spur to drive one into the arms of the Lord, who alone can satisfy the deepest desires of the heart of man.

PART THREE: Brindisi — Athens

The chains creaked as the anchors of the ferryboat Poseidonia began to be lifted off the bottom of the harbor at

Brindisi, and took their place just above the water level on the bow. The motley group of passengers who had paid their $12.00 for this passage of 150 miles from Brindisi across the strait of Otranto to Greece looked like a group of refugees as they scurried about to check over their few precious belongings for the umpteenth time to make sure they had not forgotten or misplaced anything. Many appeared to be young Americans out to "see Europe on $5.00 a day," but here and there one also could see a business-suited traveler.

While many passengers went top-side to get one final glance of Italy — a land they loved as home or had just come to know after a shorter or longer visit — the pilgrim stayed in his cushioned chair on the lower deck. He was thankful for the well lit, heated sitting room where he had several hours in which he could write one of his long letters home. Being always on the move and being too cold to write outside now on his rest stops, he found this the ideal situation for writing and reflecting on the experiences of his last two months in Italy.

After a brief stop on the Island of Corfu (called Kerkyra in Greek) the ferryboat made the last 25-mile leg of the journey and brought its passengers onto the mainland of Greece at Egoumenitsa. Here the pilgrim put on his steel-framed backpack with the blue lightweight sleeping bag and set out on foot to cover the land which he knew had nourished the roots of the Western civilization of which he was so very much a part. He felt he had to stop in Athens, and along the way at Corinth because there St. Paul had founded a Christian community which occasioned two precious letters from his hand — which letters formed part of the New Testament Scriptures. From there on he would be walking in the footsteps of the great Apostle to the Gentiles (and to him). That thought brought great joy to the pilgrim and made him feel unworthy but privileged, as he hoped it would prepare him for the final grace of walking in the footsteps of his Lord and Master Jesus Christ.

Before he left Egoumenitsa though, the pilgrim did what was by now routine when he entered a new country and that was to exchange about $30.00 of his American Express Travelers Checks into the local currency, which in this case was "drachmae". This would enable him to buy his daily loaf of bread, which was his main source of physical sustenance and pay any ferry tolls or fees for room and board.

Having still fresh in his mind the bitter experience of crossing the interior of Italy and running into so much cold and snow, the pilgrim clung tightly to the Mediterranean coast so as to benefit from its warmth. He did this even though it would mean he would have to take a boat here and there instead of walking the whole way. Thus he headed straight south through Margariton, Parga and onto Prevaza where he got a small boat across a two-mile stretch to Vonitssa on January 9. From there he joined up with the main route (19) again to Antirrion where he got another ferry over to Patras on the Peloponnesos.

During this first week of travel in Greece, the pilgrim was so thankful for the beautiful warm weather and sunny skies, especially after so many chilly, rainy days in Italy. But during this time he also experienced what he judged to be a slight case of dysentery. Though it was an inconvenience, it did not weaken him to the point where he could no longer spend the day walking. His solution to the problem was to fast and not eat or drink anything for several days. All he took each day was one orange (they were lying all along the road under the trees from which they had fallen), section it off and eat one piece at a time over the whole day. Eventually his system returned to normal.

It was within the first few days of his walk through Greece that the following incident happened, reminding the pilgrim of the dangers which lay along his path as well as the Lord's faithful provision for his welfare. It was well into the evening one day and though darkness had fallen, the pilgrim continued walking, both because to go to sleep now would make the night too long and also because he did not find a suitable spot off the side of the road in which to spend the night. As he was walking he began to hear dogs barking in the distance. At first this did not bother him, but then the barking seemed to get closer and louder as a pack of dogs was coming up on him from behind.

Earlier in the day, the pilgrim had seen what he took to be sheep dogs, which looked much like German Shepherds. But they had iron collars around their necks, studded with 4″ long iron spikes. He had guessed that these collars were protection from wolves that the dogs might have to fight off so they could not be injured around their necks. But it made the dogs look even more ferocious and it was this image the pilgrim attached to the sounds he heard growing ever closer behind him.

He felt really helpless. Here he was alone, out in the country, with no one around to help him. He had no weapon, not even a stick with which to defend himself. He did not think it wise to try and run and there were no trees nearby to climb. So he cried out to the Lord in his heart to save him. As he did he reached into his coat pocket and felt a small flashlight that he had bought in Italy a few weeks before so he could read the Psalms in the Bible at night if there was no electric light handy. He had just bought new batteries for it before he left Italy because he didn't know if Greece would have the same size batteries or not.

Then the Lord gave him the idea that was to save his life. He slowed his pace till he was hardly moving. He allowed the dogs to approach to within what he judged to be about 15 feet. Then he crouched down, wheeled around directly facing the menacing pack of 10-12 dogs, shined the little light directly into their eyes and at the top of his voice, let out the loudest scream he possibly could. Thanks be to God the dogs immediately turned around and fled into the night. The pilgrim breathed a great sigh of relief and thanked the Lord for saving him from peril as he continued to walk on into the night.

After only a few days in Greece, it became apparent to the pilgrim that the people of Greece were quite a friendly and inquisitive lot — though not as threatening as the dogs. People were constantly stopping and offering him a ride: from the bus driver who indicated "ride free — no money", to the fellow on the motor bike who did his best to persuade the pilgrim (back pack and all) to climb up behind him on his seat for a ride. And this happened so regularly that it almost became annoying. So the pilgrim had to learn how to say "only on foot" or "to Jerusalem" till they understood that it was necessary that he walk and not ride.

The pilgrim crossed over to the lower peninsula, the Peloponnesos, at Patras on January 14, in order to be in line to visit Corinth on his way to Athens. Patras was a thriving metropolis and seemed to share something of an international flavor. One particularly well dressed gentleman spoke English and showed quite an interest in the pilgrim and what he was doing. After about 15 minutes of conversation (which was quite long in terms of what the pilgrim was used to), the friendly gentleman wished the pilgrim that "his feet might always be able to take him as now, wherever his heart desired to go." The pilgrim was greatly edified by such a perceptive and thoughtful prayer and knew that he would always remember and treasure that particular encounter.

On January 17, the pilgrim arrived in Corinth. It was the ruins of the ancient first century city that was the focus of his visit. Though he was approaching it from the opposite direction, this site became the pilgrim's first link (other than Rome) with the great Apostle Paul. It would be his journey the pilgrim would now follow step by step for the next three months, as best he could reading from the New Testament letters and the Acts of the Apostles.

The pilgrim only spent a few hours among the ruins but was glad to find a marker on the spot called the "Beria" where Paul was brought before the magistrate and accused of sedition (Acts 18:12ff). The pilgrim reflected on the cost of discipleship

111

evidenced in the life of Paul who apparently lived in almost continual danger from one source or another because of his commitment to preach the Gospel of salvation to Jew and Greek. His example gave the pilgrim renewed courage to continue on his own journey, not so much as one preaching the Gospel, as one totally dedicated to seeking to experience it with his whole heart, mind and strength.

In three more days the pilgrim came to Athens. Here he needed to do more than just visit and pray at the Christian shrines. He needed to make use of certain services provided by its modern culture. His first destination was the American Express Office where he hoped to find some mail from home waiting for him. This was made easy for him on the third day when he was about 10 miles from Athens. He felt it would be best to get into Athens as soon as possible, so he decided to take the first ride offered to him that day. It wasn't long when a long-haired American youth in a van hailed him down, told him he knew where the American Express Office was, was going there himself and would be glad to take him along. So he hopped aboard, not in the least considering it a betrayal of his vow to walk, but rather as the Lord's provision for what he would need.

Two other services he would be seeking in the capital city of Greece were a dentist and a vaccination for cholera. Good information for both of these needs was also provided by his traveling friends. In all he made three trips to a woman dentist for three fillings for the reasonable price of $12 total, and got the first of two shots against cholera as he would soon be going into Turkey and the Near East.

It took two days to finish his business in Athens so the pilgrim had time to visit the ancient Acropolis on top of the hill overlooking modern Athens. Here he got a firsthand view of the Parthenon, a structure originally serving as a pagan temple and then for centuries as a Christian church. This was another one of those images indelibly impressed upon his memory through dozens of pictures he had seen during his classical and liberal arts studies in the Seminary. It stood for all that was prized by Western civilization in the field of architecture. The glory that was Greece had certainly faded now, or at least it was transported to other lands and new forms. All that remained of the ancient splendor were some broken stone pillars, lintels and frieze works.

But the Lord seemed to put His stamp of approval on it all by arranging a natural special effects event. It had been raining most of the day. But just as the pilgrim was ready to come down off the Acropolis, the sun broke through and a perfect rainbow formed over the mountain with both ends visible in the city below. It was as though the Lord was saying he accepted man's (and the pilgrim's educational) efforts to use and develop the gifts of art and architecture, because these gave Him glory as long as one recognized the Giver of these gifts. For He was the Lord of nature and could create in a moment a vastly more beautiful and awe-inspiring work of art with light (the sun) and a few drops of water (the rain).

There was, however, one more monument which captured the pilgrim's attention and that was the bronze plaque on the Areopagus, halfway down the Acropolis. This was where Paul had tried to win the Athenian philosophers to Christ by telling them he knew the unknown God they were worshipping (Acts 17:22f). Though most laughed at Paul, thinking the Gospel about the resurrection of the body to be mere foolishness, some believed, and Paul moved on to more fertile soil in Corinth. So the pilgrim reflected that the wisdom of the Greeks had hardened them to receiving the revelation of Jesus Christ, just as all his seminary studies had not brought him to a saving relationship with Jesus Christ. Indeed it is not knowledge with its attendant power that saves one, but rather the surrender of faith with its attendant weakness which fills one with the life of God. The following are the reflections of the pilgrim during these first three weeks in Greece:

JANUARY 4, 1971 — THOUGHT — Is it not believed in the States that a man is poor only because he does not work? Does this not imply that man can MAKE HIMSELF rich by his own power? Does this not ignore the more ultimate reality of our poverty and weakness before God and Christ's advice to follow him in his poverty and humility? It also shows an awareness of our weakness and helplessness without the human structures which support life.

COMMENT 1987: The pilgrim here is not only looking through the shallowness of the popular belief that people are poor because they are lazy, but is touching the roots of why people choose to believe this untruth. That is, faith in this adage covers up one's own weakness and poverty for it takes well-being and material security as a sign of goodness and power. Having let go of the ordinary structures which support one's life, the pilgrim has come face-to-face with man's inherent weakness and thus can more easily grasp Jesus's command to follow him for He is meek and humble of heart (Mt. 11:29).

JANUARY 6, 1971 — THOUGHT — As only a sick man will consent to the doctor's order to fast, so only a man who recognizes his spiritual sickness will consent to do penance.

COMMENT 1987: The pilgrim, having taken on a penitential lifestyle, understands the meaning and purpose of fasting and self-denial. But he also sees that no one else will be inspired to take it on unless they admit they are sick and need such radical surgery. If one does not perceive one's desperate situation, he is not likely to be convinced of the need of taking a painful cure.

JANUARY 14, 1971 — THOUGHT — What is life but one long waiting for the Lord. Our little waitings in life should be our most precious moments for they are reflections on the ultimate meaning of our lives.

COMMENT 1987: This realization came to the pilgrim one day as he had a two-hour wait in a courtyard before morning Mass was to start. He saw how it was an image of a Christian's whole life, from an eschatological perspective. It corresponds to Christ's teaching about being ready at any moment for the return of the bridegroom. Thus, a Christian's life is one of constant expectant hope for the fulfillment of Jesus' promise to complete the building of His Kingdom.

JANUARY 17, 1971 — THOUGHT — Prayer is now the only thing which gives my life the meaning I require.

COMMENT 1987: The pilgrim has found the pearl of great price (Mt. 13:46) and has sold everything to obtain it. That pearl is communion with the Lord in prayer. It is his sole preoccupation. It has filled the void which he had experienced even after obtaining all the knowledge that 20 years of Catholic education could give him. In light of this gift, everything else looks like straw (Ph. 3:8).

SAME DAY — THOUGHT — Only a wise man can pronounce a true blessing.

COMMENT 1987: This reflection was sparked by his meeting with the man in Patras who wished that he would always be able to walk where he desired to go. Thus he sees that blessings come from a deep experiential knowledge of the ways of the Lord, and especially of his desire to bring grace and life to his people. Therefore blessings are not just some magic words or hocus-pocus. They are signs that point to the ultimate truth of God's love and presence in very particular situations.

JANUARY 18, 1971 — Modern man lacks a heart. He has only a body and a mind. The heart is that which longs for that which is not and is scarcely possible to attain by human effort: those ideals which one considers worth striving for, knowing full well they will always be just beyond reach.

COMMENT 1987: The pilgrim had always wondered what Scripture meant by "the heart". Now he is beginning to understand. It was a part of him that had practically lain dormant most of his life, as his training and education had so much concentrated on the physical and the mental. Thus here as he be-

gins to discover this third dimension to life, he defines it as that which surpasses the physically and mentally attainable. It is his heart that contains a living faith, and this puts him in touch with the living God in a way his mind and body could not possibly do, for this is the realm of the spirit.

JANUARY 20, 1971 — THOUGHT — Daily I am growing in the power of the Lord. It is not my power but his. For of myself, I was weak and powerless. To the extent I make myself weak, to that extent is there room for the Lord to come with His power.

COMMENT 1987: The pilgrim had tried the way of power the first 26 years of his life, when he tried all of man's schemes to make himself happy by acquiring knowledge, power and position. When that failed him, he chose the way of weakness, and there, to his complete satisfaction and happiness, he found the Lord came in with His power and met all his needs and desires. Thus he found the Gospel prescription about giving up everything to find everything to be absolutely true (Mt. 16:25).

LATIN	ENGLISH
Christus vincit;	Christ conquers;
Christus regnat;	Christ reigns;
Christus imperat.	Christ rules.
Christus ab omni malo plebam suam defendat.	Christ defends his people from all evil.
Ecce crux Domini; Fugite partes adversae; Vicit leo de tribu Juda.	Behold the cross of the Lord; Flee all foreign powers; The lion of the tribe of Judah conquers.

—Rome, December, 1970

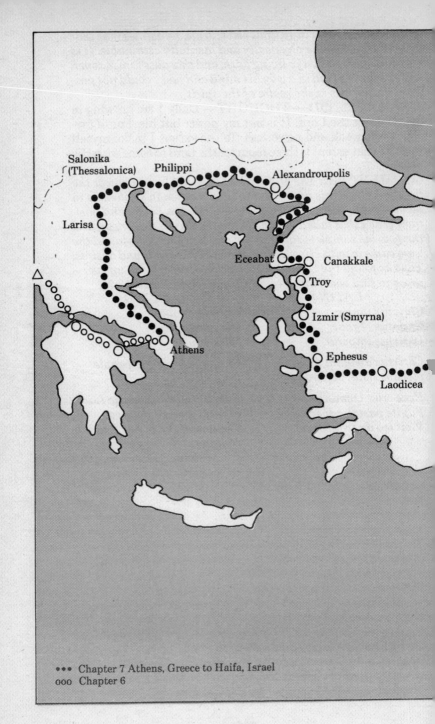

Salonika
(Thessalonica)
Philippi
Alexandroupolis
Larisa
Eceabat
Canakkale
Troy
Izmir (Smyrna)
Athens
Ephesus
Laodicea

••• Chapter 7 Athens, Greece to Haifa, Israel
ooo Chapter 6

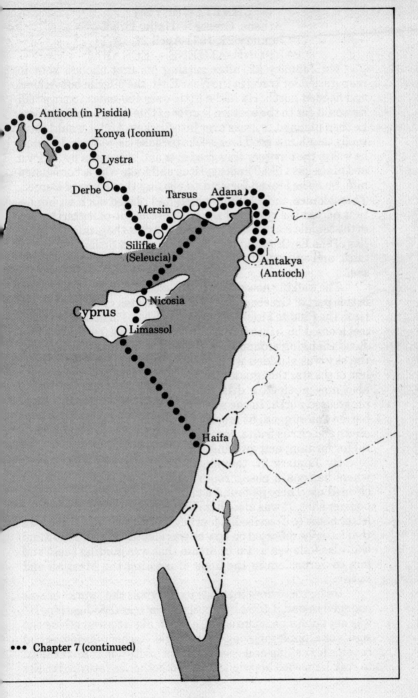

Antioch (in Pisidia)

Konya (Iconium)

Lystra

Derbe

Tarsus   Adana

Mersin

Silifke
(Seleucia)

Antakya
(Antioch)

Nicosia

Cyprus

Limassol

Haifa

••• Chapter 7 (continued)

117

CHAPTER SEVEN
Athens, Greece — Haifa, Israel
January 22, 1971-April 27, 1971
PART ONE: ATHENS — ECEABAT

On January 22, after getting his first cholera shot in preparation for travel in the Near East, the pilgrim left Athens and headed north. He had a little over 400 miles to cover till he would get to the eastern border of this little country where he then planned to cross over into Turkey. And it would eventually take him a good four weeks to make the journey. But now he was in the territory traversed over and over again by St. Paul and his helpers like Timothy, Titus and Luke who accompanied him. So as he looked forward to visiting the towns of Beroea, Thessalonica and Philippi which had played such an important part in the spread of the Gospel outside of its birthplace in the Middle East, the pilgrim prayed that these mighty apostles of the Faith would accompany him now on his journey of faith, and enkindle in his heart something of their apostolic zeal.

The walking now was just fantastic. It was Spring already in this part of Greece so the fields were a lush green. On the horizon the Pindus Mountain range with Mt. Parnassus at 8,000 feet loomed high into the clear blue sky, with a few fluffy white clouds hanging around their peaks. The nights were clear and the sky was studded with brilliant stars shining, reminding him of the star that guided the Magi to Bethlehem. The pilgrim also now noticed a difference in the countryside as he progressed north. In the west and south, the land was rather barren and rugged, fit mostly for grazing sheep and growing olives and citrus fruits. Now the land was rich and fertile, useful for farming and growing wheat.

By January 27, the pilgrim reached the city of Larissa where he took a cheap room for $1.25 where he could get cleaned up. There he found a clinic that gave him his cholera booster shot. It was also there that he wrote his eleventh long letter home to describe his journey since landing in Greece. In that letter he reflected on how he was identifying with the Magi who also followed a star or dream that was guiding them and him to Jerusalem in the hope of meeting the Messiah and Savior.

He further wrote that this journey was the "work" he was engaged in and it took his total strength and dedication. He was not out for pleasure or enjoyment, like a tourist seeing the sights or a hippie grooving on the world. Rather *pilgrimage* had become his calling and vocation — an invitation from the Lord to seek Him with his whole heart. Whether he returned to the

States or not was not his immediate concern, for he no longer made plans for the distant future. His whole effort was to surrender his life into the Lord's safekeeping and let Him dispose of it as He willed.

Leaving Larissa the pilgrim's journey now took him to Beroea, Thessalonica and Philippi, which cities were the first in Europe to hear and respond to the saving message that Jesus is the Messiah and Savior of the world. Here the pilgrim began to experience a real strengthening of his faith as he was able to place himself physically on the very site where St. Paul and his companions had testified by word and deed to the Good News of Jesus Christ.

Thus, for example, in Philippi he visited the excavated first century city. Finding an inscription marking the place of the jail and Paul's imprisonment and miraculous deliverance (Acts 16:25f), he sat himself down and slowly prayed through the whole scene. Here the pilgrim experienced one of the unique graces of his year of pilgrimaging. In the midst of this pile of broken down stones, where no church had been built, no worshipers prayed, no clerk had set up a souvenir shop, the pilgrim came into touch with the apostolic faith and zeal of that great proclaimer of Jesus, Paul. In the pilgrim's willingness to believe, shown by his walking the journey on foot, plus the grace of this geographical site made holy by the suffering of the chosen Apostle Paul, God's gift of faith found a firm place in which to be anchored in the heart of the pilgrim.

Again the Lord was faithful to his promise, "Those who seek shall find" (Mt. 7:7). He didn't have to wait till he got to Jerusalem. The Lord was free to reveal Himself when and where he chose to. Once again for this pilgrim, it was alone in a deserted place, through the written word of God, in architectural space which bore direct testimony to the faith of an Apostle who was a foundation stone in the Church of Jesus Christ. (Eph. 2:20). The pilgrim was coming alive spiritually, and himself becoming a living stone (I Pt. 2:4ff).

Upon leaving Philippi, the pilgrim's days in Greece were drawing to a close, and he began looking ahead to picking up St. Paul's trail again in Asia (modern day Turkey). But he had to make a decision whether to go the long way through Istanbul or take a shortcut by boat across the Dardanelles. Having heard from other travelers of all the thievery in Istanbul and remembering St. Paul did not go that way, he decided to also go by boat and by-pass that ancient capitol of the Eastern Roman Empire.

But before he crossed the border of Greece and Turkey and headed down the peninsula to Eceabat, one more interesting incident happened to the pilgrim. As he was walking along the road one day, a police car stopped and motioned for him to get in. None of them spoke English but they seemed quite friendly and it didn't at all appear to be harassment or arrest, so he consented, (even though he was not happy to be riding over a stretch of land which he had committed himself to walk). But at this point he did not seem to have much of a choice.

After about a ten minute ride, they brought him to their headquarters and asked him to wait in a sitting room, while they made a phone call. Eventually a young woman came in who spoke very good English and said all they wanted to know was "Could they do anything for you? Do you need anything?" Coming from a police department, this took the pilgrim somewhat by surprise, but it pleased him to see in action this branch of the government going to such lengths to assist a total sranger. Of course had he been preaching the Gospel like Paul and stirring up the citizens, it might have been a different story. But for now it was an amiable relationship and the pilgrim said, no, he was fine and would be on his way.

One thing the pilgrim did learn though during the time he spent with his friendly captors was the Greek word for bread was not the classical word *artos* which he had been using all these weeks with little comprehension, but *psomi*. Now, when he was almost out of Greece, he finally learned how to correctly ask for the staple of his daily diet. Anyway, it brought home to him in a graphic way the difference between the Greece of New Testament times and the Greece of the 20th century. Much indeed had changed. Nevertheless, one thing had remained the same — the Good News that Jesus Christ is Lord — and that would stand the same forever. Praise God.

By February 15 the pilgrim was in Kavala, only about 75 miles from the Greek border. Here the pilgrim became a "tourist" for awhile. That is, he did some shopping and souvenir hunting — not for himself but for his Mom. He bought a small $4'' \times 5''$ icon depicting St. George slaying the dragon. He bartered with the merchant who came down from $2.00 to $1.50. Then he scouted around for some paper and string to wrap it for mailing and took it to the Post Office. There he convinced the teller to send it for 60¢ rather than the $1.75 which he originally wanted to charge.

The pilgrim had carefully selected this particular icon as he had seen others like it in various parts of Greece. He felt that his patron saint, George, was very much a part of his present pilgrimage and was helping him do battle, not with some imaginary dragon, but with a very real and very strong enemy within.

The enemy within was his lack of faith in the living presence of the Lord Jesus, which kept his heart cold and locked, preventing him from submitting to his loving Lord. By the grace of God, since his encounter with Jesus in the desert in Spain, the pilgrim was now aware of what the problem was. Now he knew there was an enemy to be overcome. The mere fact of exposing him to the light was the first step in an ultimate victory, for the enemy seemed much more powerful than he really was as long as he could hide in the darkness of the unknown. Now, with the Lord's help, day by day, the pilgrim's faith was growing stronger and the enemy weaker. The battle would continue to rage for many years, of course, but having his patron saint and many others in heaven assisting him, gave him new hope and courage.

In five more days, on February 20, the pilgrim arrived in Alexandroupolis, the last major city in Greece before the Turkish border. It was evening. As it had rained most of the day, he was soaking wet and so decided to take a room for the night. Here he found a most quaint arrangement. Each little hotel room had a pot-bellied stove which the manager would light for an extra 15¢. And there was a bucket of wood nearby which one was free to use to keep the fire going after that. The pilgrim saw this as a special gift from the Lord, for the fire meant he could have hot soup and coffee in addition to his normal diet of bread, cheese, olives and raw vegetables. Also the fire meant he could dry out his things and get a fresh start in the morning.

On the next day he left Alexandroupolis and the following day crossed into Turkey. Two days after crossing the border, February 24, the Church's Liturgical season of Lent began. The pilgrim had not planned it this way, but the Lord of history sure would take advantage of these circumstances. For just as Lent is a time for the Christian to identify with Christ's forty days' fast in the desert, so the pilgrim would experience a real desert during his next six weeks of walking through Turkey. And to make the fast more complete, he would not even have the strength that came from receiving the Eucharist, for he was now in Moslem territory and would have to travel almost 200 miles before he found his first Catholic Church.

Since he had decided not to pass through Istanbul, he headed south down the long peninsula that borders on the western side of the Dardanelles. After a few days he reached a small port opposite Canakkale on the other side. He sat down to wait for the next small ferryboat to take him across the strait and onto the mainland of Turkey.

As he sat, he pondered his past seven weeks in Greece. Then as he looked up he saw a parable in action that helped him put it all together so he could begin to better understand the meaning of it all. The parable was acted out by an elderly lady, who all alone, was also waiting for the ferry. She was quite oblivious to being watched and was in no way conscious of being the Lord's instrument of teaching for the pilgrim. She was only doing something that was natural to her day to day life. It was this.

She had two bags and a hammer. In one bag she had a large chunk of bread. In the other a couple dozen black walnuts. She would take a walnut — the kind that have extremely hard shells — lay it on a rock and then, without smashing it, hit it with the hammer just right so it would crack and fall open. Then she would pick out the meat of the nut, pop it in her mouth, bite off a mouthful of bread, and chew it all up together. Wow, thought the pilgrim — the original nutbread!

But how did this help the pilgrim better understand what the Lord had been showing him the past two months? First it confirmed the great delight he found in observing things in their simplest and original forms, not only in the area of nutbread, but especially in the area of the bread of life — faith in Jesus. Here in this land, the Messiah of the Jews would be offered to the Greek-speaking world and nourish a hunger that could not be satisfied by the most brilliant logic of the philosophers or spectacular victories of its generals. It had been offered in the same way to the Jews to nourish a hunger that could not be satisfied by the most rigorous observance of the Law or possession of a history filled with acts of God's saving intervention.

So, too, the pilgrim. He had to come to this land to walk in the footsteps of that great Apostle Paul in order to get to what lies behind the legal codes, the philosophical systems and all the accumulation of what Western culture had added to the pristine Gospel. He was, as it were, going back and picking up the nuts in one hand and coarse brown bread in the other and learning all over how to be nourished by God's gifts as they came from the earth rather than as they appeared at the end of man's clever working upon them and adding to them. His walking was the hammer which was breaking up the hardness of his heart and allowing it to reveal the treasure of faith that had been locked up there since his infant Baptism. Now, practically for the first time, he was beginning to learn how to be nourished by this bread come down from heaven — the Word of God — Jesus made flesh.

Thus he thanked the Lord for this simple woman going about her primitive task and allowing him to experience the raw power of the truth of God's word and its ability to change his life, inspire zeal and build him into a person of God. It was such a precious gift and he saw how all these years he had been deaf and blind. Now the light was beginning to dawn. His prayer was that it continue to grow brighter and brighter till it enlightened his whole life. In Jesus' Name.

The following are the pilgrim's journal entries for these weeks:

JANUARY 24, 1971 — THOUGHT — As long as all that one experiences is his OWN power and the power of OTHER MEN and their MACHINES, I do not see how one can experience the power of God.

How much of the clergy's desire for further education is really inspired by a realization that they have lost some of their old power and authority and are seeking new power. Have they forgotten that their only real source of power is Christ and that of themselves they are weak? Are they afraid to admit this weakness? Have they lost faith in the power of God which can only come with an admission of one's weakness? Are they changing the Gospel of foolishness into one of WORLDLY wisdom?

COMMENT 1987: As the pilgrim continues through his desert/pilgrimage experience, he continues to face his own basic poverty and weakness. He uses this as a basis to think back on his experiences in the seminary, and now from this new standpoint questions his motivation for seeking knowledge and education. He wonders if his former classmates had fallen into the same trap as he had without knowing it.

SAME DAY — THOUGHT — It is good that the Catholic Church is freeing its members from LAWS, for they were becoming a curse, engendering a meaningless slavery (Gal. 5:16ff). But now the danger is that its members are becoming slaves to their own desires and passions rather than to the Lord in a free obedience and loving servitude.

COMMENT 1987: Having come through his last few years in the seminary during a time of relaxing the rule (replacing them with guidelines) and experimentation with new freedoms, the pilgrim sees how uncritically that was accepted and demanded. He also sees that it opens up another grave danger and that is of doing one's own thing, even when this means going against God's laws and plan. He doesn't mention here yet that this passage from LAW to FREEDOM can only be safely traversed when one is guided by the power of the Holy Spirit. Otherwise it is like all political revolutions which merely exchange one tyrant for another.

JANUARY 27, 1971 — THOUGHT — To know a reality for the first time by way of a picture is to rob it of most of its power.

COMMENT 1987: Once the pilgrim comes into firsthand contact with the things and places he had known up to that time only through pictures, he sees how far the reality surpasses the image. And so he begins to understand why his life, built almost entirely on images and words, came to be so "unreal" to him, and why he sensed his faith could not stand the test the world was about to throw at him.

SAME DAY — THOUGHT — Someday things will become so centralized that all the bread in the world will come from one bakery — what a fantastic symbol of unity. Though it possibly won't be bread but a pill for a day.

COMMENT 1987: The pilgrim here engages in some science fiction fantasizing. As he observed the waning of homemade bread in favor of mass-produced bread, he just took this trend to its ultimate conclusion, which, though by no means necessarily true, does offer an interesting image for the true bread of life, Jesus, and his one sacrifice on Calvary becoming now the sacrificial bread of life for every member of his body as they gather around the table of the Eucharist.

JANUARY 31, 1971 — THOUGHT — Since the advent of modern communications, men no longer meet each other singularly or in groups (cafes) to exchange NEWS face-to-face, by word-of-mouth. Rather they get THE NEWS individually through impersonal instruments. While there is a gain in accuracy, there is a loss in power. So they no longer have much reason to come together, except to work or socialize, and these being routine and required, lack much meaning and spontaneity, so that men are losing the ability to communicate and relate deeply to each other.

COMMENT 1987: Modern communications have helped in the breakdown of authority insofar as the reader or viewer has no way to personally test the veracity of the one handing on the news, whereas previously when one lived with the bearer of the news he could know from the rest of his life how to weigh and judge what he was saying, and could do something about it if the news turned out to be exaggerated or false. The pilgrim here is trying to uncover the reason for the lack of real communication in his technological world, evidenced by the constant talk of dialogue and communication skills which point to the lack of significant sharing of human lives. Is it any wonder that if men begin having difficulty communicating with each other, that then they find it difficult to communicate with God?

FEBRUARY 1, 1971 — THOUGHT — Part of the crisis in authority in Western society must be tied in with the fact that people, things, relationships, are no longer SYMBOLIC of anything else but are seen just for WHAT THEY ARE. Things and people in themselves are NOTHING: so all men are evil, ignorant and foolish. Therefore no one has any right to rule over another as though he were somehow better. Authority among men only makes sense as symbolic of the authority of God who alone is good, all-wise and all-knowing.

COMMENT 1987: The pilgrim here is reflecting on how the modern process of demythologization, overturning of traditional values and interpretations logically leads to anarchy. For if people are just what scientists say they are (a bundle of physical, psychological, social drives), and not children of God destined to eternal life with Him, then there is really no good reason for establishing order on this planet for it is all temporary and will soon end in ashes anyway.

FEBRUARY 4, 1971 — THOUGHT — Fasting is a preparation for death. If all through life the only thing we ever do is CLING to life and grab for more, we will not know how to let it go whenever we reach the end.

COMMENT 1987: Pilgrimage brings one face to face with death. And so it puts one's whole life into focus from that ultimate standpoint. Realizing that death will only be successfully handled by the one who can freely surrender himself into God's hands as He calls him in that moment, the pilgrim finds fasting in all its various forms a key instrument to learning how to live so as to be able to die a happy death.

SAME DAY — DREAM — I am working with my Dad on a scaffold. He is on the top. I am up and down — mostly on the ground for it appears to me to be very wobbly and unsafe. I am involved in trying to shore it up according to my Dad's directions. He nevertheless, remains on top and does not fall.

COMMENT 1987: This dream could refer to the pilgrim's earthly father or his heavenly Father. If it is his earthly father, he experiences his Dad living a superficial life that is not too well grounded while he, the pilgrim, is busy about restoring the foundations. If it is his heavenly Father, then it is similar to the instruction St. Francis received at San Damiano where the Lord told him to rebuild his church, for it was falling down in disrepair.

FEBRUARY 9, 1971 — THOUGHT — Modern man's life is filled with "unknowns" but not with mysteries. He does not know WHO bakes his bread, but he neither fears not respects the one who does for he knows it is a man or a machine and if he took the time he could trace it back to its source.

COMMENT 1987: The pilgrim here reflects on how mysteries disappear as one gets further away from the origin of one's daily basic necessities. The one who bakes bread is much more likely to be caught up in contemplation over the working of the yeast than the hurried shopper picking a loaf from the shelf or a drive-in customer unwrapping a hamburger at a fast food restaurant. So, too, if modern man is satisifed with religious products, ceremonies and thoughts made by others, he is going to miss the wonder of knowing the Lord who is behind it all.

FEBRUARY 10, 1971 — THOUGHT — Modern man is growing less sensitive to life and death, just as he no longer knows how to prune a tree, so he is becoming less capable of raising children; either he lets it all grow wild or he cuts off too much. *COMMENT 1987: Here the pilgrim identifies one of the results of losing contact with basic life experiences as also losing the ability to properly guide new life in their children. Because parents have become separated from basic life processes, they now need courses on parenting, for they do not deal daily with growing natural things. Nevertheless, this is something that cannot be learned from books, but must be gained on site through experience, trial and error, and humble, careful observation.*

SAME DAY — THOUGHT — If one is to maintain the distinction from the world that is essential to the follower of Christ, one must either live with a community of fellow believers a great deal of the time or live in the world alone and very aloof from its ordinary affairs. *COMMENT 1987: The pilgrim is beginning to compare what he has experienced on his pilgrimage with what he experienced when he was still in the world — before he left it in a literal way to follow Christ. And he sees that he cannot just return to the world and live there as he did before. So he is beginning to think of ways he might return to the world and yet remain faithful to what the Lord has shown him.*

SAME DAY — THOUGHT — Man tends to personify those powers, whether threatening or beneficent, which are REAL to him. Thus, there is a growing disbelief in the devil as well as in God. The only powers known by modern man are the impersonal powers of large numbers of men or of machines. *COMMENT 1987: As man loses touch with the transcendent, he finds his focus limited to the things of the everyday world around him. Caught up in his petty projects to subdue and organize the world to serve his own pleasures and whims, man creates new gods and myths in his own image and likeness. In this way man loses his true identity as a son of God, and falls into the fatal web of being just a number and a disposable part of the larger mass.*

FEBRUARY 11, 1971 — THOUGHT — The astronauts are the epitome and even exemplary model of the modern man. They are more directly conscious of the power of countless numbers of men and machines which support and control the mission, than they are of their dependence upon God. The reading of Genesis from space was little more than a nostalgic gesture. These men have actually become conditioned NOT to be sensitive to or enthralled by the wonder of creation, for such ecstasy would interfere with their work.

COMMENT 1987: The pilgrim may be exaggerating here and not completely correct in his assessment of all astronauts, but he is again making a point by taking a tendency and drawing it to its ultimate conclusion. Thus, he once again finds fault with his technological society for its tendency to eliminate wonder and ecstasy in favor of practical results and concrete time-bound achievements.

SAME DAY — THOUGHT — Those who live in darkness half of each day, have a tangible symbol of evil in the world. With the increase of the use of artificial lighting, people tend to feel that all evil has been overcome. The distinction between day and night being blurred, the evil one is now free to prowl about in full light (or total darkness).

COMMENT 1987: The pilgrim has now been living for eight months by the rhythm of sunrise and sunset, practically without the benefit of artificial lighting. It is February when it is dark 15 hours a day. This physical and psychological experience has helped him to experience spiritually the reality of evil, and also to understand Jesus' command to walk in the light (John 12:35). When man begins to walk in his own artificially created light, he can easily begin to lose touch with the True Light of the World which is not his creation.

FEBRUARY 12, 1971 — THOUGHT — If one considers his very first origin — nothing — and his ultimate state without God — nothing — then man truly is NOTHING.

If one considers his present condition — a creature of God, called to eternal life — then he is something and truly has an inestimable value.

COMMENT 1987: The pilgrim is searching for a way to express the basis of man's dignity and meaning. He can only find a satisfactory answer by relating it to God as his Creator and loving Father.

FEBRUARY 13, 1971 — THOUGHT — Not an idle word shall go unpunished (Mt. 12:36). An idle word is one which is unnecessary. Unnecessary for what? For the Kingdom of God. How many of them are there in the noisy world today!

COMMENT 1987: The pilgrimage puts the pilgrim in the world of silence, not only as he walks alone through the countryside, but even in the cities for as a foreigner he understands neither the talking nor the writing that is all about him. And this has the advantage of proving to him how little of what man ordinar-

ily thinks is normal or necessary is all that important. It gives a new importance to the precious gift of speech.

FEBRUARY 14, 1971 — THOUGHT — Fasting seems a more appropriate symbol of true life than eating, which is more a symbol of THIS life. If anything, a symbolic meal of simple food would be appropriate.

COMMENT 1987: Part of pilgrimage is fasting, for this helps take the focus off satisfying one's own appetites. By just getting along on the essentials one can more easily develop one's appetite for the things of the Lord and focus on Him rather than on self.

FEBRUARY 16, 1971 — THOUGHT — Man no longer has the old physical images of his poverty and helplessness that he used to have: images like darkness, sickness, threat of famine, war, dependence upon a strong lord or king, cold, rain, heat, labor (tiredness and exhaustion), insecurity as to the future. Nor does he have the old physical images of strength and life, like light, health, etc.

COMMENT 1987: Continuing on the theme of technology banishing darkness, the pilgrim's modern world seems bent on eliminating every possible reminder of weakness and fragility, and thus sadly losing important aids in coming to know and rely upon a loving Lord. The pilgrim found that only by going back to a more primitive way of life and experiencing the basic realities that all men up to the present experienced, could he come into contact with the spiritual truths that his teachers and fathers in the faith had been trying to hand on to him, and had framed in this universal language.

FEBRUARY 17, 1971 — THOUGHT — Those who are physically poor have this advantage over those who are materially well-off or rich, that they have physical images and reminders of their interior poverty and poorness that the rich do not have. Eating only simple foods, COULD be an excellent reminder that one is striving to be INTERIORLY simple, pure and humble.

COMMENT 1987: The pilgrim is beginning to catch a glimpse of Gospel poverty and the meaning of the first Beatitude "Blessed are the poor in spirit, for theirs is the Kingdom of Heaven" (Mt. 5:3). He understands better why Luke adds to the Beatitudes "Woe to you rich" (Lk. 6:24). Riches and middleclass living tends to camouflage one's real nakedness and poverty, so one begins living a lie and even believing it oneself, saying "I'm OK, I'm doing all right for myself, I'm able to provide all that I need". In the whole process, the rich easily forget the one thing necessary for happiness which one cannot provide on one's own but must accept as a free gift — a personal relation-

ship with the Lord Jesus Christ.

SAME DAY — THOUGHT — Pleasure can be a symbol of eternal life as well as pain, but it is more ambiguous a symbol because it can much more easily be misunderstood and taken as an end in itself, rather than as pointing to another life.

COMMENT 1987: By pain the pilgrim here means self-denial, as manifested in practices of penance and mortification as practiced in Catholic circles up until the 1960's, when preachers and teachers in general stopped preaching about these means of sanctification and at the same time no longer took as their themes the Four Last Things (Death, Judgment, Heaven and Hell), but instead began emphasizing love of one's neighbor, social concern, and in general making this life a more pleasurable experience.

FEBRUARY 18, 1971 — THOUGHT — Unless one KNOWS the dark, rainy, cold days, he cannot really KNOW the joy of bright, sunny, warm ones. Unless one KNOWS death, he cannot really APPRECIATE life. The same with evil/goodness, slavery/freedom.

COMMENT 1987: The more the pilgrim experiences of the difficult, painful, negative side of human life, the more he comes to appreciate the joyful, vibrant, positive side. Having been so shielded from this harsher reality all of his first 29 years of life he had not properly matured and so was unable to withstand the testing that naturally comes with facing the challenge of living a meaningful human life. As he applies the same principle to his spiritual life, he comes to value the discipline, asceticism, and focus on eternity typical of Catholic Christian life up until the modern age.

FEBRUARY 23, 1971 — THOUGHT — In the technological world we no longer "touch the hands which bake our bread, sew our clothes, or build our houses." "Hand-shaking" becomes embarassing and a mere formality.

COMMENT 1987: The pilgrim has observed in more primitive cultures the warmth of greeting between fellow human beings and relates this to the intimate contact that each person has with just a few others who supply very immediate and critical needs: food, clothing and shelter. As the origin of these products becomes more remote and more impersonal, so one's sense of the importance of the other people and other hands that touch the product along the line diminishes.

SAME DAY — It is true that most of the modern world's physical problems (poverty, crime, war, pollution, etc.) stem from the fact of rapid population growth. But birth control may not be the best or even a partial answer, for there is a deeper cause and that is the misalignment that is accompanying the untold massing together of so many people. It is a problem of human interrelationships and this is getting closer to the ultimate spiritual cause of all these problems and that is SIN.

FEBRUARY 24, 1971 — THOUGHT — Should the parish priest be like the quarterback of a football team, engaging in the battle with his team and taking his share of hard knocks, or should he (the monk) be like the coach (bishop) observing the contest from the sidelines, offering his advice from time to time-out?

COMMENT 1987: The pilgrim is still thinking about the nature of the priesthood especially because this is what he had been considering for so many years. But he has not yet penetrated into the real essence of the priesthood in terms of being another Christ and offering his life along with that of Jesus to the Father for and with the people. Thus his images of quarterback and coach deal only with the externals and job description types of questions.

SAME DAY — THOUGHT — In the world of mass communication, there is no longer any telling the news. There is only reporting the facts. There is no communication of events, only compilation of information.

COMMENT 1987: From his current perspective the pilgrim is able to see that what his culture calls news is not at all what men of other ages and especially of the Gospel age, called news. Modern news has all the life taken out of it because it is not alive — it's bare bones. To be news that communicates it must be impressed with the personality of the communicator who puts his whole self into it, appending, exaggerating, stretching, illustrating the story so that it is more than bare facts, but carries his human input and personal faith. This is especially critical for communicating faith in a person, as, for example, when the person is none other than the Lord Jesus. The scribes and Pharisees made poor communicators; Jesus "taught with authority" because he shared what he experienced as true with His Father in heaven.

FEBRUARY 26, 1971 — THOUGHT — When we don't see things "wear out" anymore, but go and buy new ones all the time, we lose a symbol of the fleeting and temporary nature of all created things.

COMMENT 1987: The pilgrim here uncovers one more subtle assumption of his culture, and this is a kind of technological immortality; the quick disposal, out of sight, of anything showing signs of age and decay, with immediate replacement with what is new. Thus man becomes blind to the fact of death and the finiteness of life and he becomes totally disoriented when he comes face-to-face with something he can't overcome, like cancer or death.

SAME DAY — THOUGHT — Before we can preach about the resurrection, we must first convince people that they die. For the constant production and use of new things creates a kind of "secular immortality" and before that we must again make them aware that they have BODIES for they are forgetting how to sing and gesture and walk and breathe. They are becoming all mind.

COMMENT 1987: The pilgrim continues in the same line of thought as the previous reflection, only now he takes it into the realm of the Gospel. He also sees how modern man tends to lose touch with his earthliness as he becomes so focused on just one of his faculties, namely the mind. Thus, the imbalanced emphasis of education and the overflowing of mental hospitals.

PART TWO: Eceabat — Izmir

After getting off the ferry, the pilgrim took a route heading south along the Agean Sea in the direction of Izmir, the Turkish name for the ancient city of Smyrna. The first site he visited in this part of Turkey was Troy, which he came to on his second day out of Canakkale. Here, where archaeologists claim nine cities have been built since the Stone Age, the pilgrim got in touch with ancient history. Here, where the Trojan war had been fought and the ruse of the wooden horse filled with soldiers that delivered the city into its attackers hands, the pilgrim recalled his study in Latin of the epic stories of the Illiad and the Odyssey. Here had lived heroes of the Greek and Roman world whose fame endured in Western culture even to the present day. But the pilgrim had to acknowledge that while these men and women had achieved an enduring fame and a type of immortality, their brave deeds did nothing to answer the ultimate questions of the meaning of life for him. The pilgrim needed more than ancient tales of military courage to satisfy the deepest longing of his heart.

More to the point in the same area, though, were the New Testament cities of Troas and Assos. It was at Troas (Acts 16:8ff) that Paul had the vision of a Macedonian beseeching him to come over to Macedonia (Greece) to preach the Gospel there. This led Paul to sail for Neapolis and Philippi where he made the first converts to Christ in Europe. It was at Troas (Acts 16:10) where it seems Luke joined Paul and from that point, faithfully accompanying him, thereafter eventually setting down in writing the Gospel and Acts of the Apostles. And finally it was at Troas about the year 51 A.D. (Acts 20:5ff) when, returning from his second missionary journey, Paul gave the speech that lasted all night and occasioned the young man Eutychus to doze off and fall out the third story window. The pilgrim was pleased to read that Paul had left Troas and walked the 30 miles by land to Assos (Acts 20:13) where he again boarded the ship.

The pilgrim would not be boarding ship at any of these ports, but he did sense a oneness with the great missionary who had walked these same lands some 1,900 years before. What saddened the pilgrim was the fact that all these early Christian communities, established with so much sacrifice and prayer and which for many centuries prospered, had now completely disappeared. The pilgrim would not find a single church in all of the 200 miles till he got to Izmir. He prayed for a new wave of evangelization to sweep the country so that once again the praise of Jesus and not the name of Allah might be lifted up by every heart and tongue.

Yet to the pilgrim's great amazement, the present inhabitants of the land, Moslems, were a very friendly people. As a matter of fact, they even surpassed the Greeks and the southern Italians in hospitality. They would come together in crowds to look at him as he passed through their towns. The pilgrim would notice in almost every crowd a few with clear, sparkling eyes. They seemed so simple and intent with beautiful souls open to the world about them. The children especially had that pure, wholesome quality one always notices in the faces of children who grow up protected from the rape of their innocence by the immorality and violence portrayed for them on the television screen, and who experience the security of being around Mom and Dad on the farm the whole day.

Thus, for example, one day the pilgrim walked into a small village early in the morning and began asking for bread as he usually did. However, instead of taking him to the bakery (possibly they didn't have one here) they took him to the home of the leader of their village. Here all the men of the village — about 20 in all — came together. Taking off their shoes they entered a large unfurnished room and sat down on rugs along the four walls. The master of the house had his wife prepare something to eat as the pilgrim tried to explain with pictures, maps, signs, and some words in German that they understood, that he was walking to Jerusalem.

Very soon the meal was served (on the floor). It consisted very simply of large thin flat breads that one tore into smaller pieces and dipped into various kinds of sauces (curries) made of vegetable or milk products. The pilgrim felt like an honored guest and it caused him to reflect, for he was pretty sure these were all Moslems. Their genuine hospitality was beyond anything he had ever experienced in Christian circles.

He further reflected: here he was a Christian, being cared for by Moslem Turks, whom his Christian brothers and sisters had fought against in the Crusades in the 12th and 13th centuries. But he had come among them in the humble form of a pilgrim, not in the shining armor of a knight. He came to be refreshed at the shrines made holy by events that took place 19 centuries ago, not to deny the present people of the land the right to live there in peace. And finally, he came to preach the Gospel not so much in words, and arguments — at least not just yet — as by simple living and walking.

During the first week of his walking on the mainland of Turkey, the pilgrim experienced quite a lot of wind, rain and light snow. This was true even though he kept close to the Aegean Sea which he hoped shared something of the Mediterranean Sea's reputation for providing warm temperatures all year round to its shores. Then on March 6, a warm breeze sprang up from the south and to the pilgrim's great joy, won a definitive victory over the chill of winter. It was such a dramatic change that the pilgrim experiencd it as though the earth had suddenly tilted on its axis and lifted its face to the sun, ushering in a while new season — namely, Spring.

And indeed all creation seemed to rejoice in the change. To celebrate the occasion the frogs, in one gigantic chorus, croaked their praises all night long. Likewise the flies and gnats came alive and the fields began taking on color with tiny little red, white, yellow and blue flowers. The pilgrim picked a few of these colorful flowers pressed them in his Bible and eventually sent them to his Mom in the next letter home.

Around noontime on March 11, the pilgrim arrived in the bustling city of Izmir. Like all other poor travelers, his first destination was the American Express Office where those on the road could pick up personal mail which the Agency graciously held for at least a month before returning it to the sender. Here the pilgrim received welcomed letters, with pictures and news from his family back in the States. These would serve to renew the ties that kept the life flowing which had nourished and sustained him all the years up to the present. Though he had definitely struck out on his own, he was not so foolish as to think he could accomplish his goal without a grateful awareness of all that had come before. So about once a month he wrote home and at a major city in each country he received letters from abroad.

The American Express Office was also good for other information the pilgrim needed and could only find in a large city, like a cheap hotel room, a Catholic Church and a dentist who understood English. The dentist was quickly found and his tooth was filled. Then he looked up the bishop of Izmir whose address had been given to him in Rome by Cardinal Wright. This was a most rewarding contact. The Bishop, the Most Rev. John H. Boccella, TOR, was a native of Philadelphia, PA, so the pilgrim could speak with him in English. Also he was a Franciscan and so had a better than average understanding of a pilgrim's way of life.

Sitting down to tea, the bishop gave the pilgrim about two hours of his time and greatly encouraged him to persevere in his pilgrimage. The bishop gave the pilgrim a beautiful large National Geographic Map of "The Lands of The Bible Today" which would be very valuable in locating historical sites that were mentioned in Sacred Scripture, from Greece all the way to Egypt. He also gave him names and addresses of three priests in three cities he would pass through in the next 400 miles of his journey through Turkey. And finally the good Bishop wanted to "make him a loan." But this was quickly refused as the pilgrim explained he wished to travel poor and the Lord had shown He could take care of him day by day. The pilgrim thanked the bishop for his generous hospitality and asked for his priestly blessing. With that the pilgrim departed.

The pilgrim left the presence of the bishop with such a joyful and renewed spirit. The genuine interest, understanding and concern he had experienced from him, confirmed in the pilgrim's heart that he was in God's will on this pilgrimage. His advice and information regarding where Catholic Churches could be found were seen as guideposts directing the pilgrim's footsteps. And so he thanked the Lord for this beautiful servant who had given his life to Him in a mission field far from home and exemplified in such practical ways the ability to be available for someone in need — even though he dropped in unannounced.

Since the pilgrim would not for the world miss the opportunity for Mass and Holy Communion the next morning, he decided not to continue on his journey, but rather take a cheap room in the city. As he made his way along the streets of Izmir, he noticed a lot of Americans there and they did not look like the typical tourists who gawk at things they are looking at for the first time. These Americans were acting like this was their home. And in a way, if was, for many had settled here because of the NATO headquarters in the city.

In a way the pilgrim was glad to be able to speak his own language with others again, but the conversations showed him something quite unexpected. He experienced their talking as so speeded up, that at times he could not even follow their train of thought. He had to ask them to repeat themselves. It seems he had become so used to thinking and observing at a slower pace, that it was now painful to change gears and get into another speed. Actually he had no desire to change his pace and return to the more superficial, less sensitive level of living as he had once experienced it. He would continue on at the slower speed.

Returning to the area of the American Express Office and train terminal, the pilgrim found a cheap room. As it turned out, it was the most primitive yet. For 50¢ he got a tiny private room with a bed, table, chair, clothes hooks and lots of framed pictures on the walls. For another 15¢ he could take a shower and wash out some clothes. The room had an electric light but the switch was on the outside. Later the pilgrim took advantage of shelter and light to do some writing and he was up rather late. So the hotel manager twice turned the light off on the pilgrim and he had to go back out and put it on.

There was no heat in the room, though one could join the other guests and local townspeople gathered around the pot belly stove in the center of the large hall on the first floor if one desired the warmth and companionship. But the pilgrim preferred his privacy where he could take a simple meal alone, pray, do some sewing, hang up his wet things to dry and catch up on his writing. Actually though, it was chilly (maybe around 55 degrees). It was not unbearable and the pilgrim had learned how to accept more primitive, less comfortable situations than he was used to in the States. Finally, taking every advantage possible of what was provided in conveniences, the pilgrim turned in for a good night's sleep. He wanted to be fresh for the next leg of his journey in the morning that would take him through Lent and up to Easter. Here are some of his Journal entries during his first three weeks in Turkey.

FEBRUARY 27, 1971 — THOUGHT — Words have become so plentiful with mass communication that they have been cheapened and have lost their former power. Pictures are following the same route.

COMMENT 1987: *The pilgrim had experienced in his seminary education how words could bury one in a deep hole. Instead of leading one to the truth and to life they could suffocate and kill the life of the mind and spirit. Seeing in a more primitive culture how words were more scarce, more valued and more important he was able to make this comparison. He notes that pictures, from the little holy card with the picture of a saint on it, to the daily newspaper, were taking the same route. Thus he saw the need for discipline and fasting in both areas in order to recapture the true beauty of these means of communication.*

SAME DAY — THOUGHT — We used to say that human

suffering was "due to sin". Since we are "suffering less" today, because of our "higher standard of living", it is concluded that we are sinning less than our fathers!

COMMENT 1987: The pilgrim here is trying to lay bare an unexamined assumption of his fellow Christians in the technological cultures, where the good life is the easy life and this is seen as a blessing from God and sign that all is well. This assumption is false because it is based upon an illegitimate transfer from the realm of the material to the realm of the spiritual. Amassed material goods are no sure proof that one obeyed God's laws all along the way.

SAME DAY — THOUGHT — All the problems and limitations the modern man experiences, can, he believes, be overcome by human effort (engineering, technology). He knows no "goals" beyond the achievable. There is no preset divine order. Man can plan and achieve whatever he can imagine.

COMMENT 1987: The pilgrim here clearly points out how modern man has imitated the sin of Adam. That is, refusing to submit to a divine order, he follows the dictates of his own weak, limited, human mind and imagination. Thus man's achievements become his god, created in his own image and likeness, and he believes he can save himself if he just has enough time, energy and money.

FEBRUARY 28, 1971 — THOUGHT — Until one experiences the limitations of his own power and that of all other men and institutions, it is not likely that one will seek out or pray to another power, namely that of God and His saints.

COMMENT 1987: The pilgrim is generalizing from his own experience. When he bought the philosophy that one could make oneself happy if he knew the right things and pleased his teachers, he did not experience any severe limitations and so did not seek God. But when it came time to make a commitment for life which required more than knowledge but also faith and love, he faltered. Only then as he explored this terrible chasm within, acknowledging his own emptiness and poverty, did he have any reason to seek the living God.

MARCH 2, 1971 — If one loves God with all his heart, and all his mind and all his strength, then he has nothing left with which to love his neighbor. I now understand the second commandment to mean that I can despise my neighbor to the extent that I despise myself.

COMMENT 1987: The pilgrim begins by showing the logical conclusion of putting all one's love into one relationship. But of course love does not follow logic of this sort, for love is expansive, and God does not hoard man's love for himself but directs it outward toward his other creatures. The pilgrim has not fully understood the command to love from the Gospel yet, but he has begun to penetrate the mystery by his reflection on the word "despise". He uses it in the same way the Scriptures counsel us to "hate" our mother and father, brothers and sisters, wife and children (Lk 14:26). That is, our total focus must be on the Lord and we must strive to let Him direct us in how to love and care for those around us.

MARCH 3, 1971 — THOUGHT — Peace is had only to the extent that one is single-minded (in all things having only one and always the same intention) towards God. This is only possible to one who can see all things as symbolic of God. If pleasure or anything created is the end, then "peace" is only possible to one who is able to be constantly satisfying his intention with specific concrete objects.

COMMENT 1987: The pilgrim here shows the difference between the peace that Jesus came to give by the power of the Holy Spirit and the peace the world tries to give which requires a constant and ever-increasing intensity of finite, limited objects.

MARCH 5, 1971 — THOUGHT — The Judeo-Christian faith seems to be based upon "the fidelity to a word", "the sacredness of a promise", "the inviolability of an oath." Could this not be the continuing basis of the Church's attitude towards "permanent commitment", "indissolubility of vows", etc.? Modern man is capable of the most thorough going despair. If he can find no meaning or satisfaction in the present life which is offered to him, he does not have the capacity to look back to the promises of the past, nor forward to the possibility of a new future (that is an ultimate past and an ultimate future). The best he might manage is a nostalgia for the way things used to be.

COMMENT 1987: The pilgrim is here putting his finger on one of the root causes of technological man's deep frustration, despair and atheism, namely the unwillingness to make a permanent commitment. Taking his clue from the constant change and flux he experiences in his daily life, he makes a fatal leap from this into the realm of the spiritual, and concludes that God may change his mind, character, will, too. Not able to trust man's word, he is unwilling to trust God's word, and so he is cut adrift on the sea of endless change. Lacking all direction and purpose beyond the immediate, life fails to render up any ultimate and deeply satisfying meaning.

MARCH 6, 1971 — THOUGHT — In the old world, the fathers passed on to their sons all the knowledge that was accumulated over the centuries and necessary to suppport, continue and serve as a basis for further advancement of life. So also they handed on their knowledge and experiences of God. The sons were grateful for these treasures, without which they could not have lived and they honored and respected their fathers and traditions. They had little or no reason to doubt or question their religious heritage for the material heritage proved itself to be true and this served to confirm the spiritual.

COMMENT 1987: Taking the example of the farmer, the pilgrim here sees how a father could pass on to his son all he knew about planting, growing and harvesting so that his son in turn could support the life of his family. If the farmer lived in a closed universe (and most did until the present) — that is, the outside world did not challenge or threaten the way of life of farming — the son would have little reason to question, doubt or change anything his father handed on to him. Not so in a technological world which is inundated with new ideals, patterns of behavior and ways of thinking. In a technological world the past is not accepted unconditionally, and so this is transferred to the realm of the faith and has its deleterious effects insofar as it sets man's critical mental faculty above and in judgment of the supreme authority of God.

MARCH 7, 1971 — COMMENT — Beware of the nut which cracks too easily. It will probably be rotten inside. Beware of the person who opens his deepest self too easily to another. It may be very shallow or empty. The hard nut can be rotten too, just as the totally closed person could be guarding an empty tomb.

COMMENT 1987: The pilgrim here continues to ponder the meaning of the woman cracking walnuts back in Eceabat on February 27. This, plus his own experience of testing nuts with a hammer has taught him a spiritual principle, namely that if something is easily attained, it probably has not near the value of something difficult to attain (like the meat inside a nut that has a solid, hard protective shell). Yet he does not make this into an inflexible rule, for he realizes that one cannot go just by outward appearances, for these can be deceiving.

MARCH 10, 1971 — THOUGHT — The average modern man's powers of observing and reporting have diminished because he no longer exercises them as he once did, but leaves this up to specialists to whom he then listens.

COMMENT 1987: The pilgrim is here returning to one of his favorite themes, and that is the importance of firsthand observation and personal concrete experience. He continues to decry the limitations of secondhand information and the insufficiency of relying on someone else to do one's thinking and analysis. Although a technological society, because it is so complex and interdependent, requires a great deal of reliance on other people, when it comes to the realm of faith and the experience of God it is fatal to be satisfied with anything less than a per-

sonal relationship with the Lord.

MARCH 11, 1971 — THOUGHT — God is man's last refuge. When all else fails to support him and give him strength and meaning, he experiences his true poverty and turns to God in hope that He might help.

COMMENT 1987: The pilgrim here points out the basic condition necessary on the part of the creature if he is to come into a personal and living relationship with his Creator and Lord. Only when one acknowledges his inability to meet his own deepest needs does he open the door of his heart and allow the Lord to come in and have a real fellowship with him.

PART THREE: Izmir — Mersin

On the morning of March 12, the pilgrim attended Mass and then left the sprawling city of Izmir. He was now two weeks into the liturgical season of Lent. His next four weeks which would bring him up to Easter, would be a true desert. He got out his map and plotted a course that would take him to Ephesus, Laodicea, Iconium, Lystra and Derbe, all cities that St. Paul had evangelized or written to in the middle of the first century. What he didn't realize was that this meant he would be leaving the coast line and its warmth, and heading into the interior of Turkey where the grip of winter still made its icy fingers felt. This would cost him dearly in terms of physical suffering.

The pilgrim's first place of pilgrimage was the ancient city of Ephesus which he reached on the evening of March 13. Here he was inspired by being able to walk amid the ruins of the fourth century Cathedral of St. Mary which church historians say was a second century Roman building turned over to the church shortly after Constantine's Edict of 313 allowed Christians to come out of their home gatherings and worship together in public. This site was also significant because in 431 the Third Ecumenical Council was held here with 200 bishops whom the Holy Spirit guided to teach that in Jesus there were two natures (human and divine) but only one person (the Son of God). Therefore it followed that Mary was truly to be called and honored as the Mother of God *(theotokos* in Greek). Thus the pilgrim was brought once more under the influence of the dignity, love and protection his heavenly mother, Mary.

But the most personal experience and unique gift from the Lord to this pilgrim was his visit to a mountainside shrine just beyond the ruins called *Meryemana.* This is the Turkish word for "House of Mary" and it was based on the tradition that John the Apostle brought Mary the Mother of Jesus here to live after the death of Jesus and dispersal of the Apostles from Jerusalem.

The pilgrim found here at this shrine a beautiful brother who spoke English. He was a member of the community of the Little Brothers of Jesus who follow the inspiring early 20th century French priest Charles de Foucauld who lived the most fruitful years of his life in the desert of Northern Africa. Of all the things the pilgrim heard from the brother, the thing that most impressed him was his telling of another of the little brothers whose life vocation was to be a pilgrim. This brother at present was traveling in South America. The American pilgrim immediately felt a great closeness to this little brother who had been called to wander the earth, for though the pilgrim did not know what the Lord had in store for him after Jerusalem, he did know that one possibility could be a call to a life of pilgrimage. And so he came to love and admire from a distance this little brother in the Lord.

From Ephesus, the pilgrim stopped heading south along the western coast of Turkey, and began walking directly east for 100 miles along the Maeander River, through Aydin, Nazilli and on to Denizli. There he would be able to visit the ruins of the ancient New Testament cities of Laodicea and Colossae. Laodicea was one of the seven churches in Asia addressed in the Book of Revelation (1:11, 3:14-22) which was known for its great wealth, due to its location in the fertile Lycus valley, on a major trade route. St. John had reprimanded it severely with the graphic image of being neither hot nor cold (like the warm springs still to be seen in the vicinity) and the Lord vomiting it out of His mouth.

The pilgrim saw how appropriate it was for his own reflections to visit this city. It definitely paralleled his own Western culture which was so filled up with material well-being, proud thoughts, and boisterous noises within, that it could not hear the Lord knocking on the door of its heart seeking entrance. Likewise, the pilgrim had come to understand the wisdom of acknowledging his own wretched, pitiable, poor, blind and naked condition (Rv. 3:17). This made room in his heart for the Lord to fill him with the gifts of his Holy Spirit like love, joy, peace, patience, kindness, etc. The pilgrim knew firsthand the chastening hand of the Lord and His love which motivated this treatment (Rv. 3:19) and the victory of the Lord and His love over fear, confusion and doubt which those enjoyed who surrendered totally to the Lord (Rv. 3:21). The pilgrim did not know how the original Laodiceans had responded, though he saw their glorious city now laying in ruins. Nor did he know how his own technological society would respond to this same call to repentance. But he knew this was the truth they needed to hear and the Lord was calling him in some way to proclaim in their midst.

The pilgrim did little more than spend a few minutes walking around the ruins of the ancient city of Laodicea and then followed the signs pointing the way toward the ancient city of Colossae. This city had a flourishing Christian community in New Testament times and not only was the recipient of one of Paul's canonical letters, but also very likely the home of Philomen who owned an early "house-church" and received a personal letter from Paul which is also part of our New Testament Canon.

The pilgrim walked into the little town of Honaz early in the afternoon. As was typical in all parts of Turkey, he found a number of men sitting at tables along the sidewalk drinking tea. They always greeted him with "chi" which he took to mean "do you want some tea?"

But the pilgrim was not out for socializing and even at the risk of offending his hosts' feelings, he refused to sit down and join them till he found out where Colossae was. By this means he hoped to communicate to them that he was a pilgrim visiting the ancient Christian sites, and not just a tourist, wanderer or hippie out to see the world. When they finally consented to his request and gave him directions to Colossae, he sat down and shared a cup of very strong tea with lots of sugar in it — for that's the way they drank it — and explained as best he could, the pilgrimage he was on.

That quickly taken care of, the pilgrim was soon up and on his way to the ruins of Colossae. Arriving at the place, the pilgrim was greeted by just a large mound of dirt with a few trenches dug through it. Obviously very little excavation had been made at the site and nothing was identifiable to him. However, there was one other individual there, a young boy in his early teens.

This young fellow came up to him and held out his hand. At first the pilgrim thought he might be asking for money, but then he saw that the boy was offering to sell him ancient coins that he had found digging around this mound that comprised the ancient city. The pilgrim said "Thank you, but I'm not interested. I'm not a tourist collecting souvenirs — even possibly authentic artifacts — but a pilgrim who has come to pray." And so they parted and the pilgrim found a place to sit down and read the letter Paul wrote to the Colossians.

Of the four short Chapters that make up the book of Colossians, the passage which seemed most applicable to the pilgrim's own life came from Chapter 3, verses 1-7. There Paul encourages the Colossians to "seek the things that are above, not the things on earth . . . put to death fornication, impurity, passion, evil desires, covetousness . . . in these you once walked but you have died and been raised with Christ and now your life is hid with Christ in God."

The pilgrim had indeed left behind his former way of life, seeking meaning first in knowledge and then in sensible pleasure. And his pilgrimage was like a new birth. He would never be the same again. He experienced as being hidden with Christ. The world considered him as good as dead, and hardly paid him any attention. So now he would "continue steadfastly in prayer, being watchful in it with thanksgiving" (Col. 4:2) . . . till Christ who is our life appears and then you also will appear with him in glory" (Col. 3:4).

From Colossae the pilgrim now headed towards Pisidian Antioch which lay another 100 miles to the northeast. During this stretch of the journey the pilgrim needed much inner strength and grace from the Lord to continue on. For he was passing along lakes and 8,000 foot mountain peaks in the interior of Turkey where winter still held sway. One morning he awoke from his spot along the side the road and was surprised to find an inch of snow had fallen upon the plastic cover he had thrown over himself in his sleeping bag.

During this week of walking the pilgrim's endurance was taxed to its limit. He would be so cold he would walk to try and generate some warmth in his body. When he got too tired to go on, he would sit down to rest till he couldn't stand the chill and chattering of his teeth any longer. And so he would start walking again till he got tired. There would be days on end when the tips of his fingers never did warm up. It was only by the Lord's protection that he did not get frostbite.

Pisidia of Antioch was important in the ministry of St. Paul (Acts 13:13ff) because there it was the rejection of the Gospel by the Jews that caused him to say "Since you thrust it from you and judge yourselves unworthy of eternal life, behold, we turn to the Gentiles" (Acts 13:46). There was no Catholic Church in Pisidia Antioch although it was a fair-sized modern town. All that interested the pilgrim there was the Jewish synagogue where Paul preached, as this is still pointed out. The pilgrim did not "shake the dust from his feet" against this town as Paul had (13:51), but he did follow the same road that Paul and his companions took to Iconium which lay about 100 miles to the east.

Along this route the pilgrim became very familiar with shepherds out watching their sheep. Most of the shepherds were men, not women or young children as he often imagined. They wore long, colorful, thick capes with hoods apparently made of dyed wool. This made an excellent protection against the cold and against the damp fog that hung over the land in the early morning. The pilgrim loved to observe how the shepherds tended their sheep, talking to them, threatening them, throwing stones beyond the ones that strayed too far to scare them back into the fold.

The pilgrim also noted in this part of the world and in this culture, when one entered a little village in the morning, one was greeted with sounds, not of cars, horns blowing, motors running, etc. but of sheep bleeting, bells dangling from their necks clanging, and the voices of people driving their flocks through the streets and out to pasture. Actually the pilgrim came to realize later that it would be here in Turkey rather than in modern Israel, that he would experience better what Nazareth and the towns of Galilee were like in Jesus' time, for Palestine today is well on its way to a being a technological society. And so through these experiences, the pilgrim was better able to understand Jesus' calling Himself the Good Shepherd and calling us His sheep.

It was about 100 miles from Pisidia Antioch to Iconium and involved walking south, then north and then east. The pilgrim was eager to arrive there for he had not received the Eucharist or attended Holy Mass for the past two weeks — since leaving Izmir. But his beautiful brother, the bishop of Izmir, had given him the name of the Catholic Church (Katolik Kilisesi) in Konya (Iconium), St. Paul — how appropriate, as a desert oasis. It had truly been a desert, this Lent, and he came to appreciate in a new way the availability of daily Eucharist in countries like Europe and America.

Although Paul and his companions stayed a long time (Acts 14:3) preaching the Gospel in Iconium, the pilgrim was there only a few hours. It was another modern city with Western fashions, automobiles, stores, etc. But the one thing which interested the pilgrim was the fact that the Gospel preached there was still alive, and 1900 years later Jesus was still being called Lord by his followers and disciples. So after being refreshed at the table of the Eucharist at St. Paul Church in Konya, the pilgrim departed and set his sight on his next important stop, Mersin.

This fair-sized city lay 200 miles to the south and right along the Mediterranean Coast. It had a Catholic Church and the pilgrim hoped to spend Holy Week there amid his fellow Catholics. By walking about 19 miles a day, he should be able to arrive there by Tuesday of Holy Week. Hopefully he would be welcomed by the priests whose names Bishop Boccella had given to him and he would spend a refreshing and spiritually

143

rewarding time celebrating the Paschal Mysteries of his Lord and Savior Jesus Christ.

On his way south from Iconium, the pilgrim came close to Lystra where Paul healed a man crippled from birth, was first proclaimed to be the god Hermes, and then was finally stoned and left for dead. Rising up as his brethren gathered around him in prayer (Acts 14:1-20) he passed through Derbe where he met Timothy (Acts 16:1) who became such a faithful disciple to him and was eventually entrusted with pastoral responsibilities at Ephesus. The pilgrim did not have the benefit of Paul in his personal presence to train him in the way of the Lord, but he prayed that the Holy Spirit, through Paul's written instructions and through his continued prayers and intercessions in heaven, would assist the pilgrim in knowing clearly and following faithfully the same Gospel he preached in this land and for which he suffered and laid down his life so many centuries ago. The pilgrim rejoiced to think that though physically removed from the scene, Paul's ministry continued to bear so much fruit to the glory of the Father.

The pilgrim followed his daily routine of obtaining a supply of bread in the morning and eating some of this at each rest stop after reading a few psalms or the Gospel of Luke. One particular morning, however, the pilgrim began asking for bread in a small village where there obviously was not a public bakery which sold bread. So a very obliging man took the pilgrim under his wing and led him from house to house, explaining to each family the pilgrim's need and obtaining a few very thin pizza-like breads from the lady of each house. Finally he led him to a canvas teepee-like structure, pulled back a heavy curtain and revealed three women sitting around a small charcoal fire which had an iron griddle on it which served to quickly bake the paper thin bread dough which was placed upon it. He gathered up a handful of these treasures and handed them to the pilgrim with a big smile as if to say "Here, this should keep you for the day."

This simple act of hospitality deeply impressed the pilgrim. Here this Moslem was practicing the corporal work of mercy to feed the hungry. It was as if he intuitively understood that the pilgrim was on a sacred journey and to not supply him with fresh bread would have been a serious offense against his love for Allah and against his brother in need. The pilgrim wished him well and asked the Lord to fulfill His promise in Mt. 10:42 where He says "He who receives a righteous man because he is a righteous man shall receive a righteous man's reward."

By Palm Sunday, April 4, the pilgrim had passed through the last of the snow-capped Taurus Mountains and reached the ancient port of Seleucia on the Mediterranean Sea. And though the pilgrim was not able to celebrate this Feast with palm branches and with his Catholic community, he certainly was united in spirit with every band of pilgrims who had ever journeyed toward Jerusalem, from however near or far, to acclaim the Lord with glad hosannas and proclaim Him alone as King.

Now, within three short days, he would conclude his Lenten journey and reach the Catholic Church in Mersin. The weather was glorious with temperatures in the 80's and signs of Spring everywhere. Due to the light showers the grass and wheat fields were luxurious. The fragrance of Spring flowers and orange blossoms was a welcomed reminder of new life after the bareness of Winter. But the pilgrim was not yet ready to celebrate the resurrection of his Lord. He still must share with Him his passion and death and so he would subdue the urge to dance and sing, till he had completed the journey of Lent.

As a matter of fact, this attitude of serious reflection became most obvious to the pilgrim himself one day. As he was walking along one morning in the bright sunshine, he heard the melodious voice of a young woman calling out "Parlez-vous Francais?" The pilgrim looked to his left and saw partway up a gentle slope, a smiling young woman in her 20's with long black hair, drawing water from a well with a bucket. Without a moment's hesitation — without even giving a second thought to how nice it would be to share with this young girl, even if the common language had to be French — he called out to her in a firm tone of voice "No," put his head down and kept walking. As he thought back on the incident, his firmness and determination not to be distracted or sidetracked from his commitment to journey on to Jerusalem (and more immediately to the site of Calvary at the Catholic Church in Mersin) surprised himself. He could only count it as a grace from the Lord. Just one year ago at this time he would have been eager to get to know such a pretty young maid. It seemed to him to be similar to the Lord's attitude reported by Luke 9:51 "When the days drew near for him to be received up, he set his face (like flint — Is. 50:7) to go to Jerusalem."

On Wednesday afternoon of Holy Week, April 7, the pilgrim arrived in the seaport town of Mersin and quickly found the Catholic Church. Although he was not led there by a jeering rabble as was Jesus it would truly be his dying with his Lord at Calvary. (*See "The Prosecuting Attorney", p. 158.) He found the Church was enclosed by a very high stone wall and so although it lay well within the business district of the city, it was like a world apart. He was met by two hospitable Capuchin Franciscans, Fathers Gregorio and Francesco. They welcomed him, immediately making him feel at home, giving him a private room and allowing him to share their table for the next five days. Of course he had free use of the church as often as he wished. It was such a perfect arrangement — one like only the Lord himself could have provided.

So for the whole of the Triduum, the pilgrim had practically nothing else to do but pray and meditate on the Lord's Passion and Death. Being a foreigner he didn't have to engage in extensive conversation. Being a guest he was exempt from the daily work that had to be done. Being a layman, he didn't have to prepare for or put on the liturgy, but could just relax and become deeply caught up in it as the Holy Spirit led him.

With the help of Latin and French rituals (his Mom had sent an English one but it was being held at the Mersin Post Office) plus his past years of experience with the Liturgy, he was able to follow the ceremonies without much difficulty. Of course the most useful preparation was the six weeks (and before that the eight months) of walking he had just completed. That was like the work the Lord had given him to accomplish, just as the Father had given Jesus a certain amount to do (Jn. 17:4), and then the climax. There would be no more journeying about — just more deeply within. Now came a rest and a struggle or agony that would bring completion to all that had gone on before. This was the time for offering the sacrifice of one's total self: body, mind and spirit, as they had been cleansed and purified and were now ready to be handed over to the Father in a radical and complete fashion.

All of this combined to create a deep fellowship between the pilgrim and the priests and people he prayed with. Although they had some customs he had never seen before — like four men carrying a plaster statue of Jesus laid out on the stone slab with flowers sticking out of holes all over his body and everyone trying to pass under the statue seven times for good luck or a special blessing. The pilgrim felt like part of the family. For those who wholeheartedly pray and worship the Lord together, eating of the one bread — Jesus the Christ — empowered by the same Holy Spirit, cannot but experience the deep unity of the Body of Christ, no matter what tries to separate them, whether it be language, country of birth or political philosophy, etc.

And so when the pilgrim stepped out of the enclosure for the first time on Easter Sunday to continue his pilgrimage, he felt like he had been living there for a lifetime. He had the sense that he knew the priests as long-time friends. The church building was like home after spending so much quality time there. And the celebration of the death and resurrection of his Savior had focused and renewed his faith to the core. The following are some of the pilgrim's reflections during these last three weeks of Lent.

MARCH 18, 1971 — DREAM — Looked at a tree at the top of our drive near the walk at home which my Dad had "pruned" as he explained why he had cut it the way he did. But I did not understand, for it was not pruned at all like the fruit trees I had seen in Europe. It appeared rather to be cut for convenience, because part of it had been in the way of the car and of the walk.

COMMENT 1987: The pilgrim recorded this dream because he sensed that the Lord was trying to teach him something about spiritual pruning, that is cutting away parts of his life which, though perhaps not bad in themselves, needed to be curtailed in order to produce more and better fruit in the future that the Lord had in store. And he was learning that this pruning was not to be left in the hands of those who only knew how to prune or discipline for convenience sake or from mere human wisdom. One needed the divine wisdom of the heavenly Father who was the true vinedresser (Jn. 15:1).

MARCH 19, 1971 — THOUGHT — INFLEXIBILITY as regards one's FINAL GOAL: FLEXIBILITY and SPONTANEITY as regards INTERMEDIATE GOALS AND MEANS.

COMMENT 1987: The pilgrim is beginning to learn that there is a time for inflexibility and a time for flexibility. The plant that never bends will soon break in a violent storm; the plant that is always bending will never grow tall or bear much fruit. Or the pilgrim could compare his life to piloting a sailboat: he's heading for a definite goal but he may have to tack back and forth according to the direction of the winds and current. What is new for the pilgrim is having a definite goal, for the few years preceding he just let the winds of circumstances and feelings toss him whichever way they wanted.

MARCH 20, 1971 — THOUGHT — Whereas once we had to say "Don't worry, these hard times shall pass, they are only a symbol of what the next life would be like without God, for with Him all shall be rest and joy;" now we must say "Don't worry, these easy times shall pass, they are only a symbol of what the next life will be like with God, they are not all there is to life (for if they were, we would be led to a terrible despair and hopelessness)."

COMMENT 1987: The pilgrim here is reflecting on the change in the way we point people to the next life according to their experiences in this life. The pilgrim sees that up to very recent-

ly, man's life on earth was physically very difficult. In that context Christian hope was clothed with words about "there will be no more tears or sorrow in heaven". In a technological society where physical hardship is at a minimum, the Gospel must be clothed with words reminding us that one should not mistake this for heaven — they are only a pale image for the rest that God has in store for those who love Him. Without this message, men would be led to despair when they found that all the physical comfort this present world can offer cannot satisfy the deepest longing of the human heart.

SAME DAY — THOUGHT — Why do I distrust all men? Because everyone I have ever met has tried to sell me a "false bill of goods".

COMMENT 1987: The pilgrim is using the word distrust here in a special way: to be wary or on guard, not swallowing the bait hook, line and sinker. He has found by experience that the world does not offer true happiness, and so like Jesus he no longer trusts himself into their hands (Jn. 2:24).

SAME DAY — THOUGHT — Most jobs in the modern world require so much attention and dedication that it is very easy to fall into the trap of idolatry and think THEY are what gives life its final meaning.

COMMENT 1987: The pilgrim here indicates that he probably will never be able to take a "job" in the future because it will distract him from his chosen goal of prayer and contemplation. In this way he hopes to avoid the possibility of falling into attachment again to mere creatures to the detriment of his commitment to his Lord. He has known too many people whose whole lives so revolve around their jobs that great harm is done to their relationship to the Lord Jesus.

SAME DAY — THOUGHT — Modern men no longer ask "Where (family and city) do you come from?" and "Where are you going?" but "What do you do?". Neither the past (family, source) nor the future (destination) are important today — only the present (the now).

COMMENT 1987: The pilgrim has come to experience the vital importance of getting in touch with his roots and clearly knowing his goal. This has caused him to see the superficiality of modern man's preoccupation with only the present, rejecting or neglecting the past and failing to consider the ultimate future.

MARCH 23, 1971 — THOUGHT — If truth itself was so misunderstood, mistreated and thrown out as refuse by the society of that day, then it would seem to be necessary in every age to seek the truth amid the poor, the discarded, the despised. The truth is that as Christ appeared to people of his day (an insane fool not worthy to be called a man or deserve to continue living), so all men appear in the sight of God.

COMMENT 1987: These two statements do not seem to be all that closely related. The first one is one of the undergirding reasons why the Church has always had a deep concern to minister to the poor, for there is a privileged place to discover and personally meet the Lord Jesus who said, "Whatever you do for the least of these you do for me" (Mt. 25:40). The second statement highlights the fact that the crucified Jesus shows us the effects of sin and the horror with which God sees it insofar as it alienates one from God, the Source of his life and leads to eternal death.

MARCH 25, 1971 — THOUGHT — As once suffering had to be given meaning, so now pleasure must be given meaning. This is only done by making them symbols of another life.

COMMENT 1987: This is a continuation of the thought expressed on March 20. Again the pilgrim opts for the eschatological perspective and wants all of our present reality to point to that ultimate reality. That is, the full meaning and purpose of the things around us is not to be sought solely in the thing itself, but rather in its symbolic relationship to the ultimate plan God has for our lives.

SAME DAY — Total non-violence is a symbol of and witness to the ULTIMATE truth of life. Christ chose it only in the last 24 hours of his life.

COMMENT 1987: Though not choosing it for himself, the pilgrim had thought much about non-violence because he had a number of friends who avoided the draft because of their beliefs. The pilgrim could not adopt this philosophy completely for he was engaged in doing violence to himself in terms of self-denial and discipline for the sake of the Kingdom. In looking at the life of Jesus, he does not see Jesus choosing non-violence as appropriate to his task given him by the Father, until the very last day of his life when he allowed his enemies to vent their hatred upon him.

MARCH 30, 1971 — THOUGHT — My lifestyle now — dropout — is very similar to what it was four years ago in California. Only then it was adopted because of a LACK of meaning in life. Now it is used because of knowing the TOTAL AND ULTIMATE meaning.

COMMENT 1987: The pilgrim is here noting that externally his life as a pilgrim does not seem all that different from that of a drop-out from society or a hippie. But the interior motive is altogether different. Thus, to know really what kind of a statement someone is making with his life, one must talk to the person and get to know the inner reasoning. Perhaps also the pilgrim is hinting at the fact that the Lord can take a purely secular lifestyle and give the person a new heart, thus redirecting the same life to his glory.

APRIL 2, 1971 — THOUGHT — The man who is dying of hunger and thirst may not be able to utter more than a weak croak. But this may be more acceptable to the Lord than the loud voice of a fully satisfied man's prayer to the Lord.

COMMENT 1987: The croaking man dying of hunger and thirst is of course the pilgrim. The comparison seems to parallel Jesus' parable about the two men who went up to the Temple to pray, the publican and the pharisee. The publican could do nothing more than bow his head and repeat "Lord have mercy on me a sinner." But he went away justified. Thus the pilgrim puts himself in the lowest place, trusting his Lord will see his heart and hear his prayer.

APRIL 12, 1971 — THOUGHT — Order is the first rule of heaven, yes, but in heaven order corresponds perfectly with the divine order, and what is order on God's level may look like spontaneous, unique, unpredictable disorder on man's level, e.g. the line of promise in the Old Testament.

COMMENT 1987: The pilgrim is here trying to state a truth he has discovered, namely that God's ways are not man's ways. As he has broken out of man's accustomed ways of thinking and acting in an effort to escape the suffocating boredom he experienced by keeping all his rules, he has discovered something of God's freedom to act according to his wisdom. Thus in the Old Testament God was free to depart from certain rules by choosing the secondborn rather than the firstborn, choosing women rather than men, choosing the sinner rather than the righteous, etc.

And so concludes the pilgrim's reflections up through Easter Sunday. This would be his last journal entry for the next two weeks. He would write nothing more until he got to the Holy Land.

PART FOUR: Mersin — Haifa

At noon on Easter Sunday, the pilgrim left the happy and secure enclosure of the Catholic Church in Mersin, and continued on his way. He was now more alive than ever with the peace and joy of the risen Lord. Having in a very dramatic and concrete way, given up his own plans and wishes by committing himself to this pilgrimage (and so dying to himself) he was able to experience how startling and exciting the event of Easter really is. Thus he now had branded in his heart the truth that only through suffering can one come to new life — if one does not die he cannot rise (Jn. 12:24).

The pilgrim's intention now was to walk along the south-eastern border of Turkey, along the Mediterranean Sea, until he came to Syria and there go directly south towards Israel. The Turkish border lay about an eight day walk away from Mersin, or about 160 miles. These last days in Turkey would be most glorious weather- and scenery-wise and reflected well his inner buoyance resulting from Easter, along with the growing sense of anticipation due to finally nearing his journey's end. He had no inkling at all of the difficultues which lay ahead.

Of course Spring was in full bloom now. As he walked along the coast with the deep blue Mediterranean to his right he only had to glance to his left to see the towering Taurus mountain chain paralleling the coast about 20 miles inland. These mountains were green on the lower slopes and capped with snow on their peaks. Often shrouded with huge billowing white cloud formations, these magnificent creatures spoke to the pilgrim of the grandeur and majesty of their Creator and his Lord. The deepness of the blue sky and cleanness of the white clouds spoke of the depth and infinity, the pureness and the holiness of the Lord and Maker of the heavens and the earth.

The pilgrim also delighted in observing man once again coming forth and going about his assigned task of caring for the earth: tilling the land, planting the fields, shearing the sheep. He also noticed the visiting tourists traveling in their mobile home campers and recording it all with their ever ready cameras. In the cities men were buying and selling, bartering and bickering, chatting and, of course, drinking tea.

The Turkish people he compared in some ways to little children in their inquisitiveness and fascination with anything which was new — like people from the Western World. They would holler, shout, whistle, or hiss at tourists to get them to notice or talk to them. They thought nothing of just staring and staring and staring. When possible they would come right up close to examine such strange phenomena and even touch and search and pull at it as if they just couldn't trust their eyes.

Also, still being a primitive people, they delighted in giving and receiving gifts. They were always offering the pilgrim something for his journey — hoping of course he would give them something new and exciting in exchange. Most of the time he has to just ignore all the attention and continue on his way.

On Monday of Easter Week, the pilgrim passed through Tarsus, the ancient city which was the birthplace of the great Apostle Paul and which, being a Roman provincial town with the right of citizenship gave Paul his Roman citizenship. There

151

does not seem to be any evidence that Paul had any success preaching the Gospel in his hometown and now again today, though a fairly sizable town, it does not have a Christian community. To find this the pilgrim would have to continue on to the American Air Force Base at Adana.

He arrived at the base the afternoon of the following day and looked up the priest chaplain whom he had met in Mersin over Easter. After much clearance and paperwork, he was permitted to stay with the chaplain overnight. Also he was able to assist at Mass in French later in the afternoon and then was treated to a large American style supper. It was a welcome sign of hospitality and a spiritual and physical preparation for the next few days which lay ahead.

While at the Air Force Base the pilgrim wrote his thirteenth long letter home. As he closed the letter he made a statement which was indeed prophetic. He said: "The end now is within sight — perhaps within a month. Then I will need guidance to discover what He (the Lord) wishes me to do next. I know help will come and I suspect His "new assignment" will appear in the eyes of most to be an even harder task than my present one. But if it is HIS will, the burden will be light to me, as He promised." How true those words would be.

Two days after leaving the Air Force Base, the pilgrim reached his furthest point east and rounding the northeast extremity of the Mediterranean Sea, he headed south towards the land of his faith. Now, however, he was in an area that was much more war conscious as he was drawing near the Syrian border. Thus, one day as he walked through a small village an angry man came up to him waving a shot gun and making threatening gestures, seemingly demanding his passport. Since he was not wearing an official uniform the pilgrim felt free to refuse to show him his passport and risk not getting it back, so he just kept on walking. Very soon the villagers around pulled the angry super-patriot, or whatever he was, back into their midst and waved the pilgrim on with knowing expressions. The pilgrim thanked the Lord for rescuing him from his enemies and continued confidently on his way.

Soon the pilgrim passed through the famed Syrian Gates between two mountain ranges and came into the important New Testament town of Antioch. Here the pilgrim eagerly visited the cave and spring pointed out as the original meeting place of the first Christians in Antioch (Acts 11:19ff). He sat down and prayed here for awhile and reflected on some of the reasons why this was such an important community of early Christians. Here was the first city in which the Gospel was preached to and received by Gentiles. Here the followers of

Jesus' way were first called Christians (Acts 11:26). This became St. Paul's home base as he began first serving the people of God here with his gift of teaching. It was from here he was sent out on his missionary journeys and it was back to here that he came to report on what God had done through him (Acts 14:26-28). From this point on, for many centuries, Antioch became one of the main centers of a vigorous Christianity in the east, being called a Patriarchal See and giving the world scholars, bishops and saints to the equal of Alexandria and Constantinople. Yet since the 16th century, the area has been occupied by the Moslems, and Christianity is hardly visible. Actually, on this visit the pilgrim did not meet a single brother or sister in the Lord in Antioch.

But as he began walking through the streets of the downtown business area, he did meet some interesting people. For example, there was the young man who came up to him and in English began to ask him why he was walking. During the conversation, the young man said they were taught in school Jesus did not really die on the cross — He only swooned and then was resuscitated. Therefore he was not really God. The pilgrim surprised himself as he found himself speaking very loudly and forcefully, "If Jesus did not die, then we are still in our sins and everything is still spiritual darkness." It was just the opposite of what he had to say most of the time when objectors took the stand that Jesus died and never rose. But it brought home to him the necessity of proclaiming Jesus' death as well as his resurrection.

Also the pilgrim was accosted by a local news reporter who wanted to get a picture of him and do a story in the town newspaper. The pilgrim agreed and when the interview was over, he asked the reporter if he would be so kind as to send a clipping of the story to his parents. He said he would as he took the address, but it never did arrive.

But the most interesting visitor the pilgrim encountered was a young Muslim husband and father of three children. This man came up to him as evening was approaching and without being able to speak any English, communicated to the pilgrim he was inviting him to his home for dinner and to sleep for the night. The pilgrim, sensing a pure and honest motive in this most unusual offer of hospitality, said yes. The pilgrim was surprised at his own yes. Normally he would make excuses and be off in order that he might remain alone to be more attentive to the Lord. But somehow here he felt the Lord wanted him to have this experience and learn an important lesson in what it means to share one's home with a total stranger.

The pilgrim was led by his host to a side street and a very

humble mud-brick dwelling in a whole row of similar single storey homes. As they entered through the front door, they came into a large dimly lit room about 16 feet square where the whole family was already gathered. As it turned out this was the only room there was — it was the whole house.

His host's wife was tending to the open fire by the chimney where a pot containing their supper probably had been cooking for many hours. The children were together in a corner quietly playing by themselves. His host motioned for the pilgrim to take off his pack and make himself at home. This meant taking off his shoes and sitting on some blankets on the dirt floor. There was not a single piece of furniture anywhere in the room.

But the pilgrim felt truly blessed to have been so trustingly invited into the intimacy of this simple family's life. They apparently were not unduly concerned that he might be a murderer or a thief. They lived so close to the earth and basic necessities of life, that they could "read" another's need for warmth, food and shelter even without being asked or sharing a common language. And out of that basic love and willingness to share the little they had, they gave the pilgrim the beautiful gift of their lives. It reminded the pilgrim of the story in the Old Testament where Lot invited the two angels in from the street to spend the night with him. (Gn. 19:1ff)

When the simple but delicious meal which resembled a stew was enjoyed and finished, it was time to clean up and get ready for bed. All that was involved was unrolling the mats and blankets which were placed along one wall and which served as the bed clothing. So all activities of the family were carried out in this one room: sleeping, cooking, eating and recreating. The pilgrim was invited to roll out his sleeping bag right along with the rest of the family and given some extra covers too. The children went right off to sleep while the adults stayed up a while to share and the pilgrim to pray some Psalms by the light of the oil lamp. Soon all retired and had a restful sleep.

The next morning the pilgrim was up with the rest of the family and soon on his way. This was an experience that he would never forget and he thought again about why God so much loves the poor in spirit who are so ready to give all they have to one in need. He wondered if such openness could be recaptured in a technological society. As far as he was concerned it definitely had been lost, for his experiences in America and in central European countries were the same. People were so preoccupied with a myriad of projects, always going somewhere so fast that they did not notice; or if they noticed, they did not reach out to him in any depth. The pilgrim saw the change as he came south out of France, Switzerland and into Italy. Italy itself showed the transition from a more industrialized less-caring north to a more rural and hospitable south. Then coming into Greece and Turkey, the pattern was repeated, namely that the more simple and primitive the culture the warmer reception he experienced.

When the pilgrim left Antioch, the Syrian border lay a mere 25 miles more to the south. He proceeded on hopefully and blissfully, not in the least expecting the reception he was about to receive at the border. Nothing had prepared him for it — no one had forewarned him of the possibility. Probably realizing how stubborn and determined to walk the pilgrim was, the Lord knew how useless it would have been to try and redirect his steps in any other way.

On the second day, April 20, the pilgrim arrived at the border station. He paid his toll and passed through Turkish customs. But when he got to Syrian customs he got a flat no. It was explained he had two strikes against him: 1) he was American and Syria was at war with Israel which was supported by the United States, 2) he was on his way to Jerusalem and Syria was at war with the owner of Jerusalem. There was no use appealing the decision to higher authority. He would have to turn back and find another way into Israel. And so without any disappointment or bitterness in his heart, the pilgrim accepted the rebuff and decided to retrace the last 150 miles of seven days of walking, back to Adana where he hoped he could get a boat going to Israel.

It did not take the pilgrim seven days to return to Adana, for he did not hesitate to take rides when offered now, since he figured he had already paid his toll in walking, so he got back in three days. Once there he could not find a boat going to Israel, but he was told that twice a week, on Wednesday and Saturday, a plane flew to Nicosia on the Island of Cyprus for $21.00 one way. From there he could get a boat at the port of Limassol which would take him to Haifa for $18.00. This did not seem exhorbitant, and the pilgrim still had enough money, so that became his plan.

For this brief part of his journey, the pilgrim once again was back in the environment of the world with its schedules, rules, crowds and noises. But he had to endure it for the sake of the greater goal. He even thought that perhaps while he was on Cyprus he could follow the journey of St. Paul to Famagusta there. But these hopes were dashed upon his landing at the International Airport of Nicosia.

There he was met by the police who escorted him and another fellow with a backpack into a side room where they were specially questioned. It wasn't a search for contraband, but an assessment of how much money each had to spend. The other traveler had $200. That was OK, he could go. The pilgrim had $60. That would allow him to stay for only two days and then he would have to be gone. So a two-day visa was stamped on his passport. Obviously if one did not have money, one was not welcome to visit this beautiful island in the Mediterranean.

Actually the natural beauty of the Island was marred in other ways, especially by the evidence of war everywhere. In the city of Nicosia, one could see whole areas sectioned off with barbed wire and armed soldiers on patrol. The United Nations peace keeping force was evident everywhere.

The pilgrim did read the appropriate passage from the Acts of the Apostles (Acts 13:4-12) which recorded Paul's missionary endeavors on the Island when he proclaimed the Word of God in the synagogue at Salamis and to the proconsul Sergius at Paphas.

But the pilgrim could not visit these sites for they lay in the eastern region and on the western coast respectively, and he had to travel from the central (Nicosia) to the southern (Limassol) part of the Island — a distance of about 54 miles.

Once in the port city of Limassol, the pilgrim immediately set about booking passage on a ship to Haifa. This accomplished, he sat down to await the 8 p.m. time for sailing. He tried to prepare his mind and heart for what was about to be the culmination of a year's worth of walking — setting foot on the land on which Jesus had walked.

During this part of the past two weeks he had only one journal entry — a kind of poetic statement on the Resurrection.

APRIL 13, 1971 — POEM

> Earth shaking;
> Stone rolling;
> Soldiers falling;
> Power disarming;
> Angel speaking;
> Women babbling;
> Men believing;
> Christ alive!

SNOW

> Oh snowfall deep,
>   so pure and white:
> Falling from,
>   an unseen height.
> With gentle touch,
>   you change the earth:

First hiding death,
  then giving birth.

— Turkey, March, 1971

DARK CLOUD

I am a dark cloud:
People don't like me:
I dampen their spirits,
And chill their bones.

I am a dark cloud:
When I appear
People seek shelter
And hope I pass by.

I am a dark cloud:
Thundering and flashing;
Tearing the earth,
Washing the land.

I am a dark cloud:
Unleashing death;
But only through me
Will new life appear.

— Turkey, March 1971

LONE EAGLE

I am a lone eagle:
  soaring high above the earth.
I see what others miss:
  my view is of the whole.
The thoughts I think are rather strange:
  not like those down below.
For there's a total difference here:
  'twixt what is high and low.

The air I breathe is clean and pure:
  free from dust and dirt.
But oft' I wish I could enjoy,
  the fragrant smells of earth.

The sounds I hear are different, too,
  mostly calm and quiet;
Though now and then I'd like to hear,
  another speak and sing.

I am a lone eagle,
  soaring high above the earth.

For me there is no other life,
though others there may be.
— Turkey, March, 1971

THE PROSECUTING ATTORNEY
(the pilgrim stands trial)

Ladies and gentlemen of the jury —
the man before you is on trial for his life —
the charge is insanity.

He maintains that we must change our lives:
he says we are on a dangerous path and that if we continue on it,
we will completely fail to reach the happiness we seek.

He says that we have been misled
and that the goals that have been set for us by our leaders
are not worth the effort we are putting into them.

He holds that if we continue to spend all our time and effort
in trying to achieve a more and more comfortable life
we will eventually find no comfort or happiness at all.

He says that we must give up thinking that work and leisure
are the most important things in life
and realize again that there is more to life
than what we see on our TV's
read in our papers
or buy in our stores.

He says that real happiness is not found in such material things
but only temporary pleasure
because like them the temporary pleasure they give us will pass
just like they break and wear out and are thrown out.

He would have us believe that we must aim for something
    beyond all these things —
that there is a goal for us which alone is worth so much time
    and effort —
that to follow the path to his goal means a change in life and
    giving up of much that we now call life.

The man would change our whole style of life:
he would have us not put so much trust in our
    life insurance policies,
bank accounts and credit cards:
he says these give us a false security —
that they will all eventually fail to satisfy us
or give to us the real happiness we are all seeking.

Now this may be partly true:
but what does he propose we do instead?

158

Not only give up our present way of life
but follow a path of self-discipline and hardships,
doing without many of the comforts we now enjoy
in order to have more time to think
and live in the reality of this other goal which he proposes.

He says that we are so busy with passing things
    that as it now is,
we have almost completely forgotten where our true peace and
    happiness lies;
to him "the good life" that we are all working to create
    is not so important as we think
and he would try and tell us we must begin thinking
    more about
and living more in the awareness of this other life.

                        — Turkey, April 1971

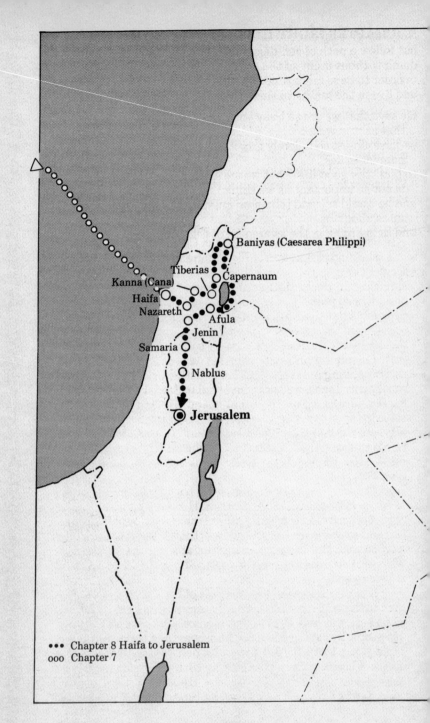

Baniyas (Caesarea Philippi)

Tiberias

Kanna (Cana)

Capernaum

Haifa

Nazareth

Afula

Jenin

Samaria

Nablus

Jerusalem

●●● Chapter 8 Haifa to Jerusalem
ooo Chapter 7

It was Sunday morning, April 27, when the pilgrim caught his first sight of the land of his faith as the ship came into port at Haifa. He thought of how many thousands of other such pilgrims he resembled who came this way over the centuries in their desire to touch base with the roots of their faith. He thought of the boatloads of crusaders who in the 11th and 12th centuries came pouring into this land to give up their lives in an effort to win the sacred shrines associated with the life of our Lord Jesus back from the hands of the Moslems. But he also thought of the pious pilgrims who only came to pray; pilgrims like Francis of Assisi and the Carmelite hermits.

The pilgrim knew that his coming into Haifa was not an accident or merely because that's where his boat from Cyprus happened to dock. Rather he believed it was part of God's providential plan. It only remained for him to be open to discovering what the Lord wanted to show him through it all.

One of the goals that the pilgrim had kept in mind from the day he left the States on his way to Jerusalem, was to meet with a Seminary professor from his days at St. Vincent's who was now living in Israel. This Benedictine priest whose name was Father Isaac, was very involved in Jewish/Christian dialogue and was a close personal friend. He had just recently come to Israel to set up a Benedictine/Kibbutz type of community and the last the pilgrim had heard, he was living in Haifa. So this would be the first place the pilgrim would set out for — after, of course, visiting a bank and exchanging some currency.

The address he had for his priest friend was the Carmelite Monastery on the top of Mt. Carmel. However, upon his arrival there, he was told his friend Father Isaac had moved to Jerusalem and so was given his new address there. That reunion would have to wait. But the pilgrim was not about to leave this place without first seeking some guidance from the Holy Spirit in this holy spot.

The pilgrim knew that this area of Mt. Carmel was important to the ministries of the Old Testament prophets Elijah and Elisha. It was here that Elijah vindicated Yahweh's rule over his people by calling down fire from heaven to consume his sacrifice (I Kg. 18:19ff). And it was also here that in the early 13th century the first Carmelites, along with St. Simon Stock who was given the Scapular by the Blessed Virgin on this spot, began to live a community life. So the pilgrim prayed that he might receive even just a portion of the tremendous graces poured out on The Lord's servants, the prophets, on His mother Mary and His beloved hermits.

By mid-afternoon, the pilgrim was heading east out of town on the Haifa-Meggido road and following the Kishon River. Before he had gone very far through the Plain of Esdraelon (Jg. 1:8), however, he took the road to the left which kept close to the southern slope of the mountains of Galilee and which would eventually take him to Nazareth. His plan was to begin in Jesus' home town, follow his public ministry around the Sea of Galilee and finish his journey in Jerusalem, just as Jesus did.

Since he had got a late start walking, he only made about six miles before darkness came on. So looking for an out of the way place off the side of the road, the pilgrim ended his first day in the Holy Land. He thanked the Lord for bringing him this far. This night he would rest his weary body on the same earth upon which his Lord and Savior Jesus walked and rested almost 2,000 years before. He already began to sense a new gift of faith coming into his heart from the Lord and His land.

DAY TWO

The next day the pilgrim was up bright and early. He read the Psalms and Scriptures for Matins from the Latin Breviary he carried with him, and set out toward Nazareth. He was not at all in a hurry. He had no timetable to meet and no one was waiting for him. His only responsibility was to pray and listen to the Lord.

As he was walking this day, rejoicing in the workers harvesting the fruit (itself a sign of God's messianic blessings — Is. 9:3), a young man came up and introduced himself. He said he lived on a kibbutz by the name of Canaan Cid in Lebanon. Apparently the kibbutznik felt the pilgrim looked like a possible candidate to join this type of community living and contribute to the prosperity of the nation of Israel. Although the pilgrim was personally interested in this type of community venture, he sensed a greater call to pilgrimage and prayer. So he politely declined and continued on his way.

This was the day the pilgrim discarded the lining to his army overcoat. Parting with a cherished possession when one only has a few things to call his own, was not that easy. But it was so warm and the pilgrim judged there would not be much cold weather anymore at this late date. He found himself folding the warm inner lining and hanging it up on a fence rail alongside the road for someone else who might have use for it.

As darkness set in, the pilgrim had almost come to

Nazareth. So he decided to stop short of the village and find a quiet place to sleep so he could be up early and into the town the next day for a possible early Mass. It was amazing to him how much the Lord had brought him through to allow him now the privilege of visiting the very site where Jesus lived most of his earthly life. He had seen so many pictures of the town during his years of study. But tomorrow, the Lord willing, he would walk into those pictures and they would no longer be mere colored images on thin paper or canvas, so imperfectly conveying the reality. Now he would personally enter into those pictures and look at them from the inside. It had to be a singular grace. In Jesus' Name.

DAY THREE

Waking with the rising of the sun, the pilgrim offered his new day to the Lord. He prayed the assigned psalms with a greater attention because of the realization that these very songs were no doubt sung by Jesus Himself in this very locale. Walking the last few kilometers into Nazareth, he began looking for a church where he could assist at Mass.

As he began exploring its streets, he was happy to find Nazareth still very much retained the physical appearance of a Middle Eastern town. Its narrow streets were lined with houses of cut stone; its skyline was studded with domes, minarets and towers; and its inhabitants were dark-skinned Arabs. Making his way along, he found himself drawn to the top of the hill overlooking the city to the Church of Jesus the Adolescent. Here he went to Mass.

Also here he found a large technical school for training young boys from the neighborhood in a trade. It was run by the Salesian brothers, whom he found to be very hospitable. After Mass they invited him to join them for breakfast and then showed him around briefly. Thanking them for their kindness, and promising to pray for them and their apostolate to youth, the pilgrim was eager to be back on his own.

Before descending the hill back into the city, he sat for a long time outside the Salesian School and just looked out over the town which Jesus, the Son of God chose to call home for almost 30 years. He thought of how He had chosen to live in total obscurity, hidden away as it were, in the life of an ordinary Jew of the time. Here He was the Messiah, sent to save the world, and He's spending his days and years in a humble carpenter shop fashioning a few wooden objects to help his neighbors' lives be a little more convenient. Oh, the mystery of it all. No wonder Charles deFaucald, the early 20th century hermit from France (whose life inspired the flourishing community of the little brothers of Jesus as well as the little sisters of Jesus) spent a few years of his life here as a simple gardener at the Poor Clares Convent.

By early afternoon, the pilgrim had descended into the city proper. Here he found the Basilica of the Annunciation which honored the spot on which, at the message of the angel Gabriel, the Word of God became flesh in the womb of the virgin Mary. He found here a very splendid and modern edifice, whose roof swept up like a huge cone overshadowing all the other buildings in the area. It was as though the secret was out — the fact could no longer be hidden — the Good News of Emmanuel was being broadcast to the whole world.

The pilgrim entered the holy shrine along with other tourists and pilgrim groups and soon found the grotto cut in the rock which over the centuries, has been venerated as the home of the Virgin. He himself knelt in prayer and gave thanks to the Father for the gift of His only Son sent to earth to rescue men from their sin. He asked Mary to obtain for him something of her grace to say yes to the Father's will for his life. He knew that this rock and dirt was like what could be found anywhere on the face of the earth. But somehow, it had become special, consecrated by the presence there once of the Son of Mary who, though God, lived like a man among the men of his day. He was not even set apart like his cousin John who lived an ascetical life as a Nazarite. He was known to His fellow townspeople simply as "the carpenter, the Son of Mary" (Mk. 6:3) and "the carpenter's son" (Mt. 13:55).

From here the pilgrim took his own tour around the modern edifice and viewed the many stone carvings and pictures of the life of Jesus to direct his thoughts and prayers to his Lord. It seemed to him a very easy place to pray and keep his mind on the Lord. Finding this such a favored place, he decided to go out into the open portico on the south side of the Basilica overlooking the valley and write his 14th letter home. In it he shared about his coming to the Holy Land from Turkey and promised to ask God's blessing on all his family as he visited the Holy Places. He hoped to hear from them in about two weeks when he got to Jerusalem.

When the gatekeeper came around to lock up for the day, the pilgrim took this as a sign that it was his time to move on and leave this holy city of Nazareth. He sought out the street which would lead him to Cana for he intended now to follow Jesus' footsteps to Capernaum and the Sea of Galilee.

Although Cana lay only five miles northeast from Nazareth, darkness came on before the pilgrim arrived. So he looked for a remote place to spend the night. Not being gifted like his master who would spend the nights in prayer, the pilgrim spent most of this night in sleep. But he was thankful for a day so rich in memories and experiences of his Lord. In Jesus' Name.

PART TWO: Nazareth — Capernaum
DAY FOUR

Upon waking, the pilgrim immediately reflected on the fact that he was in the land of Jesus. His Lord and Savior had walked this way, passing between Nazareth and Cana. Maybe He and his disciples had come this way. Perhaps they themselves had stopped and rested where he had spent the night. These were the places where they had talked together. And most importantly, this is where He had shared with them the truth of His heavenly Father's love.

It was only another mile till the pilgrim arrived in Cana, that privileged site of the first miracle of Jesus' public life (Jn. 2:1-11) where "the water saw its maker and blushed" (Gerald Manley Hopkins, SJ). He made his way to the Latin Church cared for by the Franciscans and he got there in time for Mass. He could not imagine a more fitting way to celebrate the coming of the long-awaited Messiah who made available a true feast and real joy through the pouring out of the Holy Spirit, so well-symbolized by the abundance of wine at the marriage feast. Here he was, drinking of the life-giving waters of salvation in an even deeper way than those wedding guests, and even the apostles in the time of Jesus. Here he saw Jesus as the Vine which changes water from the earth into wine from heaven.

After the Mass, the Capuchin priest who celebrated the Liturgy which the pilgrim had attended, spoke to the pilgrim briefly. And so the pilgrim shared something about his pilgrimage. When the friar saw the scallop shell fastened to the pilgrim's backpack, he understood immediately the significance of it; namely, that the pilgrim had been to Santiago de Compostela in Spain. He was so eager to have it that he asked the pilgrim to send it to him once his journey was complete.

Setting out from Cana then the pilgrim headed towards the Sea of Galilee, which, of course, was the main place of Jesus' public ministry until his departure for Jerusalem. On the way, he passed through magnificent wheat fields and was reminded of the incident in the Gospel (Mt. 12:1-8) where Jesus' disciples were caught plucking some of the wheat berries on the Sabbath and were condemned by the Pharisees. It provided Jesus with just another opportunity to teach the truth that the heavenly Father was more pleased by men showing love and mercy, than in the uninspired keeping of human regulations.

Passing by the unusual geological formation called "The Horns of Hattin" because it resembled the two ends of an Arabian saddle, the pilgrim recalled that this was where the Crusaders suffered the first disastrous defeat in 1187 which eventually led to the demise of the Latin Kingdom of Jerusalem. He could identify with the noble thought of giving one's life to make the shrines of the Holy Land safe for Christian pilgrims, but he wondered how much of this effort was really directed by God. What men could not do with force of arms and diplomatic maneuvering, God did very simply centuries later, when, as it were, He Himself opened the hearts of the Moslems to allow Christians to once again come and pray in their Holy Places.

Finally, just as the sun was setting behind him, he came to the edge of the plateau where an immense hollow begins to drop away, affording a breathtaking view of the lake that had witnessed so much of its Creator's activities. No longer was it just a picture in a book or a blue patch on a map. He was now really present to and part of the stage on which was acted out the exemplary and saving life of the second Adam. He fell asleep that night realizing Jesus and His disciples had also slept on this very hill.

DAY FIVE

As the pilgrim awoke this morning — now well below sea level according to signs posted along the road — the first thing which greeted his eyes was the beautiful Sea of Galilee with the sun rising over the hills of the Golan Heights along the east shore. To think how many times this very sight greeted the Lord Jesus' eyes was enough to inspire a prayer of thanksgiving. Here in a very personal and concrete way, the pilgrim was able to do what Jesus did when He was on earth. In this small and simple way, at least, the pilgrim was able to be like his master. He beheld the beauty of this part of creation and thanked the Father for His gift.

The pilgrim continued on towards the Sea and came to the city of Tiberias. Historians say this city was actually only built by Herod in the years Jesus lived in nearby Nazareth. Jews refused to visit it for centuries since it had been built on a cemetery, though today they wholly occupy it as a kind of resort area. Since it is never mentioned in the New Testament that Jesus visited it himself, there were no special shrines or holy places to visit there. But seeing that it was the only inhabited city along this side of the lake at present, the pilgrim did go into the city to get his day's portion of bread.

166

From there he set out to walk north along the western shore of the lake towards Capernaum which lay at the extreme northern end. Today, aside from a few restaurants, bathing beaches and fruit tree orchards, this area is abandoned and devoid of human activity. In Jesus' day it was apparently much different as a number of thriving towns like Magdala, Bethsaida, Capernaum and Chorazin are mentioned in this area. But since it was now such a desolate area, it made it easier for the pilgrim to reflect on what the Gospels record as having occurred here in the time of Jesus.

As he walked along, the pilgrim thought: here was where Jesus taught us about the Kingdom of God from a boat moored at shore. Then he had Peter launch out into the deep for a catch of fish so spectacular it caused the boats to sink and Peter to exclaim "Depart from me O Lord for I am a sinful man" (Lk. 5:8). It was from this experience that Jesus called Peter to catch men and he responded by leaving everything and following Him.

Continuing along he thought: here was the scene of the violent storm in which Jesus was awakened by his fearful apostles and rebuked the storm and the sea became calm (Mt. 8:23-26). This was where Jesus came in the middle of the night to his apostles, walking on the water, and learning it was not a ghost as they first suspected, but Jesus, professed "Truly, you are the Son of God" (Mt. 14:33).

The pilgrim passed the supposed ruins of Magdala, the city from which Mary who had seven demons cast out of her was named (Lk. 8:2). It was this Mary who became such an ardent and devoted follower and servant of the Lord, that she was the one to remain at the foot of the cross (Mt. 27:61) and seek the Lord at the Tomb (Mt. 28:1). It was in this area also that an incident happened which the pilgrim never did fully understand. It was this.

As he was walking along the right side of the road, a small car passed him going the opposite direction, tooting its horn. The pilgrim made a small sign of acknowledgment, not really knowing if the sounding of the horn was meant for him or not. Nevertheless, he continued on his way without even breaking his stride, keeping his thoughts on the words and deeds of Jesus.

As he continued on, the pilgrim sensed that the car had pulled off the road a distance behind him. Turning around he saw the car slowly backing toward him on his side of the road. Still not certain it was meant for him, he continued walking. When after a few minutes he did not sense the car any nearer, he turned again and saw in the distance a car turned upside

167

down on its roof with the four wheels slowly turning. Not sensing any urging to investigate further, the pilgrim turned and continued on his pilgrimage.

Looking back on this incident, he did not know if the people in the car were interested in seeing him or not: whether they were friendly or hostile. Was this the Lord's way of protecting him from getting hassled? Was this a test to see if he would be distracted from his chosen pilgrimage? Had he failed to take advantage of an opportunity to practice a corporal work of mercy and help a brother in need? He experienced no great anxiety over it and resigned himself to the fact that he probably would not know anything more about it till the last judgment. He prayed for the victim of the incident, which was probably more embarassing to him than harmful anyway.

Soon the pilgrim came into one of the few plains which surround the Sea of Galilee called the "Little Ghor" which is known as "The Land of Gennesaret" and which was possibly the site of Bethsaida. John says this was the native town of three of the twelve Apostles: Peter, Andrew and Philip (Jn. 1:44) though Mark gives Capernaum as the home of Peter and Andrew (Mk. 1:29). The fact that this town cannot even now be accurately located shows the efficacy of Jesus' curse upon it "Woe to you, Bethsaida: for if the mighty works done in you had been done in Tyre and Sidon, they would have repented long ago in sackcloth and ashes" (Mt. 11:21). It was a sober reminder that one cannot base his salvation on the mere fact that he has known and experienced the power of the Lord. One must act upon that experience, repent and produce good fruit.

As night came on, the pilgrim found himself in the region of Et-Tabgha or place of seven springs. In this area Christians apparently have especially commemorated three significant events in Jesus' ministry: The Discourse on the Mountain, The Multiplication of the Loaves and Fishes, and Apparition of the Risen Jesus to His Apostles. Because the area is rather low-lying and close to the Sea, it was hard for the pilgrim to imagine the first two events as happening there, but the third, one of his favorites (as a matter of fact one he had duplicated on the shore of the Atlantic Ocean in Spain near Santiago de Compostela) seemed very appropriately placed.

Not investigating any of these ruins, the pilgrim decided to start up the mountain lying off the left side of the road and look for a place to sleep. In the morning he would climb the hill to the Church of the Beatitudes on top and hope to find a Mass there. That seemed like a much more fitting place to reflect on the Sermon on the Mount and the multiplication of the loaves and fishes. And so again, lying on the very ground trod by his master and which "heard" His words and "witnessed" His miracles, waiting for the very rocks to shout out his praise (Lk. 19:40), the pilgrim took his rest on this holy ground.

DAY SIX

The pilgrim this morning awoke in the spot the Lord had provided for his night's rest. Not only was it at the foot of the Mount of Beatitudes, but it was only a few hundred yards from the Sea of Galilee. The whole area lay quiet and still in the morning dew. The only sounds were those of birds and sheep. Nothing of trucks and cars; no roaring of engines, honking of horns or other manmade din. It was as though the very countryside and atmosphere itself did reverence to the memory of its Master having once walked, taught and healed in these hills.

Having sufficiently recollected himself as to where he was, the pilgrim began his climb up the gentle slope to the church of the Beatitudes built near the top and looking out over the Sea of Galilee. All was peaceful and still. Only a single farm dwelling broke the pristine beauty of the place. Every few hundred feet the pilgrim would turn and look over his shoulder to catch a glimpse of the whole of the Sea of Galilee. And he would remember: here is where Jesus taught us "Blessed are the poor in spirit, for theirs is the Kingdom of heaven; Blessed are the meek, for they shall inherit the earth" (Mt. 5:3,5).

Arriving at the top of the Mount the pilgrim made his way into the church of the Beatitudes and shared in the Holy Eucharist. What a privilege to be able to be fed the bread which came down from heaven (John 6:51) in the very spot where Jesus had anticipated this meal by multiplying the five loaves and two fishes. And then later, in nearby Capernaum, he had explained "He who eats my body and drinks my blood, has eternal life and I will raise him up on the last day. For my flesh is food indeed, and my blood is drink indeed. He who eats my flesh and drinks my blood abides in me and I in him" (Jn. 6:44). The pilgrim thanked the Lord for the great gift of faith that enabled him to believe in these words, for as Jesus himself had said: "No one can come to me unless the Father who sent me draws him" (Jn. 6:44). It was because the heavenly Father had introduced His Son to him that made possible his being in this place, to have his faith deepened and renewed.

The pilgrim was so much in a spirit of thankfulness for the gift of the Lord's presence, that he hardly needed to notice that the church itself was octagonal in honor of the eight beatitudes and that one beatitude was inscribed on each window. In such privileged moments one hardly needed the aids of architecture and language to keep his thoughts directed to the Lord. It was enough to be caught up in the Lord's presence which pervaded the entire scene, even centuries after His passing on. He then spent some time in the ambulatory under the open arches running along the eastern side of the building. This afforded a perfect view of the lake and made an "excellent place for him to read the whole of Matthew's account of the Sermon on the Mount (Chapters 5-7).

Around noontime the pilgrim set out to descend the hill and make his way to Capernaum, which was only a half hour walk away. Still finding no human habitation, stores, or anything but open fields and simple roads, he came to the gate of the enclosure that had over its entrance the word "Capernaum." Here he found that today it is no city at all. It is merely a museum piece, though a small community of Franciscans lives here to pray and care for the pilgrims and tourists who come by that way. He paid his small fee to enter and view the ruins.

There were two main attractions. One was the ruins of a second century synagogue which archaeologists believe was built over the synagogue that stood there in Jesus' time and in which he cured the demoniac (Mk. 1:21-28), spoke at length about Himself being the bread of life (Jn. 6:6 50) and healed the man with the withered hand (Mk. 3:1). The other main point of interest was what appeared from early second century construction, to be the house of Peter where Jesus seems to have taken up residence (Mk. 1:29) through John 1:44 says Peter's home was in Bethsaida. Here at any rate, Jesus healed the sick (Mk. 1:34), forgave the paralytic his sins (Mk. 2:5) and spoke at length with his disciples (Mk. 4:10, 9:33).

The pilgrim's final reflection on this former city so favored by the mighty words and deeds of the Savior, was its hardheartedness. After pouring out His love upon this city, as He was about to depart for His final trip to Jerusalem, Jesus had said: "And you Capernaum, will you be exalted to heaven? You shall be brought down to Hades" (Lk. 10:15). And how accurate these words proved to be. Ancient Capernaum today is but a pile of rubble, with just a few stones set up here and there to indicate something of its former glory. It is a silent but vivid testimony to the fact that even the personal presence and ministry of Jesus Himself cannot assure a receptivity and positive response to the truth of God's love. Whether in Jesus' day or in one's own day, faith is always a free gift and it can be disastrously refused.

Considering his next immediate goal, the pilgrim decided not to head directly toward Jerusalem, but to follow the footsteps of his Lord and go north towards Caesarea Phillipi (Mk.

8:24-27). It was with great reluctance that he left the area around the Sea of Galilee, so rich in memories of the Lord. But this three-day detour to the north would afford him an opportunity to reflect further on what he had experienced so far and identify more closely with Jesus' instruction to his disciples about his coming passion and death (Mk. 8:31). It would be for him also a time to consider more carefully the cost of discipleship and the necessity of the cross. So heading in the direction of Safad, the pilgrim walked about 12 miles before darkness set in and he found a quiet place to rest for the night.

PART THREE: Capernaum — Tabor
DAYS SEVEN — NINE

The next three days the pilgrim found himself walking through the eastern side of Upper Galilee — that is the northern end of the Jordan Valley. Roughly, he would be following the main tributary of the Jordan River which flowed down from the Lebanon Mountains and Mount Hermon. This was the ancient land of Naphtali (Jos. 19:32), the tribe of Dan in the farthest out-post of the land of Israel (Jg. 20:1), and the lush grazing land of Bashan to the east occupied by the flourishing half-tribe of Manasseh (Dt. 3:13).

For the pilgrim, it was enough that Jesus had taken His disciples on this route on a kind of retreat away from the multitudes that sought them out around the sea of Galilee. He seems to have used this as a time of deeper instruction for His chosen Twelve, especially concerning the mystery of suffering in the Kingdom and the true nature of salvation that the Messiah came to bring. It seemed to the pilgrim that Jesus had chosen this environment well according to His purpose as this was the headwater region — the place of origin — the root and source of the life which flourished in the area around the Sea of Galilee. Just as Jesus would be touching down deeply upon the footing of His life-giving Church, so here He would reveal its foundation rock (Mt. 16:18).

As the pilgrim made his way north he could at special times catch a glimpse of Mount Hermon off in the distance. He thrilled to see the snow-capped peak often shrouded in clouds. He thought, no wonder the Hebrew text of Deuteronomy 4:48 calls it Mount Sion, the Lord's chosen dwelling place. It also recalled another Mountain much further to the south, namely, Mount Sinai. For there the presence of the Lord had been manifested to Moses and the people in the form of a cloud (Ex. 19:9). He turned to Psalm 29 which extols the glory and strength of the Lord and possibly was composed by David in this very region. What a powerful poetic image to describe the voice of the Lord as making Lebanon skip like a calf and Sirion (the Sidonian name for Mount Hermon) like a young wild ox (v. 6). The poet's choice of words was certainly appropriate when he wrote "Hermon joyously. . . praises thy name O Lord God of hosts" (Ps. 89:12).

The pilgrim did not go all the way to Mount Hermon. The furthest north he got was to the modern city of Baniyas or Panias, which in Jesus' time was called Caesarea Phillipi, and this still lay in the foothills of Mt. Hermon. But it was close enough that some of the children were seen to be enjoying eating fresh snow out of paper cups. Apparently someone had been up in the mountains and brought back this little treat for such a hot day. They shared a cup full with the pilgrim who both enjoyed it in its plain and simple state and wondered to himself how long before someone would teach them how to add color, sugar and flavored syrup to it, like the "snow cones" sold in the States.

But the pilgrim's thoughts mainly turned around Mark's account of Jesus asking his disciples, "Who do men say that I am" (Mk. 8:27). This, of course, is the pivotal question for every person who ever has or ever will live, and is confronted with the Person of Jesus Christ. For one's eternal salvation rests upon one's confession of Jesus as the Son of God, the Lord's Anointed (Mt. 16:13-20). Matthew's account adds to Peter's confession, Jesus' key words "I tell you, you are Peter and on this rock I will build my church and the powers of death shall not prevail against it. I will give to you the keys of the Kingdom of heaven and whatsoever you bind on earth shall be bound in heaven, and whatsoever you loose on earth shall be loosed in heaven" (vv. 18-19).

This event was apparently a signal to Jesus that the critical moment had arrived in His public ministry. His disciples now believed He was the Messiah. Now He could reveal to them that this implied his suffering, death and resurrection (Mt. 16:21). From here He would be looking to Jerusalem (Lk. 9:51), the place where He would offer the total sacrifice of His Life for the forgiveness of sins and salvation of the world. And so from these furthest regions of the north, the pilgrim, too, turned south and set his face toward Jerusalem.

The pilgrim was headed back towards the Sea of Galilee now, but further east — in the area known as the Golan Heights. It was all so quiet and peaceful. He wondered that for miles and miles there was no sign of human activity. There was barbed wire stretched along the side of the road, and in the fields covered with flowers many boxes in which bees could make their honey. There were also signs just off the side of the road, but these were written in Hebrew and the pilgrim could not figure out what they said.

Then one afternoon, as he was walking along in perfect peace and joy, an army jeep with two Israeli soldiers in it, pulled up to him. The officer asked the pilgrim what he was doing and where he was going. After he explained, they told him that this area was off limits to everyone: that the signs off the side of the road said: "this land (the very spots where the pilgrim had pulled off the side of the road to rest and sleep) is all mined with hidden explosives". And more to the point, in twenty minutes, the area would be used as a practice field for Israeli fighter planes. They said he had better get in with them so they could ride him further ahead to a safer area.

The pilgrim obliged them and climbed aboard — not minding that he wasn't able to walk these few miles. He was very thankful to the Lord for protecting him from such hidden dangers and now providing these two angels to get him to safety. They dropped him off outside the practice zone and then sped off to safety themselves.

The pilgrim finished his walk for the day still somewhat north of the Sea of Galilee, but now especially praying for the hostilities which still plagued this land that the Son of God had made holy. If only men's hearts would be open to receiving His Love — then all such war games would cease. He prayed: "Lord send laborers into your harvest."

DAYS TEN and ELEVEN

For the next two days the pilgrim would continue his private and quiet meditations along the eastern and southern shores of the Sea of Galilee. These he found to be totally uninhabited areas at present, except for fields of wildflowers and along the southern shore, orange and banana groves.

As he came back to the northern end of the Sea of Galilee, the pilgrim referred to the Gospel of Mark which recounts Jesus curing the blind man in the neighborhood of Bethsaida Julius (Mk. 8:22-26). This is that amazing account of a sacramental, progressive cure. It was sacramental in the sense that physical material was used: Jesus spit on his eyes and laid His hands on him. It was a progressive cure in that Jesus had to pray over the blind man twice before total healing was effected. It was as though this man needed more individual attention from Jesus as if to impress upon him that this healing was not just some kind of magic but that it cost Jesus self-giving, sacrifice and intense prayer — eventually even His Death on Calvary.

Continuing down the eastern shore of the Sea of Galilee,

the pilgrim walked the road that kept close to the shore and which was only a matter of a few feet from the water's edge in many places. He first came to the area in which a mountain spur runs down to the Lake; there are caves in the hills and there is easy access by boat. The Gospels call it the country of the Gerasenes (Mk. 5:1-20). This was the scene of the powerful deliverance of the demoniac, showing that Jesus could bind the strong man Satan (Mt. 12:29) and the destruction of the herd of pigs who plunged to their death as a result of being taken over by a legion of devils (Lk. 8:26-39), showing the power and fury and destructiveness of Satan and his cohorts.

The pilgrim saw no pigs, no herdsmen, no townspeople. Only the lapping of the waves against the shore and the humming of the bees gathering the sweet nectar from the fields of flowers broke the complete silence of the hot balmy day. It was as if the Lord had delivered this place from all bondage and turmoil. Nothing more needed to happen than for each person who came by to accept this gift of freedom from sin and its harmful effects and rest in his victory.

As a sign of his own desire to identify with that life that his Savior had made available, the pilgrim decided to take a quick dip into the clear cool water of the Sea of Galilee. It would be a reminder of his own baptism as an infant. The Lord had sanctified the waters by walking on them calming them and going down under them in his own baptism. No doubt he also drank from them and bathed in them too. Like the waters of the Red Sea, they could at one and the same time be destructive and life-giving. They would destroy sin and give life to the righteous.

In remembrance of this event, the pilgrim gathered a few tiny sea shells from the shore and collected a small bottle of water. These would be more than souvenirs he would take along with him; they would be more like relics — objects made special and sacred by having been in direct contact with the Holy One he adored — Jesus, his Savior. And though he carried an even more precious treasure in his heart — the loving presence of his Lord — he would value these little objects as a kind of proof that he was there, when his faith needed strengthening and encouragement.

As he reached the southern end of the Lake of Galilee, the pilgrim found himself walking through grove after grove of orange trees and banana trees. Everything was artificially watered by huge pipes and sprinkling systems. The pilgrim could not help but think of Isaiah's promise that in Messianic times, he would "make her wilderness like Eden and her deserts like the garden of the Lord" (Is. 51:3), even though he knew this was

174

more man's doing than the Lord's. Still he prayed for the fulfillment of the Lord's promise to make empty hearts bear abundant fruit by the power of the Holy Spirit so that the land might truly be filled "with joy and gladness and thanksgiving and the voice of song" (Is. 51:3), exulting the name of Jesus the Lord.

Having completed his tour of the land around the Lake and crossing over the Jordan River as it began its meandering journey towards Jerusalem and the Salt Sea, the pilgrim had one last stop in mind before making his way to the Holy City, and that was a visit to Mount Tabor. This meant heading east a few miles in the direction of Nazareth. As nightfall of his eleventh day in the Holy Land approached, he caught sight of Mount Tabor in the distance. It seemed to suddenly rise out of the earth like a huge earthen altar, deliberately piled up. He contented himself with sleeping this night with the mountain still in the distance. He trusted that in the morning, the Lord would grant him the grace of climbing this natural sacrificial table and receiving the enlightenment he would need to make his own journey to Jerusalem.

DAY TWELVE

Waking early, the pilgrim opened his pocket New Testament to Mt. 17:1-8 and read where Jesus took with Him Peter, James and John and led them up a high mountain. The Scriptures do not give the name of the mountain, but since the 3rd century, Christians have venerated Mount Tabor as the site, and so the pilgrim put himself in spirit with this inner band of disciples and set out in the direction of the holy mountain.

As he began the ascent of the mountain, the pilgrim found the current road winding back and forth as the slope got steeper and steeper. There was no traffic on the road but occasionally a taxi or tourist bus would pass him. Thus, the pilgrim was able to enjoy the wide vistas which opened up with each turn in the road. As he looked out over the surrounding countryside, he recalled some of the events of the Bible that happened there.

One such event was the important Old Testament battle when the prophetess Deborah was directed by the Lord to order Israel's army under Barak to assemble on this mountain for a victorious attack on the Canaanites led by Sisera. The pilgrim thought: could this not have been a prophetic sign that another woman would rise to be called "mother of Israel" (Jg. 5:7) and "most blessed of women" (Jg. 5:24) and who crushed the head of Israel's true enemy, Satan himself. So he placed himself once more under Mary's protection and sang again her canticle of praise, the Magnificat (Lk. 1:46-55). "My soul magnifies the

Lord, my spirit rejoices in God my Savior . . ." (Lk. 1:46)

The pilgrim was in no hurry, so it was just after noon when he reached the plateau on top of the mountain. There he found a rather new (1924) structure for a church, which was being taken care of by the Franciscans. They showed him most gracious hospitality, inviting him to eat as their guest in a large dining hall and to spend the night in the pilgrim hostel adjacent to their monastery.

Rejoicing in how the Lord had provided for his basic needs in such a marvelous way, the pilgrim felt the Lord was calling him to spend the rest of the day in prayer on this holy spot. As he walked about, the pilgrim found the present basilica had three chapels: one for Jesus, one for Moses and one for Elijah. It struck the pilgrim as ironic, though, that while Peter's request to set up three tents and remain here was put aside by the Lord, Christians in ages after Peter did just that very thing. The pilgrim learned from reading, though, that it was not always easy for Christians to maintain this spot as a place of prayer. It seems that with the coming of the Moslem Bibers in the 13th century, all Christian shrines were destroyed and this holy mountain was abandoned for almost four centuries. Then in the 17th century permission was again granted for the Franciscan Friars to settle on Mt. Tabor.

So the pilgrim counted it a blessing to be able to pray at this holy spot without any external opposition. He learned that this very place had been visited by early pilgrims like St. Jerome and the holy women of the fourth century. Also that in the 9th century this shrine had actually been the site of a bishopric and was cared for by the Benedictines in the 12th century. But most of all, it was, of course, the meeting place and site of the holy conversation between the representatives of the Old Testament, Moses and Elijah, and Jesus. It was like the Old Testament testifying to and giving place to the new work God was doing among His people in Jesus. Here was Moses, getting his first view of the Promised Land (Jesus) from actually within the terrestrial Promised Land that he was prevented setting foot on when he led God's people to its very door beyond the Jordan (Dt. 34:1-4).

Here was Elijah, who in his earthly life had journeyed throughout these lands and knew them well, exercising his prophetic ministry of calling the people to return to faithfully abiding by the Covenant of Sinai, now seeing the New Covenant for which it stood. And all was pointing to Jesus' going up to Jerusalem to suffer and die — to offer His Life as a sacrifice and ransom for God's people. And here was the Father confirming His son's mission for the final time with the words:

"This is my beloved son, with whom I am well pleased: listen to Him" (Mt. 17:5).

And though the pilgrim did not see a cloud of glory or hear a voice from heaven, he did kneel down in worship, acknowledging the gift of the Son of God to mankind and His presence now in each believer's heart and in the Eucharist. He was privileged to be able to attend Mass here in the Basilica of the Transfiguration and receive the heavenly bread come down from above to strengthen him for his journey through the desert of this world and on his own ascent of Calvary to offer his life to the Father in union with Jesus.

PART FOUR: Tabor — Jerusalem
DAY THIRTEEN

The pilgrim was up early the next morning as he followed the monastic schedule of morning prayer and Mass. He continued to linger for a few hours on top of this solitary mountain as though it were the very gate of heaven — indeed it was that, for the Father's voice had been heard here. And by faith it continued to be heard by all who accepted Jesus as their Savior. So the pilgrim let these words penetrate deeply into his spirit, thus cleansing his heart (Eph. 5:20) and lighting the path of his journey (Ps. 119:105).

Now he set his face to go to Jerusalem, as Jesus had done (Lk. 9:5). Until this time in his pilgrimage, he had always had Jerusalem as his goal, but now he had no other intermediate goals: he would not turn to the right or to the left but would keep to the straight path south. He walked about 10 miles before nightfall came, and he arrived at a place just south of Afula — a crossroads town in the Plain of Esdraelon. But most importantly, he knew this would be his last night in Galilee.

He wondered how Jesus must have felt as He had come to that point in His Life. He would have recalled the ways he had striven with His whole might to share the good news of His Father's Love with His disciples and the people who were so slow to believe. Now He would not lay eyes upon his beloved Galilee again till after He had offered the last drop of His blood in a final gift of self in total love and was raised from the dead (Mt. 28:16, Jn. 21:1ff). It seemed an appropriate time to look over his journal entries since he first set foot in the Holy Land.

APRIL 28, 1971 — THOUGHT — My time is too valuable to spend it working at a job for the sake of money.

COMMENT 1987: The pilgrim is still dealing with the challenge from the culture around him, both in particular individuals who questioned his pilgrimage and in the thoughts which entered his own mind from earlier training. This is his way of answering those who have a problem accepting the legitimacy of his project: he sees it as a higher calling than the ordinary workaday world.

SAME DAY — THOUGHT — One is free to believe what he wants — yes, even error.

COMMENT 1987: The pilgrim's reflection of the meaning of freedom, leads him to see this particular truth. Freedom as the world defines it means thinking or doing whatever one wants, without any objective standards. Thus in this way of thinking one is free to be in the wrong — even if it leads to hell and eternal damnation.

APRIL 30, 1971 — THOUGHT — If Jesus had lived in 1970 USA instead of 30 A.D. Palestine, He would not be killed or tried or put to death, but imprisoned and REHABILITATED to an acceptable way of thinking and living.

COMMENT 1987: The pilgrim, in trying to relate the experience of Jesus to contemporary society, notices that not only is crucifying out of the question, but also capital punishment in any form is facing increasing public opposition. The world puts its faith in its ability to deal with misbehavior as shown in the various forms of rehabilitation, failing utterly to understand the punishment which necessarily flows from sin. Thus our modern world would have tolerated Jesus or merely felt some kind of pity for his weird thinking. In other words, it would have been lukewarm, neither hot nor cold. And in a sense Jesus would have been unable to give His Life as a sacrifice for sin as He needed to do.

MAY 8, 1971 — THOUGHT — FAITH: believe that God is still in control of the world and one's own life. HOPE: desire that His power may be ever more fully manifest. LOVE: act in accord with your faith and hope.

COMMENT 1987: The pilgrim here is describing the three theological virtues in terms of a Biblical faith which emphasizes trust and dependence upon the Lord, rather than intellectual assent to true statements about Him. Thus he sees his life in more personal terms than what he had known throughout his years of study. Now he understands that only a total way of life will satisfy the deepest longings of the human heart.

MAY 9, 1971 — THOUGHT — Jesus was not a wise man who spoke many beautiful sayings. He was a fool who spoke many hard words.

COMMENT 1987: The pilgrim here shows the weakness of the position of those who hold Jesus to be nothing more than a good teacher or inspiring orator. Jesus' wisdom was not of this world, and only those with faith could call it wisdom. The world has to term it foolishness.

FOUR DAYS IN SAMARIA
DAYS FOURTEEN — SEVENTEEN

The pilgrim awoke for the last time in Galilee. As he set out this morning, he identified with Jesus, who upon approaching this very border between Galilee and Samaria, had sent his disciples ahead to prepare the way (Lk. 9:52-56). The Samaritans had not accepted Jesus, possibly for the same two reasons the pilgrim had not been allowed to enter Syria from Turkey a month earlier: because of nationality (Jewish/American) and because of destination (Jerusalem/Jerusalem). The disciples had wanted to call fire down upon those who closed their hearts to their Lord, but Jesus rebuked them, for He wanted to pour down His Holy Spirit upon them as when He spoke to the Samaritan woman at Jacob's well (Jn. 4:10) and when Philip the deacon so effectively evangelized the Samaritans after Pentecost (Acts 8:5ff).

The pilgrim thought how similar today's situation in the area was to that in the time of Jesus. In our Lord's time the Samaritans were looked down upon by most Jews because when those who had been captives in Babylon returned in the 6th century, they found that those who had been left behind had intermarried with people who did not descend from Abraham. So the Samaritan was considered unworthy of inheriting God's promises. Today there live in this area many Arabs who continue to view this as the West Bank of Jordan and not really part of Israel. So they are held in little favor by the present State of Israel. In light of Jesus' mission to proclaim salvation to all mankind, the pilgrim wondered if Jesus were to tell the parable of the Good Samaritan (Lk. 10:30ff) in 1970, would He not have the one who acted as a good neighbor be an Arab?

Likewise the pilgrim thought of another modern application as he came into Jenin, the border town between Galilee and Samaria. For tradition has it that this is where Jesus cured the 10 lepers (Lk. 17:11-19). Jesus praised the one who returned to give thanks. And he was a Samaritan — unworthy of God's favor in the eyes of a Jew. The pilgrim wondered if Jesus were to perform the cure today if the one to return and give thanks would not be an Arab?

Also this day the pilgrim passed through the ancient city of Dothan, where Joseph was sold by his brothers to some Ishmaelite traders who took him to Egypt (Gn. 37) where he became second only to Pharoah. At Burka the pilgrim was amazed to find he could look to the west and see all the way to the Mediterranean across the Plain of Sharon. It was almost the day's end, so the pilgrim began looking for an appropriate place to sleep for the night.

He had been noticing all day the groves of fig and olive trees. Not being familar with these in America and knowing how much they figured in the life of Jesus and the Gospels, he paid careful attention to their every detail. One thing he noticed about the olive trees was how the older ones often had large spaces between different sections of the trunk and that actually one could crawl through them and come out the other side. Then the thought came to him: that would make an excellent place to sleep. And so that night and on several other occasions, he laid down on the ground inside the trunk of an old olive tree, having a living creature of the Lord as a roof and wall about him. That night he prayed: "Lord, anoint me with the oil of your Holy Spirit, even as it ran down the beard of Aaron (Ps. 133:2). May your life flow into me, your servant, so that I may shine as your light and witness you before the world (Rv. 11:4). May my spirit remain awake and keep vigil with you as you prayed in the Garden of Gethsemane (Lk. 23:39ff) where those ancient olive trees kept you company on that most dreadful of nights. Amen."

The pilgrim's second day in Samaria brought him to the picturesque valley between Mt. Ebal to the north and Mt. Gerizim to the south. This place had so many Biblical associations, that the pilgrim could scarcely take it all in. First of all it was here at Shechem, by the Oak of Moreh, that Abraham pitched his tent and where the Lord spoke and said to him: "To your descendants I will give this land" (Gn. 12:7).

Secondly, it was where Jacob bought a piece of land on which to settle his large family after his return from Haran where he had lived for 20 years working for his father-in-law (Gn. 33:18-20). This must have been where he had dug a well that Jesus would drink from (John 4:12).

Thirdly, this was the place where the Twelve Tribes assembled under Joshua to renew the Covenant Yahweh had given them on Mt. Sinai (Jos. 8:33-34), at the foot of Mt. Gerizim — the mountain of blessings. And at this time Joshua buried the body of Joseph that he had brought up from Egypt (Jos. 24:32).

This last biblical fact — the burial of Joseph's bones here — quite amazed the pilgrim. To think: Joseph died 400 years before the Exodus; God had revealed to him that He would visit his people and bring them up out of Egypt to the land of promise; he made them swear to take his bones with them (Gn. 50:24-26); Joseph was embalmed according to the Egyptian custom and then kept by the people for 400 years; then his mummy crossed the Red Sea with the baggage; survived for 40 years through the desert and in battle; crossed the Jordan and finallv came to rest in this spot. Wow — what a journey! No wonder the author of Hebrews praises Joseph's faith (He. 11:22). If the Lord so protected his bones — think what He has done for his soul.

But of course the pilgrim's most privileged thoughts were associated with Jacob's well and the discourse John records in Chapter 4 of his Gospel. There he presents Jesus resting by the well, tired and thirsty and yet eager to share with a person who had three strikes against her: she was a Samaritan, a woman, and living with a man who was not her husband. The beauty of Jesus' concern; his tact; his clear statement of truth: his total focus on the Father's glory — his patience with his uncomprehending apostles — all these qualities of Jesus' personality were so finely portrayed by John in this scene of the woman at the well. Jacob may have dug the well, but it was only a sign pointing to the source of true living water — Jesus, the Lord.

The pilgrim spent this night yet in the land of Samaria. Then on the following day — his 16th in the Holy Land — he passed through Khan el Lubban and climbed up to the height which marked the present boundary between Samaria and Judea. Now he felt he had set foot in that land made more special by the presence within it of the holy city Jerusalem. Here was the land which inherited the promises; the object of the prophecies; the land of David, of the Ark of the Covenant, and most of all the land of Jesus' sacrificial death. The only place holier would be Jerusalem itself and the church of the Holy Sepulchre. If the pilgrim had been brought up in an eastern rather than a western culture, he may at this point have removed his shoes and walked the rest of the way barefooted. But he hadn't, so he didn't.

Now the pilgrim began seeing signs indicating that Jerusalem lay only some 30 kilometers to the south. That was about 20 miles, or one good day's walk. To think: after nearly 12 months of walking, his goal lay only one more day ahead. He found within himself an eagerness and at the same time a reluctance to complete his journey. He wanted to attain his yearlong goal — yet he hesitated before the unknown of what lay beyond it. Passing through the land frequented by the prophets Elijah and Elisha he knew their lives testified to the fact that receiving the favor of God's grace carried with it heavy responsibilities and much suffering. What would God ask of the pilgrim whom He had called and sustained on this pilgrimage of faith?

Pondering this question, he turned to his patron once more, St. George, who had so inspired the Crusaders in this area in the 12th century, and He prayed: "St. George, mighty warrior against the forces of evil and the Kingdom of Satan: obtain from your Lord and my Lord, the courage needed to face the opposing forces within and without. Beseech our Lord to clothe his unworthy knight in the full spiritual armor necessary for anyone desiring to defend and protect the Church of Christ. May your example of fidelity unto death be a source of strength and hope as I strive to offer my life, too, as an acceptable sacrifice to God, fighting the good fight of faith. Amen."

Then, at the end of his 17th day in the Holy Land, the pilgrim came to within a few miles of the Holy City, Jerusalem. He decided to stop short of the city so as to be able to enter it by daylight. Nothing else around him mattered much now. His whole heart and mind were focused on beholding the great city of his Lord. To help give expression to his deepest longings, he turned to the songs of Ascents in the book of Psalms (120-134) which David and pilgrims to the holy city since his time, had sung as they made their way to it:

"I lift up my eyes to the hills.
From whence does my help come?" (121:1)
"I was glad when they said to me:
Let us go to the house of the Lord!
Our feet have been standing within your gates,
  O Jerusalem" (122:21-2)
"As the mountains are round about Jerusalem,
so the Lord is round about his people
from this time forth and for evermore" (125:2)
"Arise O Lord, and go to thy resting place,
thou and the ark of thy might.
Let thy priests be clothed with righteousness
and let thy saints shout for joy" (132:8-9)

PART FIVE: Two Weeks in Jerusalem
DAYS EIGHTEEN — THIRTY-THREE

Upon rising, the pilgrim climbed Mt. Scopus and got his first full view of the ancient walled city of Jerusalem. He did not pause to look or to pray any further, but continued down the western side of the hill to avoid the modern city of Jerusalem and so be able to enter from the Mount of Olives. This would allow him to walk in the path of his Lord both on his triumphal entry on Palm Sunday, and his last journey with his apostles on the way to the Cenacle for the Last Supper.

As he approached St. Stephen's (or Lion's) Gate, he was struck by the enormous wall which ran along the eastern edge of the city above the Valley of Jehosaphat. He mixed with tour buses, taxicabs, donkeys and, of course, hundreds of pedestrians as they made for the narrow passageway which led into the

Old City of Jerusalem.

Immediately upon entering through the gate, he sensed a holiness about the place which to him was almost tangible. He would also describe it as a sense of PEACE: of stability, truthfulness, rootedness, connectedness: of ages without end. This sense grew in the following days as he moved about the city and observed how the people who lived here conducted themselves.

But for the moment, the pilgrim had only one thought: to seek out the church of the Holy Sepulchre. For he wanted to keep vigil there for the first 24 hours he spent in this holy city. The place where Jesus died and was buried — although in the first century outside the wall of Jerusalem (Jn. 19:20), now lay within the present city walls. It was not difficult to find, for entering from St. Stephen's Gate and proceeding straight ahead, he soon found himself on the Via Dolorosa (The Way of the Cross), and by following the signs he came quickly to the courtyard outside the church building covering the most sacred spot on the earth.

From the outside the church building was totally unimpressive, being not very large and crowded in on all sides by other buildings. The entrance had nothing special about it to set it apart as it amounted to nothing more than a door in one of the arches in what looked like the side wall of the church building. Inside, however, was another world such as he had not experienced anywhere else. Once through the door he was confronted at every step with altars and paintings and icons and hanging oil lamps. But what most struck him was the spirit of devotion that was present. Pilgrims were everywhere: kneeling, bowing, prostrated, kissing sacred objects, carrying lighted candles, singing and praying.

The pilgrim soon found to his right the rock of Calvary, climbed the steps and entered the small Chapel of Calvary with the altar built over the hole in the rock where the cross of Jesus stood. Here he knelt gazing upon the most sacred place on the face of the earth: the place where Jesus poured out His life-giving blood. Here where it fell upon the earth and upon all men's hearts who by faith could hear those saving words He addressed to His Father from the cross: "forgive them" (Lk. 23:34). This very rock was thus a witness to the fact of salvation, to the truth that God so loved the world that He gave His only begotten Son (Jn. 3:16) to be a sacrifice for sin.

The pilgrim prayed: "O Lord. How could you love me so much? How could you find something in me worth so much pain and suffering? How could you gaze into the depths of my heart and see there your very image and likeness? I am at a total loss, trying to fathom the depths of these truths. I cannot understand. I cannot explain. I can but humbly bow down before you and say yes, Lord: here I am. Let me be your servant. I only desire to do your will, now and forever."

From this most privileged spot, the pilgrim then visited the other stations of the Cross commemorated in the church with various altars. Day wore on and night came. He found each major religious group, the Latin Catholic, the Greek Orthodox and the Armenian Orthodox, took turns carrying on their own particular liturgies in the Church of the Holy Sepulchre. About 2 a.m., this all came to an end and the pilgrim was told he would have to go outside as the doors were locked. But only for two hours, as it would begin all over again at 4 a.m.

So the pilgrim went out into the atrium and sat down at a spot against a wall. He kept vigil there for two hours, just outside the locked door but still no more than 30 feet from the hill of Calvary. And then when the door was opened at 4 a.m., he went back inside and joined the processions and litanies and went off at times to pray on his own.

At one point he was allowed to enter into the small chapel built over the place where Jesus was buried. He was able to touch and venerate the slab on which Jesus was laid. And then upon coming out of the tomb, he was led by a Coptic priest in black robes with his distinctive little square, box-like hat, to a tiny chapel at the back of the tomb and allowed to touch "the real rock on which Jesus laid," while an empty, outstretched hand was placed in front of him to receive a small donation for such a privilege.

After his 24 hours were up, the pilgrim left the Church of the Holy Sepulchre and went in search of his Benedictine priest friend, Fr. Isaac, whose address he had been given in Haifa. He soon found him living in a modern apartment in the Beit Hakerem section of the new city of Jerusalem, along with another Benedictine brother. Their vision of a Christian kibbutz was still in its infant stages as they continued to study and pray about how to proceed.

The pilgrim was grateful for the hospitality, enabling him to make this his home base for the next two weeks he would spend in Jerusalem. He lived with his Benedictine brothers and divided his time between praying and reading there in the apartment and making short pilgrimages to the different sites in and around Jerusalem. Thus he went to the Garden of Gethsemane where he saw the ancient olive trees and attended Mass in the Church of all nations, whose main altar was built over the Rock where Jesus prayed. He climbed the Mount of Olives to the place where Jesus took leave of his apostles and ascended into heaven (Lk. 24:50). He walked the streets of the Old City of Jerusalem and visited all the places marked as the Stations of the Cross.

During this time, the pilgrim recorded the following reflections in his Journal:

MAY 14, 1971 — Jesus chose MEN to be His apostles. If He wanted to choose the weak and despised, why did He not choose women and children?

COMMENT 1987: *The pilgrim is here reflecting on the divine wisdom that selects the weak and despised to confound the strong and honored of this world. Yet he notices that God does not apply this so called principle the way man would do with rigorous logic. He is still free in His choice, and man cannot completely contain Him within his own human categories.*

MAY 17, 1971 — QUOTATION — "Those who, like the friends of Job, are satisfied with the good things of this world, and find the Lord in them, cannot easily be brought to see the vacuity of the present life unless it is thrust down their throats: nothing but an experience like that of Job will ever convince them of the inescapable reality of the next life. For men do not look to another life until they have seen the futility of the present life." J. McKenzie, *Two Edged Sword*, p. 25

COMMENT 1987: *The pilgrim was reading this book from the library of his priest friend Fr. Isaac. He identified with the deep conviction of the vanity of all the things of this world. But he did not come to this truth the way Job did, at least not in having all the material wealth Job had. He came to this realization rather through the despair he reached at the end of a long path of intellectualization which proved utterly incapable of satisfying his heart. He perhaps records this thought insofar as he often wonders how to bring this truth to those who have everything — as in the modern Western world.*

MAY 18, 1971 — QUOTATION — "The Gospel should provoke in us neither naive enthusiasms nor petulant slander of the world, but awaken us to the deep truth of man's sinfulness and hardness of heart, overcome by the love of God and by His restoration of the world in Christ." T. Merton, *Conjectures of a Guilty Bystander*, p. 34.

COMMENT 1987: *This book by Thomas Merton was another the pilgrim had been reading the previous few years and now had picked up again. The pilgrim did not find that he needed to guard against any naive enthusiasms, but perhaps did have to examine his conscience on whether he was falling into the error of petulant slander of the world. This will always remain a danger in the life and ministry of a pilgrim and a prophet.*

MAY 20, 1971 — QUOTATION — "A person who realizes the

particular evil of his time and finds that it overwhelms him, dives deep in his own heart for inspiration and when he gets it he presents it to others." Gandhi, *Conjectures,* p. 59.

COMMENT 1987: The pilgrim obviously identifies with the one who realizes the particular evil of his time. He dove into his own heart and there found his Lord, Jesus. But how is he to present his treasure to the world? Not everyone is interested in such a treasure, and he doesn't want to cast his pearl before swine (Mt. 7:6). This step will require much prayer and seeking on the part of the pilgrim.

MAY 23, 1971 — "Relativism does not imply subjectivism or skepticism. It is not evident that the man who is forced to confess that his view of things is conditioned by the standpoint he occupies must doubt the reality of what he sees. It is not apparent that one who knows that his concepts are not universal must also doubt that they are concepts of the universal." R. Niebuhr, 1941, quoted by Harvey Cox in *Secular City,* p. 33.

COMMENT 1987: This particular book by Harvey Cox had been one the pilgrim had avidly read in his theology days and he now took it up again after his year of pilgrimaging. He could still find something there that spoke to his experience, though it was stated in the most abstract terms possible of particulars and universals. He seems to pick up this thought because it offers hope to one who might tend to despair because of an inability to get all the facts together and therefore always be suspended in a state of indecision and hesitant expressions.

After only a few days of prayer in Jerusalem, the pilgrim began to sense that he would not be staying there for long. This was not the place to settle down or to make any kind of more involving commitment. The journey was not yet complete. There was something more that needed to happen. He felt the Lord saying: "This pilgrimage is over but you will remain a pilgrim the rest of your life. You have journeyed through the countries of Western civilization and known something of the desert: now you must return to the city of man (New York?) and pilgrimage in this spiritual wasteland of your own country."

And so the pilgrim wired his parents to send the money he had set aside in a bank for just such a possible airplane trip. He purchased his ticket to Luxemburg via Tel Aviv and Brussels. From there he would fly to New York City and then on to Pittsburgh. His departure date was May 28. If all went well he would be at his parents' home in Allison Park in time for the family reunion on Sunday, May 30.

It was just one year since the pilgrim had set foot on Spanish soil at Barcelona on May 24, 1970, and begun his walk to Jerusalem. The Lord had brought him safely over a distance of approximately 4,000 miles and had solidly established him in his childhood faith. He had given him a perspective on life from the point of view of death, judgment, heaven and hell, and had laid the foundations of a vocation to pilgrimage and hermitage.

Many things were still not all that clear. But the pilgrim knew for certain that he was not the same person as the one who started the pilgrimage a year ago. He had died to his old self during these months of walking. He had been radically changed. He had come out of his tomb. He now lived a new life. He was reborn of the Spirit of the Lord. Halleluia.

At the time of his departure, the pilgrim did not yet have adequate words with which to express the experience he had undergone. It would be several years before he would be able to talk about it in biblical terms. But as he flew out of Jerusalem and felt himself wrenched from the earth that he had come to know firsthand, he put down his thoughts in the following manner:

THE GOOD NEWS

FOR WHOM?
— for those who dream of a fantastic future;
— for those who feel deeply the inadequacy of the present;
— for those who have experienced their own severe limitations;
— for those who are longing for a source of energy beyond that of man.

WHAT IS THE GOOD NEWS?
— that man is not alone in his struggle to create a perfect society;
— that man has a partner who is ever-calling him to a greater development of this world;
— that we need not despair in spite of our blindness, failures and regressions;
— that the ideal life is already present to the extent each one believes and hopes for its realization.

WHAT DOES IT DEMAND?
— that one never become satisfied with the present state of his life or that of his society;
— that one always be conscious of how he can help the limited present grow into the unlimited future;
— that one cooperate with all others striving for the same goal;

— that one be ready in the end to die at the hands of the forces which seem to be diametrically opposed to all he lived for.

In Jesus' Name

EPILOGUE

And so where is the pilgrim who left Jerusalem in May of 1971 now, 16 years later in 1987? How did the seeds planted in the year of walking in faith, sprout and blossom? How did the pilgrim live out the call he thought he heard in Jerusalem when he returned to the States?

The pilgrim did not go to New York City, but to Western Pennsylvania and to his parent's home where he had grown up. At first he found it difficult to share his experience with his family and friends. But he soon found fellowship and understanding with evangelical and charismatic Christian brothers and sisters. Once he was baptized in the Holy Spirit, the Lord was then able to use him to share the Good News that Jesus was alive, with others.

As an outreach, in 1973 he was led to work with a Franciscan teen ministry which evangelized through teen retreats, Jesus Rallies, prayer meetings, Bible studies, pilgrimages, street ministry, etc. In 1974 the pastor of his church permitted him to take up residence in a small abandoned pump house in a wooded area of the property. This he used four days a week like a poustinia as a place of prayer, devoting the other three days a week to his work with teens.

This rhythm of prayer and service has continued to the present, with pilgrimages varying from one week to three months' duration interspersed through the years. He found his life revolving around three elements: 1) contemplative prayer — praying always; 2) a poor, penitential lifestyle — owning nothing; 3) apostolic ministry and outreach with the Gospel. His whole life, both at prayer and on pilgrimage, amidst both affluence and physical poverty, points to the fact that the meaning of life lies beyond the immediate physical world, and that with the Lord's grace, one can trust literally in the promise that those who seek first the Kingdom of God will have all they need provided (Mt. 6:33).

The pilgrim has staked his life on the truth that Jesus of Nazareth is the very Son of God, Savior of the world and risen Lord of all. Finding the pearl of great price (Mt. 13:46), he has sold all to possess it, realizing now that it is a treasure that rests in his heart and that no one — not even Satan — can take it from him. In this supernatural confidence he receives the grace to go contrary to every normal expectation of the people and society that surrounds him, as he offers to anyone who is hungry and thirsty for real life, the only one who can satisfy the deepest need of their hearts, namely Jesus the Lord. May His Kingdom come. May He be praised now and forever. Amen. Alleluia.

GEORGE WALTER

APPENDIX I
PILGRIMAGE LOG

FEBRUARY

Thursday, February 4, 1970 —Left Pittsburgh, PA

Wednesday, April 29, —Wrote first letter home

MAY

Wednesday, May 6 —Set sail on Mar Adriatico from New Orleans

Wednesday, May 20 —Arrived at Cadiz, Spain

Sunday, May 24 —Arrived at Barcelona, Spain

JUNE

Friday, June 5 —Took room and wrote second letter home

Tuesday, June 9 —In Leon

Saturday, June 20 —Arrived at Santiago, de Compostela

Monday, June 22 —Left Shrine in Santiago

Tuesday, June 30 —Spent day on beach at San Vicente

JULY

Sunday, July 3 —Third letter home

Wednesday, July 8 —Entered France

Saturday, July 11 —Visited Chapel of Virgin near St. Geours de Maremne

Monday, July 13 —Met Pierre near Bordeaux

Saturday, July 18 —Wrote fourth letter home

Saturday, July 25 —Birthday celebration in Tours

AUGUST

Monday, August 3 —Arrived at Paris

Friday, August 7 —Wrote fifth letter home

SEPTEMBER

Tuesday, September 10 —Left Paris

Thursday, September 24 —Arrived at Enchenberg

Saturday, September 26 —Wrote sixth letter home

OCTOBER

Monday, October 12 —Left Enchenberg

Tuesday, October 20 —Visited Ronchamps

Thursday, October 22 —Crossed into Switzerland at Basel

Sunday, October 25 —Arrived at Schibli's in Zurich

Thursday, October 29 —Visited Monastery at Einsiedeln

Friday, October 30 —Climbed Mt. Mythen

NOVEMBER

Sunday, November 1	—Slept on top of Alps at Gotthard Pass
Tuesday, November 3	—Wrote seventh letter home
Friday, November 6	—Entered Italy
Thursday, November 19	—Sent eighth letter and prayer home
Sunday, November 22	—Florence
Thursday, November 26	—Entered Umbria County
Sunday, November 29	—Assisi

DECEMBER

Thursday, December 3	—Norcia
Friday, December 4	—Cascia
Monday, December 7	—Arrived at Rome
Monday, December 14	—Wrote ninth letter home
Tuesday, December 15	—Left Rome
Saturday, December 26	—Foggia

JANUARY

Sunday, January 3	—Left Italy at Brindisi — tenth letter home
Thursday, January 14	—Patras, Greece
Thursday, January 21	—Arrived at Athens
Wednesday, January 27	—Larisa — eleventh letter home

FEBRUARY

Sunday, February 14	—Philippi
Monday, February 15	—Kavalla
Sunday, February 21	—Alexandroupolis
Monday, February 22	—Enter Turkey at Canakkale

MARCH

Thursday, March 11	—Arrived at Izmir
Friday, March 12	—Wrote twelfth letter home
Saturday, March 13	—Ephesus

APRIL

Wednesday, April 7	—Arrived at Mersin
Sunday, April 11	—Easter
Tuesday, April 13	—Wrote thirteenth letter from Adana AFB
Tuesday, April 20	—Turned back from Syrian border
Saturday, April 24	—Arrived at Cyprus
Tuesday, April 27	—Arrived at Haifa
Thursday, April 29	—Nazareth/fourteenth letter home

MAY

Friday, May 14	—Arrived at Jerusalem
Friday, May 28	—Flew out of Jerusalem for USA

APPENDIX II

The following letter was written in Paris in August, 1970. The pilgrim intended it to be sent to his seminary classmates for distribution, but it was never mailed:

As one most concerned about "the glory of God and the salvation of men", I am writing to you who have been chosen to be leaders of the people of God. I hope I will not be imposing on your time by merely adding to the flood of words with which you are already daily saturated. I write in the spirit of praising God for His mercy and faithfulness to me.

The theme of these reflections will be my personal search for, and discovery of, PEACE. Beginning several years ago, when my life was mostly in turmoil, I hope that I will be able to trace the basic process and identify the contributing factors that have brought me to this peace. Possibly in this way I will be able to enkindle a small light for you.

Three years ago, when I left St. Vincent Seminary with the graduating class of 1967, I did not take the path of ordination to the priesthood and service in the parish ministry. After 12 years of seminary training, I found myself not only NOT ready and NOT willing to take up the originally planned ministry, but found myself instead involved in a deep questioning of that ministry as well as of all life. Certain changes had been made through the Church in general, and more specifically in the seminary itself, which had led me to a state of basic confusion and uncertainty.

The first 22 years of my life, up to and including my last year in college, I had been formed by all the religious structures available for Christian education as they existed before Vatican Council II — the Mass and Sacraments, a good Catholic home and neighborhood, Catholic grade school and minor seminary. Within this world I had grown up to believe that the most important thing in life was to BE SUBMISSIVE to my superiors who would direct me how to think and act. By following their counsel I would be led to a meaningful and happy life. It was simply a matter of learning what they expected of me and of my carrying out their suggestions. I trusted them and at all times cheerfully obeyed. I was comfortable, well taken care of and happy. Possibilities outside this religious world did not much interest me.

Then with Vatican II and its new perspective of dialogue with the secular world and less rigid control of its faithful, I began to hear a different message. My superiors were now less willing to regulate every detail of my life. I was encouraged to assume more responsibility for my own life. Now I began to believe that the most important thing in life was to think and act on my own. So I eagerly set about exploring new and diverse ideas, trying out new forms of behavior, questioning old forms and suggesting new ones.

As I became more and more involved in these new trends, I began to realize just how much I had been taking my life for granted up to that time, especially my life of faith. It had been a given: it was never questioned, challenged, or threatened in any serious way. Nor did it much depend upon my own personal effort. It was just there: always had been and always would be as far as I knew.

Now, however, in an effort to better understand this faith as well as to be better able eventually to communicate it to others, I began to think and raise questions about it. I was brought up against other possibilities, other ways of thinking, other ways of living. At the same time as my thinking was changing, there were changes being made in various other forms of Christian life. New patterns of thinking, speaking and acting all combined to give the Christian in general, and the seminarian in particular, a new image.

Of course throughout all these changes, it was said again and again that the *substance* of the faith was remaining the same: that just its "forms" were changing. But as time went on, I more and more began to get the feeling that we really were going beyond just the forms and were making basic changes in our identity. I, for one, no longer felt like the person I used to be. As I looked around at my fellow Christians, they no longer looked or acted or thought as they had before. If we had changed our thinking as well as our acting, how could we claim to be the same as before?

In general, it seemed like we no longer considered ourselves "a pilgrim people, passing through a vale of tears, primarily on our way to another land." You might say we were "hanging up our rough pilgrim garb" and "putting on the stylish clothes of the new city". We were learning their language, customs and manner of living. It was as though we had arrived at the land to which we as a people had been journeying for so long and now our primary goal was to "settle down", and build comfortable homes here and become citizens of this new city.

During my last years in the seminary, I eagerly participated in all of these changes, for I was finding the old unattractive, embarrassingly out-of-date, and lacking in meaning. The new looked much more attractive, exciting, and relevant. And as long as I remained within the secure world of ideas and the academic community, this questioning and theorizing was interesting, challenging and fun. When, however, the time came for me to undertake the serious work of leading the people of God,

I found I was not ready for such a responsibility.

For I was still out exploring, searching and testing the new world that had been opened up to me, and I had not yet settled this question of our identity. Had we changed that much or hadn't we? If we had changed our purpose and goal as a people, then my main task as leader would be to help the people adjust to the new life of the city by getting them to think and act on their own and encouraging them to get involved in the world around them. But this was not a significant enough task in my mind. Besides, I was not that well-equipped to do this and the "new city" was itself accomplishing this task much more efficiently and rapidly than I could ever hope to as a priest.

But if we had not changed our identity, then my job would be the same as that of priests in all ages past — to lead the people of God on their pilgrimage to another life beyond their present one in the city of man. However, I was also unwilling to assume this task, for I did not feel I had a strong enough awareness of that "other life". I did not have a sufficient "sense of direction" myself to attempt to lead a whole people.

One would have thought that after all my seminary training that I would have had an excellent "sense of direction". With my study of theology I should have been able to give a very detailed account of where we as a people came from and where we were going. And in words, I could. But this was not a sufficient knowledge for me. I needed to KNOW it in a much deeper way — with my whole heart and body, as well as with my mind. I had to experience it in a TOTAL, LIVING WAY.

And I was unwilling to go into the pastoral ministry without this deeper sense of identity, for though I did not see it too clearly then, I really wanted to make a PERMANENT commitment and to give myself COMPLETELY. But I had to have a sufficiently clear idea of the goal before I would give my life to working on a project, and if it were going to be "life-long commitment" this goal must be UNCHANGEABLE and beyond the reach of doubt. So far nothing in my life met these requirements, for I had opened up everything first to questioning and eventually to doubt.

Nor would I take the normal path of settling for a TEMPORARY commitment to limited and changing goals. I would not go the way of trying out different roles, within the ecclesiastical society or the secular society, with the idea that in time I would come to a clearer sense of this identity. These roles assumed certain principles as true and expected certain patterns of behavior. They were not open to the kind of questioning I was doing, for I was striking at the very root of all human activity. To throw myself into some "work" would mean I would either have to put aside my search, or live with the contradiction of acting as though I no longer doubted, while continuing to internally doubt.

Neither alternative was acceptable to me. My search was my primary goal and working in the "straight" way would too seriously cramp my style. My style would be to set out on my own, staying loose and unattached, looking, observing and testing from a position independent of the structures whose validity I questioned and whose meaning I sought. This would mean "dropping out" of all the major institutions of present-day society as far as this was possible.

Granted, this was a rather drastic step, and those very close to me who did not have the same need to assure themselves of the solidity of the foundations of their lives, were anxious and fearful for me. For they sensed, and accurately so, that by cutting myself off from the supporting structures of society, I was going into a "wilderness", as it were, and exposing myself to exceedingly great dangers. But as one driven by some powerful force, I was determined to explore these deepest regions of the presumed, forgotten and unknown, in spite of its many risks.

My search first took me west to California, which still seemed to be a frontier where everything "newest" was happening first. Once there, I was soon attracted by a group of "dropouts" and seekers, who were called hippies. These people seemed to be living witnesses of many of the new ideas of love, freedom, authenticity, creativity, etc., which had come to me from my reading and thinking. They, too, were looking for new meanings, questioning and refusing to accept the roles handed them by their parent societies, and at times were even raising questions about the ultimate meaning of life.

Eventually, however, I came to see that most of them were satisfied that the meaning of life lay in enjoying oneself, in "turning on", and that there was no more distant or ultimate goal in life than that. This, however, could not be the ultimate solid basis of the identity I sought. For the pleasures they offered were too temporary and fragile, even in the intensity and variety of forms they found possible in today's society.

So I began hitchhiking from place to place on my own, looking, observing, testing. But no person, no place, no project, was strong enough to elicit my total dedication. All the numberless roles and jobs to which other men dedicated themselves and which satisfied their search for meaning in life, failed to satisfy me. I wanted to know more. I sought to go deeper. I had an uncommonly strong desire to prove to myself that there was an ultimate solid basis underlying all these other various meanings.

Everyone, to my mind, was acting as though an ultimate basis did exist — even the "modern man" who denied an ultimate future and admitted only temporary goals — for all continued to find it worthwhile to support life by their daily activities. Few, however, ever seemed to give this ultimate basis much thought. Most people seemed to operate best on short range goals. But for me, to find it worth living for even a short range future, implied there was an ultimately worthwhile future. I could not find, however, even a single person who could talk to me convincingly about an ultimate future. Most of all, what I sought was someone whose LIFESTYLE was a witness to a CONSTANT AWARENESS of this ultimate and unchanging reality.

Unable to find such, I proceeded to attempt to live completely in the present: to do what those modern men claimed to be doing but actually denied by their living for even a limited future — to live as though all were relative, temporary and passing. In practical terms this meant that I make no plans, set no goals and just let happen what may. I refused to take on any responsibilities or obligations. I just did what was necessary to basically stay alive, and my only reason for doing this was to continue my search.

During this period of my life, many looked upon me as a symbol of total freedom. They envied my not having any ties, responsibilities, and worries like those with which they felt themselves burdened. But in a way, I envied their ability to be satisfied that life did have an ultimate basis to the extent that they were able to take on tasks which supported life. But I had a burden too. I had the final responsibility of searching out what others either accepted on an intuition, on the authority of others, or just plain took for granted: namely, the solid and enduring basis which ultimately made life worth living.

So I continued alone in my search. I refused to dedicate myself to building the earth if I could not find a more solid and permanent goal than either pleasure or work. If this were all that there was to life, I did not find it worth my effort. In Chardinian terms, I was threatening "to call a strike (to stop work) in the noosphere."

And then in the Summer of 1968, while camping alone in the Rocky Mountains of Colorado, with nothing on my mind and little to occupy my body, surrounded by rivers and mountains, sun and sky, moon and stars, wind and clouds, trees and grass, birds and wild animals, I caught a glimpse of God again in the world and experienced an awareness of His relationship with me. Here where the hand of man had scarcely touched, I desired to thank someone for such a beautiful masterpiece. And since no single man and no group of men could take the credit, there was no one else to turn to but the Father and Creator of all life.

Here among all these natural elements which so faithfully and harmoniously lived the life given to them, I became very aware of the life given to me. The first question and answer of the Baltimore Catechism hit me with all its concise truthfulness: Who made me? God made me. Why, that's where I came from! It was that simple. In such a context it was not a catechism lesson to memorize, an abstract thesis to analyze, or a hard truth to preach. It was just a clear statement of what was. And how wonderful that it should be so. The light of this first truth in its simple grandeur was dazzling.

This then was the deep solid bedrock of all reality. This was that ULTIMATE basis which I had so desperately been seeking. Knowing the Father to be the origin of my life, I also knew Him to be the goal and end of my life — the second question and answer of the Catechism. Here was that which remained constant from the beginning to the end of my life and to which I could attach all the changing realities of daily existence. Here was the One to whom I could make a total and permanent commitment of my life without fear of change or deception.

Having discovered a solid basis upon which I could build my life, I felt I was now able to emerge from the wilderness and return to the societies which I had left. For I now knew that my life did not really depend upon the structures of these societies for its ultimate meaning. These structures were secondary, temporary supports to man's life on earth. They could not ultimately account for its origin, nor were they the final goal of life, as I had once feared. Realizing this, I felt I was now ready to assume a part in the society of man and give witness to my life as a Christian.

Still having the order of Diaconate, I decided to attempt once again to live this in some official way. I thought that possibly here I would be able to put together again, now around this new awareness of my relationship to God, all the pieces of my Christian faith. Now that I knew "union with God" to be the ultimate goal of my commitment and all other activities and forms of service to be secondary, I thought I would be able to work out a form of witness and service consonant with both the old and new thinking and structures of the church.

Such, however, was not to be the case. For one thing the pastoral ministry expected busy, active forms of service and I was still mainly listening to the Word of God speaking in his scriptures and through his people. Also, I did not yet have a strong enough awareness of Christ as being the way to the Father and needed to grow closer to Him before I was ready to speak his word to others. The hierarchy grew impatient with my silence and slowness, so I had to withdraw for the moment from the pastoral division of the Church.

I thought I should continue my listening to the Word of God from some small corner of the "secular society" and from there possibly I could build an appropriate form of witness to God's holiness. So I chose an apartment in Uptown Pittsburgh and got a parttime job as an orderly in a nearby hospital. I also set up a regular prayer schedule and spent time each day visiting with the people living in the neighborhood.

But after seven months, nothing concrete had developed out of this. I was close now to the manmade world of the city with its noise and air pollution, brick and asphalt, crowded and impersonal surroundings, but I still did not have a strong enough sense of my Christian identity to undertake with confidence what I could label as authentic action in the inner city. I still lacked a vital awareness of the Biblical faith and so I was still unwilling to assume more than a "parttime" responsibility for working in the city of man.

Finding myself, however, still determined to pursue this "Christian thing" till it rendered up its meaning, and unable to come to a satisfactory experience of it through reading and study, through the power of my imagination or with all the ecclesiastical and secular institutions at my disposal, I conceived yet another effort. This time I would attempt a physical relocation of myself into the land of Israel — where our faith had been born and was nurtured for centuries. It would be a kind of "physical realignment," a "bodily configuration," a "total environment, experience": the kind of thing the Church tried to give its members through symbols, liturgies and rituals (though all of these in their present forms had failed to speak to me).

And since I desired this to be a total experience, this relocation must not take place by a quick easy flight of a jet plane. It must be a real JOURNEY: one which cost me much effort: one which involved every resource of mind and heart and body. I would go on foot and by boat. I would be as dependent upon my immediate environment as possible so that I could be close to the source of each action which supported my journey — the good will of people who gave me rides, food, housing, etc.

Once I got to Spain I also came to see the importance of WALKING rather than taking rides and SLEEPING OUTSIDE rather than taking rooms. Walking gave me an experience of space and time similar to that of all men up to the present: that is, measuring them in terms of one's own bodily capacities. Sleeping outside gave me a deeper sense of the earth and the natural forces of the environment. Living with the farmers and shepherds of Spain I came to realize better how they felt the rhythm of life and how they could believe that all depended upon an eternal law which guided the movements of the heavens and earth. With such an experience of life subject to powers beyond the creation and control of man, it was a much shorter step to belief in, and prayer to, the Lord of the universe.

Now, too, as never before, the imagery of the Psalms came alive as I daily experienced the warmth and heat of the sun, the cool and damp of the night, the vastness and infinity of the stars, the majesty of the clouds and snow-capped mountains, the refreshment of cool spring waters, good fresh bread and pure natural wine. With this new awareness of the heavens and earth, I came to a new appreciation of the God who made the heavens and the earth.

I came also to understand better the primitive distinction between good and evil. Living close to the earth and the forces of nature, things fell much more easily into one of two categories — yes or no — than when living in a city where basic survival is taken for granted and it is possible to make all kinds of fine distinctions. In a country environment, and even more in a wilderness, things are judged as either supporting life or threatening to life. When meeting another person, an immediate judgment must be made: friend or enemy. There is much less possibility of just ignoring each other and passing on, as there is in a city. Man is in a life and death contest with forces beyond his control. He needs to have trustworthy friends and has to know his enemies.

This kind of experience also made me much more appreciative of my own life. It was no longer so easy to take it for granted. It required effort and often depended totally on the goodwill of one or two people who were immediately and physically present to me. I understood better the Biblical sense of supernatural powers of good and evil and the psalmist's feelings of helplessness and cries for divine assistance. If one takes away all the life-supporting structures of the city of man, he comes face to face with some pretty terrifying, as well as awe-inspiring powers of life.

In this context I slowly pondered the words of the evangelists and as I did so, they, too, became more and more real. As I came close to physically living in the kind of world they and Christ knew, their witness to His life and teachings no longer seemed so distant and strange. All the words and pictures that had been given to me over the years in an attempt to help me understand his message, failed to even come close to recreating the reality as I now understood it. It was really very simple. Too simple, perhaps, for one born and raised in the complicated world of modern man.

But this is the way I have been led back, first to a vital experience of the Father as the source and origin of all life and then to Christ as the way back to the Father. This has been my passage from uncertainty, confusion and ignorance to certainty, peace and understanding. Nothing new was really added: it was just that what was there was arranged in its proper order and enlightened by the grace of truth. This, in turn, has led me to dedicate my life in a new way to growing closer to Christ every moment of my day through the mediation of His Word in all its sacramental forms.

As a result of this experience, my perspective has now become radically eschatological. It is only with this perspective that I have finally been able to find something that gives me as a Christian an identity distinct from that of a citizen of the new city. I am convinced that only to the extent that one looks beyond the goals and projects of the city of man, and places his hopes in the one Lord and God of the universe who sent His only Son to transform this city and lead it back to the Father, can one authentically claim to be Christian. That is, we still are a pilgrim people, because our primary goal does lie beyond this present city.

In day-to-day living, of course, most Christians are intimately involved with building this new city. Their lives may not appear much different from those of the citizens of the city of man and there may even be a great similarity of thinking and reasoning between the two. But there must be a radical difference of perspective. Insofar as one dedicates himself completely to the building of this city, whether it be to his work, his family or his community, to that extent does he cease to be a full Christian. And if his work in this city becomes of ultimate importance, he has ceased to serve God at all and has chosen to serve "mammon."

I know this is hard saying for those who have been shaped by the modern world and who have little experience of going very deeply into remote origins or carefully pondering long term implications — of ultimate questions — and whose lives are filled with a seemingly infinite variety of changing realities. To them such an eschatological perspective will look like a self-centered cop-out from society and a failure to take seriously the commandment to love our neighbor and cooperate in the building of the earth.

But what I am saying is that I found the incarnational perspective led me to limit my vision to the point where I was no longer able to see beyond the second commandment and came to forget there ever was a first commandment. Thus my service-to-man-theology depended more on a lack of awareness of the holiness of God than on a dedication to that holiness. In my eagerness to think of all men as belonging to the people of God, I forgot I was supposed to lead them to a deeper appreciation of God and not just leave them where they were.

Maybe others have been able to find God mainly by considering His closeness to man and man's work in the new city. But I could not. All I saw there was man and the objects of his creation. My vision stopped at the people, places and events themselves. It seemed that the city of man was the origin of life, its total support and final goal. It was not a symbol of another reality to me. I failed to discern the presence of God shining through it.

It has only been with an awareness of God's distance from and inability to be contained by man and man's work in the new city, that I have been able to come to an awareness of Him. From this perspective, man's projects and activities look tiny and insignificant, temporary and passing, superficial and vain. Only with an experience of God's otherness did I come to know what is meant by sacrifice, detachment, penance, sin, judgment and death. In the process, erotic pleasure has been replaced by reverential love: wild excitement by a tranquil joy; surface calm by a deep inner peace; and superficial brotherhood by a union of hearts. I have gone from knowing, depending upon and fearing man and the structures of his civilization, to knowing, depending upon and fearing only God.

Thus I have become determined to make union with God the all-consuming goal of each moment of my life. So far I depend mainly upon meditation on His Word in the scriptures to aid this union. Possibly some day I will receive a call to leave this wilderness and come back to the city to live some kind of communal witness to the transcendence of God or to put into practice my belief that only with an eschatological perspective can one engage in incarnational activity. For now I will continue to meditate upon the Word of God in the desert — keeping alive, at least in my own heart, this awareness of His Holiness.

To those of you who may experience a need to go this far out into the desert, I send you these words as some reassurance for your darkest and most bleak moments. To all of you I send back this witness to God's continuing goodness and mercy to those who seek Him with all their strength of mind and body. I trust all of you will continue to labor for Christ, always seeking to be ever more faithful to His Word, remembering that He said not a dot of the law shall be changed or unfulfilled, and that anyone who teaches any differently will be called least in the Kingdom of Heaven.

Amen.

APPENDIX III
THE BEGINNING OF A SIMPLE STORY

God is the beginning and end of all things; the origin and destiny of all that is.

A long time ago, before time began, there was only God and He was very happy.

But God wanted to share this happiness. So He drew up a plan whereby there would be more life that could also share in His life.

And that's when God made what we now call the universe, all the galaxies and stars. And He set everything to work according to certain laws.

And according to His plan, there would appear in time a creature called man. And when he appeared, it became possible for this new life God had created, to know Him as its origin and destiny.

But when the first man became aware of who he was, he was not satisfied with God's plan for his happiness, and decided that creation itself was all he needed to make him happy even though that meant death was the end for him.

This made God very unhappy, as now it seemed that his creation had turned against Him and they did not care to live with Him. So He decided He would come to earth in human form and show man once again the way back to Himself, so that all creation would not have to end its life with death.

— Holy Land, May 1971